NonDicCual

The Rantings of an Alleged Washed-up Diva

2n2me

Copyright © 2022 by 2n2me.
All rights reserved.
Printed and Bound in the United States of America

Book Cover Design by: Alexa Tolen

ISBN: 979-8-218-08469-1

First printing December 2022
Second printing December 2024

No part of this book may be reproduced, stored in a retrieval system or transmitted in any form or by any means without the prior written permission of the publisher—except by a reviewer who may quote brief passages in a review to be printed in a newspaper, magazine, or journal.

For inquiries, contact the publisher.

Dedication

To the owner of the footprints in the sand who carried me through this life, whom without His amazing grace and mercy, I would still be lost; who loved even a diluted heathen like me. In Jesus' name! I thank you, thank you, FATHER!

Mommy, thank you for my life. You will always be my first love. I love you unconditionally and forever. I hope I have made you proud.

Dad, I wish we had more time. I long to talk to you and tell you how much I love you and share with you all the things that fathers and daughters should. I hope I have made you proud and that you are shining down on us, witnessing everything.

Paul, my knight on the white horse who saved me from myself, I know it ain't been easy, baby. I know I'm a lot, but I would repeat every single moment with you. I can't imagine this journey without you in it. I am so happy I answered the message that day. You changed my life for the better. I love you more each day because you have my back, front, and all my sides, no matter how big or small. I am honored to be riding shotgun with you by my side. You are still fine AF!

Lexy and Layla, my legacies and my bonus baby, Manie—no words will be enough to say what you have taught me about love. I am privileged to be your mom. Thank you for everything I could ever imagine. Thank you for putting up with me while I try to be as good to you as you are to me. I am in love with you equally and separately. You have shown me how to be a grownup, and make myself worthy of your love, and you have shown me what it's like to never forget the little girl inside me because you are magical.

To my grandmothers, my aunts: Carolyn, Tina and Jerry, my cousins: Debbie, Shellie, Kathy, Pam, Deda, Karen, Reggie, Vernon, and Darny—thank you for loving me, believing in me, and always having my back. Because of you, I never felt alone as an only child.

Oprah Winfrey, I'm coming! Save me a seat on your couch, and a spot in your book club. You have been my shero, my mentor, and like family since your first show back in 1986. Oprah, you are my OZ, the Wiz, the pinnacle. I can't wait to finally meet you, manifesting my dream.

Tyler Perry, we share the same spins around the sun. You help me believe that my dreams are possible. My book will be a series on your network.

There are so many friends I want to dedicate this book to, but it would be a list so long, I would hate to miss anyone. So I will say, you know who you are. If I've ever told you I loved you, then insert your name here: _____. If you helped me in any capacity, insert your name here: _____. I love you!

Table of Contents

Introduction 1

Rant! 4

Jewels 25

A Mother's Love (Part I) 69

A Mother's Love (Part II) 111

Dreamin' 154

At Will 187

On My Own 215

Rooted 265

Homecoming 302

Goodie Bags 339

Introduction

I am the American dream. I am an American success story. I am Black history. I am Gen X 1965-1980. I am post-civil rights. I am a part of the generation who gave us *Roe vs. Wade*, Soul Train, cell phones, my beloved hip-hop music, video games, CDs, Sony Walkman, reality TV, Rubik's Cube, and blockbuster movies. Superstars Michael Jackson and Prince. Movie Stars Denzel Washington and Cicely Tyson. My favorite TV personality is Oprah. Birth control pills, home recorder/VCR. I'm claiming Double Dutch. My generation created ATMs, cable, and the Internet.

My story took two decades to finish, but it was all in God's plan. 2020 was the year I finally wrapped up my tale, and it was a work of passion. 2020 freed me from my creative slump and gave me time to finish what I started writing in 2002. Amazingly, the words just flowed from my pen. It was nice to focus on something other than the global crisis we were all facing. Now, I've always been one for a little time travel—nostalgia's my jam, so this allowed me to go back to all the moments I enjoyed and escape from my present situation.

Listening to all my old favorite songs helped me turn my memories into words. Some parts of my journey were very tough to relive, but it was healing to get them out of my mind. Mental health matters, folks! 2020 took away my job, my security, my trust, and my freedom. I will never be able to go out in public again without thinking about covering my face. But it also gave me some valuable priceless things, a stronger bond with my family, my spirit of community service, my pride in my journey, and my self-confidence. And 2020, let me chase my dream of writing a book, you are never too old to make your dreams come true. I poured my heart and soul into these pages, and I pray you feel every ounce of joy I felt while writing it. Dive in!

My Bucket List

Perform in front of a large crowd. ✓
Host a TV show. ✓
Meet Janet Jackson.
My book on the *New York Times* bestsellers list.
Audition for a girl's group. ✓
My book turned into TV series
Travel the world, Paris, London, Egypt, Greece, Italy, and Bali.
Concur my fear of flying.
Host speaking engagements.
Visit the Hollywood Walk of Stars. ✓
Guest on *The View* talking about my book.
Win some Lotto money.
Pay off my home.

NoNDicCuaL

Record an album.

Open an Arts Community Center.

Oprah's Book Club (featuring my book).

Rant!

The hungry look in his eyes met hers, and without a sound, he spoke to her with his lips. They engaged in a deeply intense, long-awaited kiss. She surprised herself by surrendering to her eagerness and curiosity without contemplation. Would it be everything she envisioned? Would reality be just as delicious as her fantasy? Her curious mind wanted to know.

Without pausing, he closed the sliding door behind him and turned her around so her back was against the cold glass. She could feel his excitement swell against her abdomen as he pressed into her. Then he kissed her again. His soft, sweet lips worked to calm her nerves, giving her time to regain her composure. She planned what she would allow him to do, pretending to be vulnerable. Now that she was in this spot—the situation she had previously tried to avoid—it was too late. He was in her lair. The sexual tension now pulsed in different physical zones of her body, like her nipples and the throbbing between her thighs.

Unexpectedly, panic erupted in the pit of her stomach. He was gaining control over her emotions. She wanted to retreat, so she attempted to free herself from his embrace and move away from his touch. The origin of her apprehension wasn't because of what he might do to her, but because of what she wanted to do to him if she allowed herself to let go of her morality and inhibitions—not just physically, but mentally. She didn't want to ruin his young mind or his view of women. He would fall in love with her sex. She couldn't have that. With urgency, she needed to break free from his embrace. She had tried to ignore the urge to take him before this moment. "All in due time," she told herself. Damn, it worked in the past—why not now?

He leaned in close enough to graze her earlobe with his lips. The warmth of his breath against her skin was hypnotic. "Please, don't refuse me this opportunity. I've been wanting to know your flavor for far too long. Don't deny me." He stroked his lips against her earlobe as he spoke. "Please… please… please…" He traced her neck with butterfly kisses. With each touch of his lips, her argument became harder to voice…STOP!

WTF! (Insert the sound of a record scratching to a halt here.)

Now that I have your attention…

DJ 2n2me, please play "Deep Inside" by my girl Mary J. while I try to explain myself. What in the funky fart was I doing, dreaming about my neighbor's son, who lived across the street, with my Roberta Kelly ass? He was barely an adult! Look, I know we can't control what we dream about, but damn! Why is it that when you have a situation, Mary J. is always involved? You wanna be happy? She's got a song for that. Are you tired of being alone? She's got a song for that. Are you in love? She's got your back. Mary J. is the girlfriend you always wanted but didn't know you needed. I love me some Mary J. Blige! She has been serenading me my whole adult life.

Okay, let me exhale.

It's important to tell you how I got to this ranting, miserable, manless, wet-dreaming, fantasy existence in 2002. Loneliness can play awful tricks on your mind; it's a master illusionist, capable of twisting reality and urging you to entertain thoughts that would otherwise never cross your mind. I was just miserably tired of being alone. Little did I know, sunshine was right around the corner. All I needed to do was persevere. This narrative isn't a chronicle of a fairytale ending; it's a testimony of my survival as a single woman. I'm dramatic, right?!

Let me start with my wild book title. It was originally *NoNDicCuaL: Sexless in the Chocolate City*. Initially, this was just a story about my first four years in Washington, DC. Twenty years later—how long it's taken me to finish writing it—now it's a memoir! (Insert laughter here.) So, I changed the title to *NoNDicCuaL: The Rantings of the Alleged Washed-Up Diva* because it includes a lot of flashbacks, details about my life, and my rantings about my single-woman experiences.

It's important to tell you a bit about my background, so some of my crazy makes sense. If that's possible. I coined the word "nondiccual," which means being intentional about what you want without allowing dick to disrupt your goals or take you in a direction you don't want to go. It's crass, yes, but it is what it is. Legs wide shut and your third eye open so you can control the future you want for yourself. Ladies, I know you can relate. You can't think with your legs open or by keeping it cute; clarity waivers when passion is strong.

Let's talk Diva. The essence of a diva is encapsulated by a crown—a symbol you must earn. The first rule: you must win it. My coronation as prom queen created a lot of artificial confidence in me. For nearly a decade, I chased the mirage of another triumph, albeit in vain. My pursuits weren't for illustrious titles like Miss Missouri, Miss Black America, or even *Jet's* Beauty of the Week, but for local pageants that lacked grandeur. Despite their predetermined outcomes, I was undeterred, drawn to the allure of the stage. As a child, pageants captivated me—not for the competition, but for the sheer luster of the beautiful crowns, the rhinestones capturing the light in sparkling success and validation. Have you ever made a crown from aluminum foil? I have, parading in my mother's heels, adorned with my makeshift crown. To me, winning a crown wasn't just an achievement; it was a defining moment. The term 'diva' is subjective, its definition varies with those who bear the title. I was never truly 'washed up'—after all, one must rise to fall. Yet I harbored a sense of having missed my shot at stardom. Locally recognized, perhaps 'has-been' is a more fitting label, though I wield it with satirical flair. I was supposed to be famous, especially coming from a performing arts school modeled after *Fame*. Well, it wasn't for lack of trying, but this prom queen became a telecom engineer. I reluctantly traded in my second- and third-place sashes for a laptop and a WFH (work-from-home) career. It wasn't the future I had envisioned, but it was the one I embraced, thanks to the foresight of my elders. The entertainment industry's elusive spotlight gave way to a thriving business career, which rekindled my passion for writing. This book, which I started writing in 2002, echoes the voice of my thirty-two-year-old self, still navigating the waters of life. I'm pointing this out because you'll see the evolution of my perspective, a maturation that time inevitably gives. I didn't figure it all out in this book. Instead, I shared my lessons learned and the person I was becoming.

    I will start by sharing my background. My family comes from the Deep South on both sides—Mom's side is from Amery,

Mississippi, and Dad's side of the family is from Prichard, Alabama. Both sides of my family moved to St. Louis for better prospects. My grandmother, her sister, and a first cousin came to St. Louis to get training for work in the medical field.

My dad's eldest two sisters left Alabama to attend college in St. Louis, where they began their careers and married. After settling down, they returned to Alabama to bring my grandmother and the younger siblings with them. My dad was the twelfth child out of thirteen.

In contrast, my mom had one brother and an older half-sister. They were both born in St. Louis. The older half-sister lived in Arkansas. My grandmother moved her parents up from Mississippi once she was married. They bought the house on Page Boulevard, where they all lived until they passed. Then, in 2016, my mom reluctantly sold our family home for something smaller.

I am an only child with a rack of cousins on my dad's side, but not so many on my mom's side. My grandmother's brother also moved to St. Louis. He had five kids, who had kids, but we weren't close, so I never really had a connection with them. However, one significant cousin operated more like a brother—Ronnie. He was my grandmother's sister's son, and we were only four years apart, always together. Thus, I was a spoiled brat, or that's what they said about me. Despite this, I never felt that way because I also spent a lot of time alone, except for the times with Ronnie, who was an only child, as well. Anyway, I was a happy kid who enjoyed being the center of attention. I was the kid the grown-ups would call into the living room to do the latest dance or perform commercials for products like Zest soap or

Crest toothpaste. Hell, I could sell these products better than the commercials themselves. I blame it on all the time spent watching soap operas with my great-grandmother. I loved the laughter, the applause, and the cheers. I wanted that approval for the rest of my life. Consequently, I decided early on that I was going to be an entertainer.

My parents separated and divorced by the time I was four, which meant a lot of back and forth, and I often found myself sitting by the window, waiting for my dad to pick me up for the weekend. They loved and hated each other, and I had to listen to their banter as they pleaded their sides, as if it would make a difference to me.

Skipping ahead because I'll explain a lot of this in the following chapters.

Who am I?

I was the one who did what my family told me to do. I'm sure I'm not alone in that. I didn't have money for college, so I got a job, like most young adults my age back then, who shared my predicament. I was working at a job that had no future for me, and I realized I needed to go back to school. So, I went back to college at twenty-four.

I spent much of my young adult time pursuing singing and modeling, my passions. These were all local projects, meaning I never left St. Louis, except one time, but I'll talk about that later. I worked hard from 9 to 5, but after that, I let loose. I liked to get cute, hit the clubs with my gang of pretty girls, and dance until I couldn't feel my toes. I enjoyed live music, laughs, and romance. I loved hanging out with my friends at the malls and the movies;

I was always at one or the other. I collected movie ticket stubs like trophies—yeah, I was that geeky. I was a chatterbox; no surprise there. I was always making connections, always on the go, always involved in social events. I was the official chauffeur for my girlfriends because I was the first one who had a car among my friends. I've always been a giver and believe in the best of people. My mom's family was a bit bougie, and my dad's family was just happy, down-to-earth folks. I embody both sides, allowing me to get along with all kinds of people. I never took myself too seriously and humbly valued the love and appreciation of others. However, I'm an acquired taste—not for everybody. My loyalty lies with my friends and family.

As a child, I had curly hair, caramel skin, almond-shaped eyes, high cheekbones, long legs, a bow-legged stance, a round head, Tweety Bird lips, and a gap between my teeth. Despite being thin, the only things that grew were my feet and my boobs. My silhouette resembled a "P" shape, lacking hips or a substantial ass, but I looked great in a bikini from the front. I had a modest little dent for a butt. I was a blossoming butterfly who didn't fully bloom until I had my first baby. My family boasts a long line of beautiful women with diverse backgrounds, including Native American, French, Irish, and, of course, African. I discovered this before doing the Ancestry DNA test later in life.

I stopped growing at about five-foot-six and a half inches. Too damn short to be a runway model, but great for print work, as local modeling agencies told me. I loved taking pictures; I was taking selfies before it became a trend. It was a bit vain for some, but it was always about proving to myself that I was good enough, pretty enough, worthy enough. Okay, enough about that.

Back to my rant...

So, let's start at the beginning of my tale. You know when folks are about to tell you a long, complicated story because it always starts with a deep breath and, "What had happened was..."

My life... If you summed up the events of moving to DC from 1999 to 2002, I guess it could be told in about an hour on a talk show. Well, forty minutes minus the twenty minutes of commercials. Okay... I'm old, so maybe a two- to three-part show, tops!

Wait a minute, full disclosure. I'm vain, so I really envision a television/cable series, maybe on Lifetime, STARZ, or OWN. Hey, I am manifesting my dreams right now.

In 1999, I made a hasty escape from the Gateway to the West—St. Louis, Missouri—heading east to the Chocolate City and cherry blossoms: Washington, DC. My life was scattered in all directions like a bag of microwave popcorn gone rogue. It was time for some soul-searching, and not just because my last boyfriend had the emotional depth of a teaspoon.

I've got Daddy and Mommy issues—shocker, right? But I'd never before dared to rummage through the family attic of disgruntled skeletons. Until now. My story zigzags through time like a time traveler with a broken GPS—not in chronological order but in themes, each with a creative, humorous twist that only my life could provide.

Fast forward from 1999 to 2002, and I'm doing a deep dive into the 'why' of me. It's like a "This is Your Life" episode, minus the celebrity guests and with more embarrassing childhood photos.

I'll tackle some tough topics too, like my relationship with my mom. I adore her, but let's face it, airing the family laundry is like dry snitching. And I'm doing it with love—grown-up style. She might not be thrilled about me dredging up the past, but hey, I've got things to say.

As I dug into my book, I chatted with the elders, uncovering tales of my ancestors' exploits. Turns out, I hail from a line of overachievers—no pressure, right? It's important because it's the secret sauce to my quirky concoction of a personality.

By now, I was supposed to be basking in the glow of fame, but the universe didn't get the memo. Dreams of modeling, singing, acting, and hosting a TV show were all packed away in my mental attic, gathering dust. Everyone else jetted off to LA, NYC, or Atlanta to chase their dreams, while I stayed put in good old boring St. Louis.

Watching my dreams do the vanishing act was tougher than a two-dollar steak. I buried the disappointment deep down after my little one came into the picture.

At the tender age of twenty-nine, I was as lost as a sock in a dryer. Who was I? What could I do? It was time to find out. There were new dreams to chase, a baby to raise, and a life to rebuild.

Enter my cousin, Mellie, my personal superhero sans cape. She swooped into St. Louis, helped me pack up my life, and gave me a crash course in DC living. I owe her big time—she's the GPS to my life's road trip. But life is like an express train—it waits for no one. Before I knew it, Mellie was Texas-bound, and I was flying solo. Like my biology teacher's, Mrs. Foster's, words echoed in my mind: "Either you get it, or you don't." Well, I was about to get a whole lot of 'it.'

And that's how I left my heart in St. Louis—but took my "scary ass" on an adventure of a lifetime.

Oh, by the way! Excuse my manners; I'm terrible with introductions. I'm 2n2me. Nice to meet you! I am a "laugh with me," not at me kind of girl. I'm extremely sarcastic and overly down-to-earth, and I think I have a great sense of humor. It can be self-defeating. I have never met a stranger—I got that from my grandmoms.

Anyway, here it is, 2022, and I have finally finished this book. I'm a lot wiser today than I was when I first started writing it. Let's just say my life experiences have changed a lot, and I have had many, many a-ha moments. That's a cute way of saying I've been procrastinating, allowing life to get in the way of one of my lifelong dreams. I've always wanted to write a book and have my thoughts read in black and white. So, I owe it to my nine-year-old inner child, who asked for and received an orange and cream-colored typewriter for Christmas in 1979, along with the Sugar Hill Gang's first single, "Rapper's Delight," and Barbie dolls. Thanks to COVID-19 and losing my job in 2020, I had time. Finally, I am happy to see this through to the end. From the bottom of my heart, thank you for reading this far.

Okay, now that I have that out of the way, I can continue my rant. I was running for my life, and before I jumped off a really tall sidewalk or slit my wrist with a plastic knife, I was happy to leave the horror show in St. Louis. This "Alleged Washed-up Diva" is extremely dramatic, with no cameras rolling. I refuse to be labeled a victim of my circumstances. I was going to have to learn how to mediate my damage, and quickly. What doesn't kill you makes you stronger, so "they" say, but "they" didn't say anything about crazy.

Truth be told, motherhood was never in my plans. Marriage was supposed to precede even the mere thought of children.

Growing up, the idea of having kids was far from appealing. Under no circumstances was I ever, ever, ever supposed to be single with a child at a mere twenty-eight years old (I articulate this with a Mariah Carey-esque flair).

I've realized that I'm not the center of the universe. The Goddess of Love and Cupid aren't conspiring against me despite their misguided matchmaking. I've returned the misfits, and I'm still waiting for my refund. They certainly owe me! No matter how much I wish there were simple answers to my personal problems, I am not unique. Everybody had problems it was 1999, see what I did there? I had just two boyfriends since turning eighteen. Two! My first love was six years. The other one, which shall remain nameless, was four. I didn't put a conscious effort into having a man at any cost. There was never a notion in my head that a man had to complete my circle. The relationships just lasted as long as they did. But I've always had a boyfriend in my life up to this point, blah, blah, blah…

It wasn't about being a devoted girlfriend; it was about discovering my identity and forgiving myself for the longevity of those relationships—well, one in particular. It was time to learn self-love and embrace my new normal. With a deep breath in and a release of air, I found solace in my faith. I persevered, and now I'm here to share my story—unfiltered, vulnerable, and mostly unashamed. Sure, there's a tinge of regret, but only about five percent.

Woo, child, I needed time to reflect and recoup before I could allow someone new to share my space. Maybe I'm a bad judge of character, or I just attract the wrong men. It's possible that I just never gave myself permission to be selective, or that I never viewed myself as worthy of options. Woah, that's deep! Uh-oh! That sounded like Ms. Iyanla! Big props to my beloved. I've encountered 'meantime' men, placeholders until I'm ready for a lasting connection. You've got to get her book to understand that one, but I'll try to articulate it. In a nutshell, it means that the next man you meet may not be with you forever. He may be just there in the meantime for a season until you get yourself together to meet your forever. It talks about the different seasons, it's a whole thing. It's worth the read, and I highly recommend it.

I was going to take my time, which involved keeping my legs closed and getting to know the person inside. All this while being more selective because I wasn't afraid of being alone—hence, Nondiccual no-dick-@-all. Real talk: I deserve the best, and so do you! Yeah, yeah, yeah, I can say that now, looking back, but it was a journey to keep those legs closed. I don't know if you can even call them "meantime"—more like "right now for the moment" on a 10-to-2 shift. In by 10:00 p.m. and out by 2:00 a.m. I was young, I had needs, and nobody knew me here in DC.

I can honestly say, "I didn't learn a damn thing" (in my Robin Harris voice—RIP! Don't know him? Google him) about men until I was single. All of my opposite-sex comprehension came from the two men with whom I had spent the last ten years of my immature young life. The only thing I learned was what I really didn't want. I was brand new to single life and DC. Well, more to the point, I was dropped off on the short bus in front of a train, and DC was willing and ready to swallow me whole without mercy, rolling right over my little country bumpkin ass, lights bright and horn blowing.

I didn't have a clue about the games people played, but I became a quick study, and it was imperative if I wanted to stay sane... Let me say I had a little practice with the last failed relationships.

Can I say I hated being single? I hate the whole dating-getting-to-know-someone representative thing. Especially in a city where the ratio of men to women was 4:10. Some may say they love a challenge, but trust me, that wasn't the case with me, with the odds being that bad. What was I looking for? Similar goals and compatibility would be ideal. Confident that his sexual orientation was heterosexual was a must, and not competing with nine other females for his attention would be appealing.

My search led me to Black Planet, one of the first Black social media sites for singles to network with the opposite sex. I stumbled on this site by accident. The option of meeting men online offered me access to a pool of alleged single men across the country that I would have otherwise never met. It seemed safe, acceptable, and, considering the alternative, less expensive. Going to a club entailed a $20 parking fee, a $20 entrance fee, and an additional $20 for drinks. I have said this explanation more times than I care to mention, rationalizing the logic behind why I wasn't completely desperate and insane for exploring this less-traveled, unpopular option in 2000. As bleak as that was, it topped the list of fun things I did for the next two years. Wait, did I say two years out loud? Two years!

Man, did I have to settle for the slim pickings, leftovers, and misfits? I swear to the good Lawd. If I met one more insecure man, I was going to walk to the busiest part of Pennsylvania Avenue, stand in traffic, and beg for change. It would be more productive than trying to build up someone else's self-esteem. Nope, under no circumstances did I want a man project!

I don't know; I assumed all the really good guys were married. Maybe not happy, but definitely unavailable. Maybe they gave them all out like government cheese, and I missed my invitation in the mail. The men that are available in the DC metropolitan area are spoiled, in my experience. I had found a lot of emotionally unavailable guys; sex was readily available but without commitment. It has been very disappointing. Did I mention I hate being single? The East Coast has a very strange and complex outlook on dating for a Midwesterner like me. For example, a friend is someone you are sleeping with, but it's not a relationship. Label me old-fashioned, but if you are sleeping with a person and he or she is the only one—from where I come from—it's a relationship. I don't sleep with my friends.

Fear of labels—maybe commitment, whatever it is—is unconscionable when relating that way. If you stayed here long enough, you got sucked in, and then it became a matter of survival—shameful but necessary. I guess I chose one of the worst places to live for a decent woman not looking for the okie-doke. Of course, this was not exclusive to men. Don't get any ideas—this opinion can be true of any sex or orientation. Please insert your mate of choice. This is an equal-opportunity kind of conversation, but I can only speak from my own experiences.

I believe the shortage of men enables the nonchalant attitude some men have toward women because they know they can be just as greedy as they want to be. It's that old supply and demand thing that gets in the way; I know it's usually defined by products and services, but it can be true in human relationships, too.

In their defense, it isn't entirely the men's fault. Some women enable their noncommittal attitudes toward monogamous sexual relationships because they tolerate it. I would even go out on a limb to say that we encourage them. Do you know why? It's simple. Something you've never thought of, or maybe you have. We give up our bodies before they have any real honest interest in or connection with us. Sometimes, in the early phase of dating, we allow way more bullshit than we should. Sometimes, we are not honest about our expectations out of fear of scaring him off or the embarrassment of being alone, dickless/nondiccual.

Here is what I know now: if I had kept my legs closed long enough to listen to what the guy had to say, assessed if his actions matched his words, and conducted a background-check mentality to ensure his stories checked out—oh yes, it takes that level of scrutiny—days of trusting without verifying are over—I would have found out he wasn't worth my time. I've gone through a lot of "no's," the long way around. I've since learned not to waste time with them because messing around with Mr. No-No may lead to not finding my Mr. Oh Yes. Of course, this revelation was the journey I was on from 1999 to 2002, and now I'm sharing it with you.

Believe it or not, I wouldn't change a damn thing about my journey. Okay, maybe I'd un-gift those coochie coupons, but nothing life-altering. Speaking of coochie coupons, one-night stands never work. Child, they're like microwave dinners—quick, unsatisfying, and leaving you wondering why you bothered. I've tried it once or twice a long, long time ago (said in my Bernie Mac voice, RIH). But me? I'm clingier than a fresh press-on nail. I need substance, a frickin' callback, no matter how much my body tells my mind I can handle it. I'm a softie. I believe in romance. I want picnics in the park, wine on the rooftop, barefoot on the beach. Yup, I want all of them shits. Someone once told me, "You give away a piece of your soul every single time you sleep with someone." It's true, in my opinion. Who wants to give away a soul, anyway? I need every bit of mine if I'm trying to make it into heaven. I long for a man to come into my life who is completely without drama, low self-esteem, and narcissistic tendencies. Is that too much to ask for?

All the good things I remember about being with a man—shoot, I could go on and on real talk! The thing I miss most is the companionship of intimacy, not sex, but the yearning for the meeting of the minds, the mental support, and navigating life together. Now, let's keep it 100: it's been a hot minute—four years, to be exact—since I've cozied up to that kind of intimacy. But hold up, because where there's good, the universe throws in some side-eye-worthy bad. Picture me in the passenger seat, sandwiched between bad luck and questionable choices in men. It's like trying to sip champagne while driving on a pothole-ridden street. I'm sure some of you can relate. Under the circumstances I was in, I just had to learn to put all of it on the back burner and focus on things I could control. So, ladybugs, let's keep our tiaras straight and our hearts open.

Another thing, if you've got your stuff together, then I will celebrate you. For the life of me, I can't understand why some people think that doing positive things in my life minimizes the success in theirs. They have one less dent in their car than I have in mine, and they are shaking pom-poms in celebration as if this were some big accomplishment. It's like they're counting my dents while I'm out here building constellations. Newsflash: their success ain't my subtraction. I've got my own lane, my own rhythm, and my own pom-poms—and I'm cheering for everyone, even if their car's dent-free.

Speaking of pom-poms, I have always been a cheerleader for my friends. They'd come to me for the pep talks and the hard-to-hear truths, always delivered in love. I could be envious of their lives. Some of my friends are well-accomplished; they've actually done things I've wanted to do. You may even recognize their names. I have lived some of my dreams through them, and I am happy for them. Hell, their success is my success, and besides, I get free stuff.

You know what? I've taken more wrong turns than a man refusing to ask for directions, for the same reason: stupid, sinful pride. I must believe I am here to serve a purpose, and I'm still discovering that purpose. I say you have to laugh about it until it hurts, then cry. This is my therapy. My goal is to inspire anyone to embrace their flaws, celebrate their accomplishments, no matter how small, and to give inspiration to others to share their story—all with dignity. Everybody has a story to tell, and this one belongs to me. Ride with the one who brought you. YOU!

There are a couple of things I want you to take away: 1) You are in control of your own destiny, and 2) You are your own best friend. I know sometimes we need to be reminded of those two facts. This is my adventure, my rabbit hole, my tornado of self-breakthrough and preservation. A challenge is only an opportunity to succeed. Control your future; make it happen because it is possible. All things are possible through Christ, who strengthens me. With an abundance of faith, a sprinkle of grace, and a whole lot of "I got this," all things are possible. My grannies would side-eye me from heaven if I forget to keep some "God in this."

Oh, one last thing before I end my rant and start my story. I have to introduce you to my best friend: music. It has been with me my whole life, serenading me through my ups and downs, nursing me through heartbreaks, and celebrating my heartthrobs. It has been my shoulder to cry on through every loss and has cheered me on through my accomplishments. Music is the confidant that never judges, the companion who knows every chapter of my life. Every song is tied to a memory, allowing me to traverse time, revisiting the scents, sights, and sensations of moments long gone. It's the soundtrack that underscores my journey, the rhythm that beats to the pulse of my narrative. To be a true diva is to live life with a soundtrack that echoes your innermost essence; a selection of songs that capture the flavor of every chapter. This chapter has all of my hip-hop favorites because I am a self-described OG when it comes to rap music. I love the fact that I was here when it all began. Yup, I'm that old, and I can debate you about all the rap classifications at the drop of a hat. I can't mention them all, but check out some of my favorite rap artist playlists below.

Playlist (I'm an OG hip-hop head)
Scan the QR code to listen to the playlist.

Freaks of the Industry—DG
Ambitionz az a Ridah—Tupac Shakur (2Pac)

Rant!

I Need Love—LL Cool J
Wild West—Kool Moe Dee
Radio—Eazy-E
Tonight—DJ Quik
Don't Let It Go To Your Head—Brand Nubian
Big Daddy—Heavy D
Captain Save a Hoe—E-40
Paid In Full—Eric B. & Rakim
Ex-girlfriend—Method Man
If I Ruled the World—Nas
Down with the King—Run-D.M.C.
This Is It—Camp Lo
Hey DJ—Word Famous Supreme Team
Brown Sugar—Mos Def
A Friend—KRS-One
Can't Truss It—Public Enemy
Five Minutes of Funk—Whodini
The Learning—Mobb Deep
Hypnotize—The Notorious B.I.G.
Mind Playing Tricks On Me—Geto Boys
Back In The Day—Ahmad
Get Down—Craig Mack
Put Your Hands Where My Eyes Could See—Busta Rhymes
Bitches Ain't Shit—Dr. Dre, featuring Snoop Doggy Dogg & Dat Nigga Daz
Elevators—Outkast
C.R.E.A.M.—Wu-Tang Clan
Can I Get A…— Jay-Z, featuring Ja Rule and Amil

NoNDicCuaL

Award Tour—A Tribe Called Quest
AJ Scratch—Kurtis Blow
The Rain—Oran Juice Jones
Roxanne's Revenge —Roxanne Shanté
Roxanne Roxanne—UTFO
(Nothing Serious) Just Buggin'—Whistle
The Show—Doug E. Fresh
La Di Da Di—Slick Rick
Brand New Funk—DJ Jazzy Jeff & The Fresh Prince
Funk You Up— Sequence
I'll Take Your Man—Salt-N-Pepa
Crush on You—Junior M.A.F.I.A & Lil' Kim
I Got It Made—Special Ed
Smooth Operator—Big Daddy Kane
Punks Jump Up to Get Beat Down—Brand Nubian
How I Could Just Kill a Man—Cypress Hill
Born to Roll—Masta Ace
Sally—Stetsasonic
They Want EFX—Das EFX
The Ghetto—Too Short
Friday—Ice Cube
One Eight Seven—Dr. Dre, featuring Snoop Doggy Dogg
Gin and Juice—Snoop Dogg
How's It Goin' Down—DMX
Fuck Faces—Scarface, featuring Too Short, Tela &
    Devin the Dude
They Reminiscence Over You (T.R.O.Y.)—Pete Rock & CL Smooth
The Man Right Chea—Mystikal

Rant!

Regulate—Warren G, featuring Nate Dogg (RIP Nate Dogg)
Bad Boyz—Shyne
Girls L.G.B.N.A.F.—Ice-T
Sock It 2 Me—Missy Elliott
Gotta Man—Eve
Oh Yeah—Foxy Brown

Jewels

If I had a dime for every time I played the fool, I'd be sittin' pretty on a mountain of coins. But let's keep it real—this chapter should've been called "Find a Fool, Bump Her Head." What does that mean? It's about those Rico Suave types who spot a diamond in the rough and think, "Easy mark." They see a heart so big and a spirit so willing that they pounce without a second thought: no conscience, no care, just take, take, take. And I was that diamond—shining bright but blind to the game.

I trusted him with everything—my heart, my dreams, and yes, even my coin. But like the old saying goes, "A scorpion is still a scorpion," I was that frog, learning the hard way that some creatures never change.

So, I sat down, put pen to paper, and thought, "How can I flip this mess into a message?" This four-year circus of a relationship is a masterclass in what not to do—call it "Bad Boyfriend 101" or "Real Relationships for Dummies." I'm laying it all out there so you can sidestep the traps I fell into.

This hot mess of a courtship? It's got all the makings of a trash TV classic. Picture it: an episode on "The Jerry Springer Show" (rest in peace) or a juicy segment on "Maury." We could headline it "He Pawned All My Jewelry, But I'm Still With Him" or hit 'em with a "You Are the Father" shocker. But the one that takes the cake? "The Lie Detector Determined that Everything You've Ever Said Since Birth Was a Lie." And let's not forget the grand finale: "He Used My Furniture as a Child Support Payment."

Now, don't get it twisted. I'm not just here to tell my story; I'm here to share the lessons. So, grab your cup, and let's toast to the wisdom that comes from wearing your crown, even when it's tilted. Funny, I could actually see him arguing about the results, just like the people did on the show. I often wondered how it was so easy to be so devious. One must really muzzle their conscience, if they have one, not to feel guilty about the people they hurt. I guess that is where the words narcissist, con artist, and sociopath come from, because if you looked it up, his picture would be right there.

In the beginning, the sperm donor (oh yes, I went there!) seemed like a nice guy who had all the correct answers to my problems. The issue, however, was that he was about to become my only problem. He latched onto me when I was at my lowest point. Since he was easy to talk to and an excellent listener, I told him all my issues—six years of dating troubles and my atrocious relationship with my mother. He manipulated the situation in his favor, using everything I confided in him about, saying and doing all the things my previous boyfriend didn't do. I unwittingly armed him with all the tools he needed to portray himself as the one for me. But here's the thing—I'm no one's fool. Not anymore. I learned to see through his charm, recognize the wolf, and trust my own beautiful, fierce intuition.

I was twenty-four, and he was twenty-nine. I believed he was the answer to it all. Being young and impressionable, I made him my pseudo-guru, thinking his age and life lessons could guide me. He had a great perspective on life and street smarts, he knew how to navigate various situations and deal with all kinds of people. I valued his opinion like it was the gospel. He was right about how to interact with my mother and validated my intentions of needing to be a good person. It was a simple thing, but no one had taught me simple consideration the way he articulated it. It felt good to learn something positive, and I was in total awe of this con man. Outside of my mother, I hadn't encountered lessons about emotional manipulation; my love for her clouded my perception.

Well, there were more exit signs in this relationship than on a cruise ship, but I plead illiterate, naïve, and hopelessly hopeful. This chapter walks through my example of a bad relationship, reflecting on the lessons I learned while keeping it light. I'm pointing out where I went wrong and where I should have walked away.

Clearly, he is not worthy of a chapter, and I shall not name him. However, my lessons are worthwhile. My story isn't even exceptional. I could have made this a male-bashing hate fest, but that would be counterproductive. I'd rather celebrate my youth, gullibility, inexperience, and nonjudgmental, sunny disposition because, without these qualities, I couldn't have become the beloved, important, valuable person I am today. Not that I'm petty, but he stole some of my twenties without my permission, and that was not cool! The thing is, he didn't even deserve me, and I know that now. My epiphany!

You know, I think he should have gone into sales; he could have sold you the shirt you were wearing back to you for double the price. No, he truly missed his calling! He should've been a corner pimp or a crooked preacher because common sense was no defense against him, and he had no issues with taking people's hard-earned money or genuine intentions of kindness.

Hold up, wait a minute! Let's put some gratitude in it. I have to thank him for being the worst possible human being on the face of the Earth that he could be to me, so I could unearth the best me that was hiding inside—the butterfly that emerged from the soiled cocoon. "Muthafucka," I say with a side-eye so sharp it could cut glass. I never saw it coming, but I invited that train that would eventually roll right over me. So, here's a shoutout to the one who thought he broke me. Thanks for nothing and everything, for the pain that made me pick up the pieces and put them back together like a mosaic—more beautiful for having been broken.

There are no dumb girls here, only love lessons to be learned. Hopefully, you only have to go through the class one time. Flunking out is optional, and you are in control of that. But for me, learning the lesson the first time around… well, that was just showing off! I'm from Missouri (ree, not rah), the show-me state, so he had to show me, show me, and show me like in the song by Glenn Jones. Practice made perfect—unfortunate for me in this situation.

With that said, I wouldn't change anything about my journey. I now know what it means to fight for self-love. Let no one ever control who you are by using your insecurities to keep you down. Be loyal to yourself!

We're taught morals, values, and virtues from the cradle, but life has a way of testing just how deep those lessons go. When love comes knocking, or sometimes crashing, we find ourselves at a crossroads. Do we hold on to our self-respect, or do we let the fear of loneliness blur the lines? Honestly, we take more time picking out a pair of shoes or a repair person than we do picking a suitable mate. Think about that!

News flash, ladybugs: we are natural problem solvers, but every problem is not ours to fix. We need to know when to stop, pick up our crayons, and walk away. Alright, it's time to mix things up. Grab your favorite drink—alcoholic or not—and let's play a little game. Every time you nod along, thinking, "Been there, done that," take a sip. If my story feels like your own, go ahead and take a gulp. We're about to bond over our shared misadventures in love and life. I've laid out fifteen jewels of wisdom from this relationship. For each one that hits home, that makes you say, "Girl, yes!"—that's your cue. Take a drink. Let's see if you end up as tipsy on truth as I did writing this.

No judgment here, just a circle of friends sharing stories and sips. Whether you're giggling into your glass or raising an eyebrow with each revelation, remember—there are no failures, only lessons.

So, let's clink our glasses to the past, to the present, and to the future chapters we're yet to write. One drink per jewel, my friends. Let's see who ends up needing a bathroom break first!

Remember:
- Nod along? Take a sip.
- Feel a connection? Take a gulp.
- Laugh or cry because it's just so relatable? Cheers to that.

Let the games begin and may the spirits—in our cups and hearts—be ever in your favor.

Jewel 1: How you meet him matters!

It was 1991, and I worked with a girl named Stacey at Brown Shoe Co. in Clayton, Missouri. I was a part-timer, and she was a full-time employee. I was the new girl, barely twenty-one, and the youngest female in the department. Before I came, Stacey was the youngest. Our interaction was cordial but not personal. Our department moved to another building, where we were packed in cubicles like Vienna sausages. I guess because of our close quarters, we got to know each other a little better. Stacey got pregnant and married the baby's father. I had only seen him in pictures on her desk.

One Saturday evening, I was at an East St. Louis nightclub. Back then, it was called Terrance on the Strip. I saw a gentleman resembling the picture on Stacey's desk. As he passed by our table, I asked him if he was Stacey's husband. Yep, sure enough, it was him. When I explained I worked with his wife, he backed up from the table, and I told him to tell her "Hi" for me. He agreed and disappeared into the crowd. The deejay put on a good club record—ironically, it was "OPP Remix" by Naughty by Nature. To my surprise, Stacey's husband asked me to dance. My mind said, Tell him hell no. I know how women are, but I think he sensed I was about to decline. He said he wanted to dance with someone who knew Stacey to keep him out of trouble. It sounded reasonable then, so I agreed. It was only one dance. I didn't even make eye contact with him, and it felt very awkward. I immediately regretted my decision. The song was over, but not soon enough for me. We parted without words, only a simple nod.

Later that night, my crazy cousin, Derrick, showed up at the club. He was a Que (Omega Psi Phi). He was my father's sister,

Aunt Cee's oldest son. Wouldn't you know it? A fight broke out on the dance floor, and guess who was in the middle of it? Yup. Derrick, with his Que brothers. I ran downstairs to find him, but they had already put them out. I found him outside the club. He explained how the fight went down, and I drove him to my aunt's house in U City, afraid that whoever he fought with would come back because he won that fight. I totally forgot all about the incident with Stacey's man and my guilty feelings.

The following Monday, Stacey was not pleased to find out that her husband had danced with me. He told her he had met me. Now, I don't know how the conversation went between them, but she was never the same toward me. We had a baby shower for her at a co-worker's house. I came early to decorate for the party and to drop off the beautiful baby blanket I had bought. I left before the party began because I had a previous engagement. When I left Brown Shoe Co. for a full-time position at a local cable company, I gave out keep-in-touch cards, and she never did—keep in touch, that is. The small lesson here: I should not have even acknowledged him that night, even if it was innocent. Not to mention, I was in a relationship and had no intentions of doing anything crazy or spiteful. He said I was going to keep him out of trouble, but why would there be any trouble in the first place? It was a bad decision.

After I left that job, I would continue to see him out all the time without Stacey. I would tease him and jokingly say, "Go home to your wife and kid."

A few years passed before I ran into him again. It was 1994, and this time it was at the newly reopened East St. Louis club in Illinois called Broadway.

We spotted each other, greeted each other with a friendly hug, and caught up. He told me he and Stacey had been separated for about two years and that he had just returned from Atlanta. He mentioned he was hanging out with his new girlfriend and pointed her out. I warmly waved in her direction, and we continued our platonic conversation. I asked about his daughter, and he said she was fine, growing like a weed, and shared a picture of her with me and all that jazz. After our hellos, we said goodbye, and that was that, or so I thought.

The following Monday, my day started like any other Monday. I was a CSR—customer service rep—at TCI Cable, on Delmar and Kings Highway, taking incoming calls. My co-worker took a weird call for me. The caller wouldn't give his name, but he told her I knew him. I told my co-worker, "If he isn't giving a name, then I have no interest; leave a message." The caller insisted, so I had my co-worker transfer the call. It was none other than, guess who? It was the guy from the club, Stacey's ex.

"Do you recognize my voice?" he asked me.

"No." I wasn't picturing anyone in my mind.

"You just saw me at the club. Stacey's ex?"

"Oh, yeah? I never knew your first name." At that moment, I remembered he said he had a girlfriend, so I asked him, "What happened to your beautiful girlfriend?" She had a low haircut like Zhane (a duo R&B girl group).

"I will explain all of that later. I know you are at work, so give me your number, and I will call you later."

I did not give him my number. Instead, I got his. That way, I held the power of deciding. I was kind of curious and nosey, but not pressed. Besides, I was still with Dimiel. I knew it was a bad thing to talk to him for three very real reasons: 1) I had a man, 2) he was my former co-worker's ex, and 3) he had a current girlfriend. I didn't feel good about the situation, but we were just talking on the phone, so what harm could it do, right? Well, I entertained it because my relationship with Dimiel had declined, and someone was showing interest in me.

Point—I have learned a valuable lesson, which is always following the girl's code. If women followed the girl code, who would men cheat with? What is the girl code? If a guy is attached to someone you know, he is off-limits, no matter what he says, even if they aren't together anymore. It's bad juju to date someone your friend dated or someone you know. What in the hell was missing in my life at twenty-four that made this okay? Excitement? Curiosity? Vanity? The easy conversations that morphed into soft, silent manipulation drew me in. If I knew then what I know now, I would have valued myself more. I deserved more than a cheater—more than a married man who did not take care of his child, had garnished checks, and was living in his momma's house, with no plans for the future. However, I didn't know all that in the beginning.

Jewel 2: If they only pay you compliments, they can't afford you.

I met him in a club; he had a wife and a kid, and later, he had a girlfriend, but he claimed she was cheating, so that was why it was okay to reach out to me. I was only hearing one side of the story. It should have been easy to walk away—a no-brainer—but no, I didn't do that. If I had observed point one, point two would be unnecessary. I should have noticed all the warning signs. At twenty-nine years old, he lived with his momma in a rented four-family flat on the north side of St. Louis. Separated from his wife, she was putting him on paper for child support. If you're a man who takes care of your child, then the child's mother will not—most times—take you to court because she is getting the money, or you are doing what you need to do as a good father. I should have sent him packing from my existence, but I agreed to go out to lunch with him. On our first date, he borrowed five dollars from me for the tip. He got away with it because he claimed he had no more cash on him. It is poignant to add here that I didn't know my worth, and his compliments were sufficient.

Point—I should have never entertained him. You teach a man how to treat you. If you pay upfront, you end up compensating a lot more in the end.

Jewel 3: Don't let the "D" fool you!

Whelp, he didn't have any money. Not that it meant I wouldn't date a guy because of his empty pockets, but the relationship started with some bad juju. What was it, you ask? Well, I am still contemplating it to myself because he didn't have a damn thing to offer. He would become the love of my life. I would have done anything for him, and I kind of did. He was tall and dark, and he had a great presence. He was Nino Brown fine. When *New Jack City* came out back in the 1990s, chocolate men were in, and light-skinned men were out like a fad. He was well-spoken, charismatic, slick like a used car salesman, and extremely sexy.

Hell, let's spill the tea: hung like a horse with a long-ass tongue; he used both with the expertise of a paid whore. Oh, yes! He was good at that. As a matter of fact, that was all he was good for—a good time and sex.

This was his truth: find a fool and bump her head with a penis. I was dickmatized. I hadn't gone out with any other man since I had been with my then-boyfriend. No one had ever wooed me the way he did. I've always been a sucker for ambiance and music. I remember little of our first encounter—thanks to the Jack and Coke I drank. Dark liquor was never my friend, so I found out. I only remember Jodeci's "What About Us," the whole *Diary of a Mad Band* album on repeat. That is the gist of it—not to mention the walk of shame to my car at 6:00 a.m.

I was not a cheater by nature, so my guilt was killing me. I wanted to break it off with Dimiel. The romance with the new guy was great while I was with him, but after I left and was alone with my thoughts, I hated myself for what I was doing to Dimiel. I started falling for him. It was hard to be with Dimiel and continue to think about him. I had to decide. I knew I needed to break it off; it was the right thing to do if I was going to keep seeing him. He pleaded with me not to break up with him because he was cool with having sex on the low. It should have been a sign! I wasn't listening. He didn't want a relationship with me! I went forward with my decision to break it off anyway. "How can I love somebody else when I can't love myself enough to know when it's time to let him go?" Mary J was telling me how to "Be Happy," but I wasn't listening. It was not the first, second, or third time I had broken up with Dimiel during our six years, but it was the first time I meant it—not just to get his attention.

Point—Beware: Never let sex be the focus of the relationship. You will not see the really important faults. Being blinded by a penis can dumb you down. Listen to the intentions of the guy. He was okay with just sex, but not a relationship. Whoever you're thinking about giving yourself to, make sure you get to know him first. Get tested together and make it a date. Make sure the sex includes condoms, and don't be afraid to bring your own or say "No" if condoms aren't involved. Don't change your whole world on a maybe, just because you get caught up in the sex! More importantly, listen to him. If he isn't interested in a relationship, believe him! You can't think with your legs open, Nondiccual!

Jewel 4: Listen to the real ones who have your back.

You know, neither my mother nor Auntie C, nor any of my older female co-workers liked him on sight. Hindsight is a motherforya. My mother actually said, "He ain't worth shit, not worth two dead flies." My mother has always had a way with words, always speaking her honest opinion about everything. Offering this advice as only my mom could, she said, "Baby, love don't make no shit." Of course, I didn't get it then, but I know very well what it's all about now. It meant that my love for him would not make him a better person. He was what he was. I thought she was being materialistic and biased because she loved my ex, Dimiel. It was more like she loved his status and the money.

She was right about my ex, you know. He was a great catch. Still is, and he hasn't gotten married yet. Anyway, he helped build a wedge between my mother and me. Once he figured out that she wouldn't be manipulated by his charm, he turned on her, making himself a better option. It was an easy enough task because we were always beefing about something—mostly about him at the time. Thanks to my mother, the control-freak regime, it was easy to be swayed to move away from that narcissistic, power-hungry tyrant and her constant drama. He talked about love, moving out, and getting married.

The first year with him was blissful; the sex was incredible, and he became my best friend. In the back of my mind, I always knew and felt I was doing something wrong. That feeling followed me throughout the entire relationship—a constant, soft nudge. Our courtship started in late 1994 and consisted of clubbing, sex at motels, Blockbuster nights, and watching *In Living Color* and *Martin* on Sundays. He didn't have a place of his own until he talked me into moving out and in with him. That sums it up in a nutshell. I swear—I don't understand, as I tried never to look directly at him or in his eyes now. What was it about him that made me think he was attractive in any form? Now I only see him from the inside out, and it makes me shudder in shame and disappointment.

Point—You've heard it before, and it's as true as the sky is blue—you can spot everyone else's mess from a mile away, but your own? It's like it's cloaked in invisibility. That's why we've got to tune into the folks who love us, who root for us, who'd move mountains to see us smile. They're the real MVPs, the ones who dish out advice not to sting, but to soothe; not to belittle, but to build up.

They're the lifeguards on duty, ready to throw you a line before you even know you're drowning. And sure, not every word will fit your life like a glove, but that's the beauty of it. You take what resonates, what clicks, what makes your heart say, "Yes, that's it!" And the rest? Let it float away like leaves on a stream.

So, here's to the loved ones, the wise ones, the ones who see our blind spots and love us all the more for them. Listen closely, take what you need, and step forward with a little less weight on your shoulders.

Jewel 5: Pay attention to the little voice in your head.

Between clubbing, we spent our weekends searching for the perfect love nest. He knew I always wanted to live in the Central West End. It was how he kept me on a string. We found the perfect one-bedroom, two-bathroom loft apartment on the 4400 block of West Pine, and it was perfect. I had to sign the lease alone and come up with the deposit. Why? Because he didn't have the money or the credit. You know, I had a premonition as I was at the ATM, withdrawing my hard-earned bonus money to pay for the first and last months' rent. A little voice in my head said, Don't do it. You are going to regret it! But "How can I turn back now?" I asked myself, knowing I was making a big mistake, but I was in too deep. I was determined to prove my mother wrong and convinced that no matter what, I was going to make this work. We moved in April 1996 to the Central West End apartment. I felt so independent, so liberated, and so damn broke. I bought all the toiletries and needed items for our new place. It was the first time I was on my own. We needed everything—I even bought the living room furniture on my credit. I didn't realize at the time that he owed more creditors than he acknowledged. Plus, he was behind on his child support, and he wouldn't be able to help me with any of the new bills because his checks were being garnished. The budget we sat down and figured out together would not be enough to pay for all our household expenses. It seemed like we should have done this before we moved in together. Duh! Somebody needed to get a second job. I was working and still going to school full-time, so that left him. He had every excuse in the world about why he didn't want to do it. He finally got me to shut up by suggesting he'd just get a new job paying more money.

Point—See, there was no reason for me to move out. I was still in school, so there was no rush. On the other hand, he needed to move. There was always a motive. He used my emotional tie to my wanting to settle down and get married to get me to say yes. Yet, he was still married. How was that going to happen? I never saw it for what it was—he was using me, just as my mother said. I was blinded by my love for him, my naïve love.

Jewel 6: Don't build them up to tear you down.

One day, I was going through the Sunday employment section of the St. Louis Post-Dispatch. He had fifteen years of background experience in dry cleaning. As I was looking for paralegal positions, I saw an abundance of opportunities in dry cleaning for many hotels, and there was a huge need for his skill set. Bingo! First, I convinced him he could take on a management position even without proper management experience or a degree. Then I created his resume to help him get the swanky job as laundry manager in a luxury hotel in downtown St. Louis. He got the job! It was the proudest moment we ever shared. He worked very long hours, and we barely saw each other during the week except in the mornings. When he returned home in the evening around eleven, I was already in bed.

The first thing he did with his first check was to buy clothes for his new position and go out clubbing with his friends to celebrate. He did all of that without me. He already had dress clothes he wore to go clubbing but insisted he needed the right look. Bills be damned! They were past due, and I was robbing Peter to pay Paul. If I brought it up, he would argue it was my fault because I didn't tell him when the bills were due, or he didn't need me putting him in a bad mood when he had to go to work. He was "working," so I was left alone to figure out the bills. We argued constantly. He said I wasn't being a good stepmom the few times he would have his daughter over or that I was gaining too much weight, and then he would storm out because he needed "to think and clear his head."

Point—He tried to play the part of a prize catch, but he just couldn't pull it off. He could only give it a shot because of my guidance, but self-sabotage was his specialty. Like wearing an old, borrowed pair of shoes that never quite fit, it just didn't feel right. With a woman like me in his corner, going above and beyond to ensure he had everything he needed to succeed, he couldn't have landed that position without my support. He was doing things he never dreamed of before me. I saw his potential. Together, we were living better and doing bigger things. However, those blessings were for me—the "me" that was driving him. I blew his high because I was holding him accountable, so he needed someone to stroke his ego, and I became replaceable. Like the narcissist he was, I became his problem; my insistence on integrity was the pin that pricked his inflated ego, and suddenly, I was no longer the muse but the mirror reflecting a truth he refused to see.

Jewel 7: It's a duck, believe it!
The shit started with the first infamous call. I answered the phone to a girl on the other end who called to inform me she was sleeping with my man. Her words were disturbing, but I didn't let on. I asked her calmly, "If you are enjoying sleeping with him, then why are you calling me? How did you get this number?" She hung up. He was sitting across from me on the couch, flipping through *Essence* magazine with his legs crossed like he was Ward from *Leave It to Beaver*. "Who was that?" he asked nonchalantly without even looking up as if he didn't hear the whole thing. I told him what she said, and he laughed it off. I asked him, "How did this girl get my number? What silly childish girl who doesn't know me is bold enough to call my house?" That was if he wasn't provoking her actions. Oh, he was good at defusing the situation as only he could. He calmed me down for the moment. He had only been at the new job for three months. A series of hang-up calls started, so I got a caller ID. I just didn't answer the phone if I didn't recognize the number. The calls continued. I complained to him about it, and he told me to just get the number changed, but I refused his solution. It had been my number for so many years; it was the only way my old friends knew how to get in touch with me. I was angry about the whole thought of it. Why should I have to change my comfort for someone else's ignorance?

Do you know he accused me of enjoying the drama and keeping the turmoil going? Dig that! Oh, and by the way, the calls were coming from the hotel. I got in touch with the management of the hotel and threatened to sue them for the harassing phone calls. The calls stopped coming from the hotel. Imagine that!

Point—If it walks and talks like a duck, it's a DOG! You know what I mean. You ain't crazy; he just wants you to think you are. He was doing something, and this silly girl wanted me to react. Don't ignore the signs.

Jewel 8: Don't let them gaslight you.

After the harassing phone calls debacle ended, magically, we were back to hanging out like we used to do, going out every weekend, and entertaining friends at our house. I also entertained his daughter when she came over for the weekend. I was enjoying our life, still in school, and hosting episodes of "The Cable Connection." On the nights when he worked late— or so he said—I hung out with my co-workers at the hole-in-the-wall spot on Kings Highway and Delmar across the street from the Nationals grocery store and next door to Long John Silver's. Life was good, temporarily. The winter holidays were our own little wonderland. The sex? Fireworks. His cooking? Great; he can burn. He was home every night before the clock struck eight, like Cinderella with better time management. We threw a New Year's Eve bash at our house. All of our friends had other plans but made cameo appearances on their way to other parties. Mom popped in too, blessing us with a drive-by 'Happy New

Year' before vanishing into the night. We rang in 1997, just the two of us.

Valentine's Day? A blur. We renewed the lease in March, and it was a perfect opportunity to get out, but did I take it? Nope! My April birthday loomed. The happy times didn't just end—they ghosted us. Petty squabbles turned into a cold war of one-syllable answers. His silence was deafening—a one-man boycott. So, true to the characteristics of my sign, Aries, I planned my own good time for my special day. I called up some old friends to invite them to celebrate with me. One of my good girlfriends let the cat out of the bag and asked me if the surprise party was off. Surprise party? What surprise party? I didn't know he had even planned anything for me; he wasn't even talking to me, so how could I think he would consider anything special for me? When he got wind that I was planning something on my own, he became irate and threatened to call all my friends to tell them it was off. Talk about the potential shame. Most of my friends didn't think he was right for me, anyway. This idiot thought it was going to be cool with me to call them and cancel my party. The nerve! He had no problem embarrassing me in front of my longtime friends. An argument ensued. It was the worst argument we had ever had. Out of nowhere, he had the nerve to ask me if I was going to move back in with my mother and continue to pay rent there. What! I was so hurt—I left the apartment this time. I called my ex, Dimiel, and through my tears, I told him the whole sordid tale. See, we had maintained a friendship without him knowing about it. His advice to me was to go ahead with the party as planned and not let him ruin my day. I took his advice, sucked it up, and went to the party. He didn't even bother to show up that night. He was nowhere to be found. It snowed, but it was just a dusting that had covered the ground when I left the club. I was more than tipsy when I left, thanks to all the birthday drinks I consumed, but sobered up on the way. Of course, being a Prince fan, the song "Sometimes It Snows in April" came to mind. When I got home, he still wasn't there. I don't know when he came home because I went to sleep. I don't believe he came home at all. When I woke up the next morning, he wasn't there. He worked Saturdays, or at least that was what he said. I still wasn't ready to quit.

Point—In this case, he was clearly trying to end our relationship with some bullshit. He knew messing up my birthday was a big no-no. He was showing me who he was, and I should have shown him the door, given him the boot, but nope; I wasn't there yet. I was still holding on to a thread of 'what ifs.' But let me tell you, when a man drags your name through the mud in front of your day ones, and when he leaves you waiting while he's out painting the town without you—that's your cue. That's the universe screaming, "Girl, enough with the shenanigans!"

It's about self-respect, about drawing that line in the sand, and saying, "This, right here, is where I stand." So, if you're reading this and nodding along, know that it's never too late to say, "I'm done." It's never too late to choose you.

Jewel 9: A woman's intuition is always right.

He became very distant. Then came the change in routine—always working late and going out without me. He would tell me he was working late; I would call his job, and the employees would say he had left hours ago. I would page him when he was supposed to be at work. It would take hours for him to call me back, and it would be from an unknown number. We started arguing about his portion of the unpaid bills because he stopped contributing to the rent while never being at home, but was always ready to go to the clubs with the boys, supposedly.

Then came the emotional finger-pointing and badgering, telling me about all the things that were wrong with me, how everything wrong with us was my fault, and this was why he was never at home. The sex had become boring, predictable, and finally nonexistent. All the signs of his indiscretions were there. I read about them in Michael Baisden's *Never Satisfied: How and Why Men Cheat*. I met Michael at the Sister to Sister Women's Expo. Of course, this was before his fame. He autographed his book, and I read it cover to cover. I even bookmarked certain passages with sticky notes. He was positively cheating on me. He was doing everything Michael wrote about in his book. Yet I still didn't want to accept it as true. I never thought he would cheat on me. It was the last thing I wanted to believe.

Point—If there's one thing he was consistent in, it was his pattern of stepping out. His M.O.? Stir up a storm, play the victim, and make his grand exit. It was a twisted performance, one where he convinced himself he was the wronged party—no longer the sun in my universe or just paranoid that his masquerade was wearing thin. He craved that ego boost like a moth to a flame, always searching for the next person to affirm his worth. And let's not sugarcoat it—he was, and likely still is, a textbook narcissist. The kind that leaves you second-guessing reality, wondering if up is down and right is left. But here's the kicker—I saw through the smoke and mirrors. I recognized the game, and I wasn't about to be played. So, to anyone out there holding the mirror for a narcissist, hoping they'll see themselves for once, put that mirror down. It's time to reflect on you, your worth, and the life you deserve—one free from the chaos of someone else's making.

Jewel 10: Always love yourself more.
One day, out of the blue, he revealed for the first time that he was discontented. It wasn't the first time; now, was it? He had been telling me for a while, but I wasn't ready to hear it. This time I heard him loud and clear. Instead of kicking his sorry ass to the curb as he deserved, I accepted the responsibility for everything wrong and tried to correct myself, even though there was nothing to correct. I don't mean I was perfect, but I wasn't the one cheating. I wasn't the one going outside our relationship. The truth of the situation was that no matter what I did or how well I did it, it wasn't good enough for him, but I kept trying like a fool. I will admit I did some dim-witted stuff as a reaction to his events, which he would use to reinforce his arguments. Although I would leave the house and stay gone as long as possible, I never cheated on him. I was trying to show him how it felt, but of course, this did not work at all. It only gave him the excuse to continue cheating and to justify his actions. It was clear that he had no plans to help me save this relationship. Our relationship and my credit were deteriorating faster than a snowball in hell. I don't even recall what the last straw was anymore. I remember it had something to do with him pawning the diamond earrings he bought me for my birthday the year before, and maybe the

fact he asked me one too many times if I was going to move back home.

The summer didn't prove any better for the crumbling relationship. An old friend reentered my life. I met Sharon at TCI; we worked together answering the phones. She went off to college, and we lost touch. She called me out of the blue, and I shared with her my current woes. Instrumental in showing me my value, Sharon told me I was a queen and didn't need to lower myself for this peasant. I was beautiful and accomplished, and didn't need to live like that anymore. She was right. I wish I could remember all the things she said. I would play it over and over aloud until I could believe it and affirm the words. She read him right away. She saw straight through his shit and shared it with me. Let me tell you, I was lower than an ant's pee. She was all about the power of sisterhood, if there is such a thing. Her face should be on the logo. She explained to me how he was walking all over me. "Game, recognize game," were her words. She was no punk, so strong-willed and ready to two-piece him if I ever gave the word. She reinforced that I was a good person with a big heart. I didn't deserve the treatment I was receiving from him and would do well to leave him alone. I had lost twenty pounds in two weeks, worrying myself to death, literally. She talked me into finally leaving him. I had cried so many times that I didn't have any tears left about the situation. Sharon and two other friends came over to my apartment and helped me pack the things I wanted to keep. They helped me move it all back to my mother's house. I gave them all the dishes and all the other things that reminded me of him, even if I had purchased them. I left him one cup, one fork, one plate, and one bowl. Do you know this man had the audacity to attempt to take back the suede coat he bought me for Christmas? He actually put it on, so I couldn't pack it. So petty! He looked so stupid because it didn't fit him.

So, I was at home with my mommy once again. She didn't spare me from her saying, "I told you so." I wish, with all my being, that it would have ended that summer. It didn't stop there. My mother's threat of my being out on the street if I didn't leave him alone didn't deter me. I was in love, but it wasn't with me. I wasn't finished allowing him to mistreat me, and I was too far from hitting rock bottom with this situation. I was strapped in on the emotional roller coaster on full throttle.

Point—You know what they say about lessons—if you don't learn 'em, you're doomed to repeat the same old foolishness. And let me tell you, I had a front-row seat to that show. If I had just listened—really listened—to what he was non-verbally screaming, and to the chorus of loved ones in my corner, I would've caught the hint. His actions were a billboard, bright and bold: "It's over!" I should've been long gone. But there I was, not wanting to believe that someone could actually treat me like yesterday's trash. It was a first, and it shook me to my core. Relationships can be cruel that way. When we don't get the closure we crave, when we're not the ones holding the reins, it feels like a desert-level thirst while the world snatches the water right from our lips. We've got to be done in our hearts before we can push away with our hands. That's the secret—the magic key. Knowing when to be done-done, when to say, "This is where my story changes." I should've slammed that book shut, but instead,

I lingered on the last page. Well, no more. I should have been DONE!

Jewel 11: Stop playing yourself.

By now, I should have had enough of his shit. It was the fall of September 1997 after the holiday, but yet there was more. Let's see: all the stuff I had done for him up to that point; all the furniture in the apartment and the lease were in my name. I co-signed on a loan for his car and paid the first insurance premium. The diamond earrings he gave me for my birthday—oh, they were in my name too—along with the first engagement ring he gave me. Did I mention he was still married, still not paying child support, and still had garnishments? I should have left him and never looked back, but I gave him something precious to me. I gave him my time. "Baby, you know if the situation was reversed, I'd do it for you," he would say. Funny, I never got to test that theory the whole time we were together. After I left him and before he moved out of the apartment, he called me saying he had to talk to me. I needed to come over. He was really upset and sad. He finally admitted what I already knew about the mysteries regarding his cheating. No big surprise, right? Are you ready? Yeah, she was pregnant! So original! Can the plotline get any more basic? Ooh, he had to tell me the truth because he still needed to use me. He played nice, admitting the truth about his cheating and attempting not to blame it on me. The girl with whom he was cheating worked with him at the front desk of the hotel. He swore it was over because he really wanted to be with me. Remember the hang-up calls? It was her playing on the phone. Clearly, he felt I played a part in him putting his penis inside another chick or chicks. He was so sorry; he loved me, and it was a one-time thing. It was over now—blah, blah, blah. He had actual tears, too. Can you see me rolling my eyes?

I refused to move back in. That was the real reason he called me. It was subtle and nicely done. This time, it didn't work. It was the first time I had ever told him no. I needed time to think. I actually thought I was done.

He got lucky; his co-manager was moving out of town and needed to sublease his studio apartment, and he said yes. A month later, after he got settled into his new place on Laclede's Landing, he invited me over for a "talk." Of course, I ran my little hot ass over instead of telling him to kick rocks. He greeted me at the door, invited me in, offered me a glass of wine, and led me to the balcony with the most fantastic view of the Mississippi River. While we were out on the balcony, there was a knock on the door. Guess who? The hotel's front desk girl—she did not look pregnant at all. This was October 1997. He closed the door behind him. I could hear them arguing on the other side of the front door. I felt dumb! Then I got angry, so I grabbed my purse to leave. They were going back and forth at the elevator. They both saw me approach and stopped talking. "Don't mind me; I am leaving. You two continue," I said, hopping on the elevator, fuming. My mind was going a mile a minute. If he was over with her before he moved out of our old place, how did she know where he was living? Oh, yes, I asked the questions, but I got some dense-ass answers that made no sense at all. We didn't speak for a while, and this should have been it for me.

Nope! Four months later, on Valentine's Day (in 1998), he called me to come over. I hadn't seen him since that October 1997 incident. I still loved him, so I went. He talked me into getting back with him; he had roses, wine, and food when I got there. We were back clubbing and hanging out like we used to. I loved his spot downtown. I bought him a dog. However, it was short-lived because one day, while there alone, I listened to the answering machine and heard all the messages. There were all kinds of messages from women. I felt so dumb, but I did it to myself. I left without an explanation, but I accidentally left a business card on the counter on my way out.

It is so true: when you do someone wrong who is pure in heart, it comes back to you in threes. He lost his job, car, and studio apartment all in one month. He had to move back in with his mother. It was March 1998. Of course, he called me. Can you believe I felt sorry for him? I should have left his sorry ass alone, running heel to ass, but no, I was "in love." I called myself being bright. I was only going to see him on my terms. Yeah, right! Funny how the hang-up calls never stopped coming. They were on my cell phone now, and guess what? Now he was getting them too—so he said! Let me tell you how far gone I was. While he was looking for another job, I would take him out to dinner, movies, and video nights, and when we went to the club, I would give him the money, so he didn't look deficient in front of his friends. He pimped me in every way there was, but I allowed it. He had a person who believed in him, someone who was in his corner no matter the circumstances and was ready to have his back, no matter what. I wonder what it would have been like if I had given myself the same care and unconditional love. I even stopped talking to all my friends because I knew how ridiculous this thing was. I had gone too far.

Point—I stood up for myself, a step in the right direction, but I didn't follow through, so he couldn't respect it. I popped his nose with a newspaper, but I went back anyway, so what lesson did he learn from me? Nothing! He had nothing to offer, and I didn't have the dignity to practice self-love. All I did was show him it was okay to cheat on me and treat me any kind of way because if he said ouch, I'd be there with a Band-Aid.

Jewel 12: Stick to the plan.

It was April 1998, and my twenty-eighth birthday was coming up. I had just received my bonus check from my employer, Ameritech. I needed to get away, and that money was right on time. I needed to do some serious thinking about my future, so I took a hiatus from his drama and stupidly financed his entertainment with his unemployed ass. I went to my beloved Houston to visit my best friend, Cindy, to mull over my life and figure out what my next move would be.

While enjoying my week-long trip to Houston, I had time to evaluate my situation. I realized my love for him was one-sided, and I needed to plan my exit. I hated being a failure, but that also meant knowing when to cut my losses. It was clear this romance was over, and I was ready to end it. I had been wooing the clown that had been playing me like a Jodeci record.

During our 'winter break-up' at the end of 1997 until Valentine's Day of 1998, I had gone back to doing normal things like hanging out with my friends at our spot, Hadley's, two-for-one Fridays in U City. I attended the now-infamous rap concert with my favorite girl, Kas—all VIP—in November 1997. I met somebody from the tour. Kas knew him, and she introduced me. While they were in town, Kas and I took them on a brief tour of St. Louis. Then we spent the rest of the night talking until the sun came up. I had the nerve to still go to work; I was so frickin' tired, but I made it through the day. That's what youth will do for you. He called me from the tour bus at all the stops during the tour. We talked throughout the holidays. I spent Thanksgiving and Christmas with my family and went out with my girlfriends, Lynne, Sharon, Irene, Kas, and Mia, who came to town for the holidays. I had such a good time with all of them, and I missed their presence in my life. They congratulated me on finally leaving that sucker. The guy I met from the tour asked me to come to NYC to bring in the 1998 New Year's in Manhattan with him. I did it. I even met a ball player with the Mavericks while I was in Houston. I had a plan. My plan was this thing was over. By the time my plane had touched down in St. Louis from Houston, I had rehearsed my goodbye speech a thousand times, and I was ready! Unfortunately, you know who tossed a monkey wrench into my plan. He called me, insisting on picking me up. I thought, Great, this would be the perfect opportunity to tell him it was over. But he met me at baggage claim, armed with a dozen roses, a copy of his divorce papers, and a diamond ring. He bought me like a cheap hoe for the night. Nothing else changed about the facts; they just looked better with blinders on. Remember, he told me the girl was pregnant? He claimed he wasn't in contact with her, so he didn't know how far along she was or how she was doing. He avoided the time frame question. Supposedly, she got pregnant in September 1997, during the time we broke up. It was now the middle of April. You do the math. Every time I broached the subject, he would get incredibly irritated.

Supposedly, he bought the new engagement ring on my credit. I didn't know it at the time, and I don't know why the jewelry store would do it without my permission. Point—All the facts were the same. All he did was spray perfume over the poop. I had no new incentive to stay. There was nothing in it for me, so I should have stuck to the plan and LEFT HIM!

Jewel 13: Put a spotlight on that bitch with receipts!
Still under the influence of his cunning deceptions, we went house hunting, like every bad thing was over. Everything seemed to be picture-perfect, right? Wrong! We were "pretend" happy as long as I didn't bring up the subject of the girl's pending pregnancy. After the new shine of us getting engaged wore off, he was back to being himself. He finally got another job—nothing exciting like before. He was back at another cleaning company, back to wearing jeans and t-shirts to work. It was a long slide down from where he had been, and I was still riding shotgun.

As if the lesson couldn't get any tougher, without warning or planning, I got pregnant. Surprise! I couldn't believe it. In the deep recesses of my mind, I believed he did it on purpose, as we had never made any mistakes in the four years we were together. I believed he felt my shift, so this was a way to keep me under his control. It must have been in my eyes. Maybe it was the way I said,

"I love you," without believing in the promise of a future together. I was apprehensive about being pregnant, and he was lukewarm about it. Now, more than ever, I needed to know the situation of the girl being pregnant. She had been pregnant long enough to have an elephant. I was about to discover the reason.

It was a beautiful August day, and my workday started like any other—with morning sickness. My cell phone was blowing up with hang-up calls, and I knew it was the girl because she had my cell number after I mistakenly left my business card back at the studio apartment. Now, I had her cell number, so I called her back. Of course, she didn't answer, so I left a message. I told her if she had something she wanted to say, then come say it, be a woman, and stop playing on my phone. I guess she worked up enough courage because she called me back and told me she was pregnant too. No surprise there, but then she said she was seven months. It was August 1998. Now, that would explain everything.

Okay, let's do a quick recap and put some context around this. I moved back home from our loft apartment in August 1997. She was originally pregnant in September 1997. She told him she was pregnant to force him into making a decision about their relationship and to prove to her that we were done. It didn't work the way she thought it would. Come to find out, it was a false alarm. More to the point, she did the okie doke—keep-a-man-baby—she wasn't pregnant that time, but I never heard that part. He never told me. Why would he continue to lie if she wasn't pregnant at that point?

Remember the incident at the studio apartment that was in October 1997? We broke up, and we didn't speak again until February 1998. She got pregnant for real in January 1998. We were back together on Valentine's Day in 1998. He knew she was really pregnant then and didn't say a word. My heart sank. It was indescribable; all the lies were running through my head. Overwhelmed with grief, I told her I was coming over to her house right then. She gave me directions. I told my supervisor something came up, and I had to leave. She made one powerful statement to me. She said, "Whatever you are thinking, don't do it. The baby didn't do it." How could she have known I was ready to go to Planned Parenthood and end this mess? Her words saved my baby's life and a lifetime of regret. Little did I know that having my child would save my life and send me places I had never dreamed could happen. A calmness came over me as I drove to the woman's house, and a little voice told me not to worry; everything would be okay. I called her on the way to her house. We talked more about it; she filled in all the empty blanks. Look, she had all kinds of Hallmark cards from him, professing his love for her during all the holidays. We talked for three hours, clearing up all the mysteries. By then, I had enough. I convinced her to go to his job to confront him. We rode in separate cars. I called him to meet me out front. As he walked up, he knew he had been busted.

I said, "I don't think there needs to be an introduction, considering you already are familiar with this young lady, so now tell me how pregnant is she?"

The only thing he had to say for himself was, "So, you are going to believe her over me?" Just like a truly busted clearance-rack play would. Then he turned around and walked back inside his job. I told her after all this shit was over, we should go out for drinks. I wasn't mad at her. He was the problem.

Did I kick him to the curb? Hell no! I was pregnant, and I still loved him. However, before he walked away,, I said, "I will see you in court."

He didn't call me right away. He had to get the story straight with her first. He thought I needed time to calm down, or at least that was what he told me. Later on, we talked, screamed, and yelled. He was so wrong; he couldn't get any worse, right? A grown-ass man caught up in this kind of mess should have just admitted his faults and claimed he was trying to make it right. No, that was not what he did. Once again, he moved the blame in my direction. I had caught him dead in his lies, and I was the one who needed to get over it. That was how he played it. I accepted it because we were supposed to get married in September. He told me that she was giving the baby up for adoption, and of course, I didn't want to have this baby alone.

This insensitive shadow of a human being talked this young girl into giving the baby girl up for adoption, and she did it. Just like that, his problem was solved. I still wonder how a woman who carried a baby to full term and delivered could give away her baby. He told her he didn't want to pay child support for a baby, that he would not be a part of her life, and she accepted it reluctantly. I should have never given in to him the last time, but it would be the last time.

Point—I loved that I communicated with the other girl. I believe in girl power. She had the receipts I needed to confront him. My relationship was with him, not her, and he was the focus of my wrath. I wasn't angry with her. She didn't owe me a thing, and the betrayal solely sat at his feet. In a small, weird way, I was relieved to know the truth. At least I wasn't making it up in my head. It was heartbreaking and validating at the same time. He had been lying to her as he was lying to me, so how could I blame her? The only difference was that she knew about me. This was why he didn't want to converse about her because he knew he was lying to me this whole time about her pregnancy. He was lying about not seeing her or talking to her, and he even saw her while I was in Houston. I mean, this should have really been the end.

Jewel 14: When violence is introduced, LEAVE!

He wore me down. He talked me into moving in again, but this time he paid for the apartment because I refused to pay for anything. Small victory! It was short-lived. He went back to his old habits of working late and hanging out with the fellas. When he was at home, he wasn't really there. Come to find out, he didn't like pregnant women. He said, "They are too needy. They think they should be treated special just because they are pregnant." His words. Well, that was the beginning of the end. We spent Thanksgiving, Christmas, and New Year's Eve apart even though we still lived in the apartment. I finally decided to leave him for good. There was one huge blow-up at the end. I had gone out to pick up my favorite Pasta Primavera from Pasta House, their famous salad with extra artichokes, and my favorite dessert, Ben & Jerry's Chocolate Fudge Brownie ice cream. YUM! I stopped at Radio Shack and bought an extra-long phone cord so I could drag it from the living room to the kitchen. We couldn't afford a cordless phone. He came home, said his mundane "Hello," took the phone, walked it into the bathroom, and shut the door. I was beyond livid. I politely went into the kitchen, got a knife, cut the cord, and placed it back in the drawer. I was so angry I didn't even care that I had just bought it. I waited for his ass to come out of the bathroom, where he was washing his dick in the sink—nasty ass! He came out cussing at me, frank and balls swinging under his T-shirt, and said, "I knew you would do something like that."

It was on from there. He got in my face, pointing his finger at me as his penis swung from side to side. I asked him to back up off me. I pushed his hand out of my face as I sat down on the loveseat because my back was starting to ache. He ignored me, bent down, and pointed that finger in my face again, still yelling at me. I pushed his finger out of my face and told him to stop, and again he continued to yell and point his finger in my face. So, I slapped his ass all the way back to Africa. The palm of my hand against his face felt so good. It was a priceless moment that made him leave the room and return with a .45-caliber, telling me I needed to calm down.

I didn't see the gun at first until he sat down next to me on the loveseat and placed it on his bare thigh. Seeing a gun didn't faze me. I was beyond that, and I told him if he planned on using it to kill his unborn child and me, he needed not to hesitate. I guess I didn't give him the reaction he was looking for, so he left the living room with the gun. He returned to the living room dressed. He left the apartment, slamming the door.

I saw my future flash before my eyes. I asked myself, "Is this all my life is reduced to be?" Panic rose inside me, the thought shouting in my mind, I can't live like this! I can't bring a baby into the world under these conditions. This place is not a home. There's no happiness, no hope, and definitely no future in this fronting.

I was six months pregnant by a microbe of a man who had little to no regard for our baby's or my well-being. He pulled a gun on me. It was the day I regained control of my destiny. My dick repellant was on. I didn't want sex with him anymore. Hell, he wasn't sleeping with me anyway—I was sleeping on the couch in the living room, so it allowed me to free my mind to come to grips with how I had wasted four years of my life with this lowlife, but more importantly now, how I was going to fix it? It was the beginning of living my life with ABC plans and forecasting my moves. He didn't deserve me or my existence any longer. Besides, he was still deceiving me with the girl he claimed he wasn't seeing anymore.

Before I could leave him, we had an enormous snowstorm on New Year's Day, January 1, 1999. It fell on a Friday, trapping me in the house with him that weekend. Yes, I said "trapping," with nowhere to run or hide from his passive-aggressive attacks. He was using the old famous silent treatment act. He knew I hated that bitch move. My mother did that to me my entire life. The silence had become intolerable, and he knew how to push my buttons.

After forty-eight hours of straight snowing, I took all I was going to take. That Monday, I put on my coat, boots, gloves, and hat, and with the shovel in hand, I headed toward the front door. I didn't actually believe he was going to let me dig my car out of a foot of snow. Not only did the asshole let me, but he watched me from the patio door. I told myself that after I dug myself out of the parking spot, I was leaving his sorry, no-class, non-goal-oriented, cheating son of a bitch ass for the last time. If I could dig my car out of a foot of snow, six months pregnant, then surely, I had the strength to leave and never look back.

Okay, I still have some fervor for it, but I called it just as it was. It was a short week because of the holiday. Every day at work seemed to pass so fast, and I dreaded going home. Having a plan made it bearable. I was moving back home. The weekend couldn't come fast enough for me. At lunchtime one day that week, I was playing on the Internet. I looked up how much he was going to have to pay me for child support. The estimated total was $500 per month based on his salary and mine. I was feeling pretty good about it. I figured at least he was going to have to pay me my due. So later that evening, when we were sitting in the living room watching TV, I asked how much he thought he was going to give me for child support.

"Nothing," he said coldly.

"Oh really? We will see about that." I smiled to myself, now realizing this would be the last time we would share the same space ever. He told me if I was leaving, I needed to pay my portion of the bills, just like that. I didn't respond to him. I wondered what I did to him to make him think he was a victim. I just couldn't understand it then, but I get it now. The mere thought of my leaving him again scared him shitless. The only time his life was good was when we were together. So, without me, he would be vulnerable, to figure it out by himself—not to mention unable to afford the place without me. His cold demeanor was all smoke and mirrors, and it didn't work this time because I was unfazed.

It was the first Saturday after New Year's. I had it planned. I didn't reveal to him I was leaving. I just waited for him to go to work. Then I called my cousin, Ronnie, who had a truck, to come down and help me move some of the big things. He was happy to do it, and he was on his way. He warned me not to touch anything until he got there, but by the time he pulled up, I had moved all of my things that would fit in my 1995 Honda Civic (on two inches of ice and a foot of snow), and I was just waiting on him. My cousin cursed me out for doing it, but the pain I had in my back was deafening. I was sorry for not waiting, even to this day. I left R. Kelly's "When a Woman's Fed Up" playing on repeat, and we were out.

Point—This relationship was a wrap. Done. Done. Put a fork in his ass. OVER! Yo! He pulled a gun out on me. No, he didn't point it at me. So what? No matter! Done! It was time for the exit plan. It's amazing how your mind protects you. I wasn't even afraid because I never believed he was going to shoot me. NBC Dateline is full of people who thought the same thing. Ladybugs, when anyone introduces a gun or physical violence, it's time to go—get your hat. Get your coat. LEAVE!

Jewel 15: Show yourself some grace.
As I was driving to my mother's house, who cheerfully said I could come home, I reflected on how in the hell I let it come to all this. I had no one to blame but my damn self. I was ashamed and defeated. I did this to myself. This time, I didn't get the "I told you so" speech. She hugged me for a long time, and I broke down in her arms. We shared a moment. I felt relieved, and it actually felt

good to be back home with my family who loved me. He didn't bother to call me for two weeks. When he finally called, it was about the debt I left him in, asking if I was going to pay anything. Now that was funny. He had no conversation about what he was going to do about his support for our child, how I was feeling, or how the baby inside me was doing. The conversation was brief, ending with my hanging up on him. Later, when I went to the hospital, he came for the birth of our child. I don't know how he knew about it because I didn't call him. I'm guessing my mother called and told him. He actually stayed with me that night and slept in the hospital chair. He signed the birth certificate. We were cordial toward each other. Our two-month-early preemie baby had to stay in the hospital for two weeks. He conveniently showed up when I wasn't there, which was rare because I was breastfeeding her via the pump at the hospital.

He became very different—ignorant, and cold on purpose. I came to find out he actually thought the baby wasn't his. Even today, I can't help but laugh out loud at this one. He told his circle it was Dimiel's. I never cheated on him, especially not with Dimiel. He wouldn't come to see his child once I brought her home from the hospital to my mother's house, even if I wasn't there. It was because I had filed for child support while I was still pregnant. I had gotten myself a good lawyer. I paid one thousand dollars, and we had him served at his job. He was livid. Can you believe it? He had the audacity to cry victim. When we went to court for the child support hearing, he never looked at me. He said I filed because I was a woman scorned. But he NEVER mentioned that he wanted a blood test, which was his right if he thought the baby wasn't his. It would have been court-ordered. He knew better. He just wanted to have a reason for being indifferent with his circle.

Imagine that! He said I was a woman scorned—he stated that in court! It had nothing to do with the fact that we created a child together. She may need to eat, poop, need a place to stay, or wear clothes. It was always about him—never about her.

I suffered from a severe case of low self-esteem. The forgiveness I really needed was for me to forgive myself. It was time to stop blaming myself and look forward. I had bigger and better things to focus on. I am very passionate about this topic. I have had a lot of time to reexamine this from every angle. Now, when I meet young women approaching the wrong conclusion to a bad situation, I feel compelled to scream, "Wake up!" I have seen how it's going to turn out. If I can save someone from a moment heartache, I'm there.

"The lips that kissed my thighs, lips that told me lies, both were on the same damn guy." I wrote that.

Point—It hit me like a ton of bricks—that man was nothing but a simple-minded, self-absorbed narcissist. Why did it take an eternity for the scales to fall from my eyes? I kept trying to lift him up to my level, to see him as my equal, not wanting to judge him by where he started. But truth be told, he was never my kind of people, never my equal. Just a sad, womanizing con artist surrounded by a choir of "yes men," tossing aside anyone who dared to challenge him. Does this ring any bells? After he wrecked what we had, he tried to replicate our shared success with a parade of others. But it was a no-go; they weren't me. The blessings I brought into our life were mine alone. And isn't it just poetic justice that he never found that same success again without me by his side? I don't mean to toot my own horn, but it reminds me of that line from *The Color Purple*: "Nothing you do will be successful until you do right by your children." I've tweaked it a bit, but the essence is the same. Forgiveness was my mountain to climb, my lesson to learn. To truly break free from his mental hold, I had to forgive him. Otherwise, he'd keep a piece of my soul locked away. I had to not only forgive but also wish him well and send up prayers for him. That's when I could claim my victory. The value of my self-worth, that's the gem I unearthed from the rubble. It's the lesson that's etched deep in my heart, the one that's shaped the woman I am today. I hope reading this will help anyone on the fence to decide to choose YOU! You are worth better. Love you more! Trust your inner voice. Lastly, and most importantly, trust God!

Whew, that was a lot! How did you do? Were you more of a sipper or a drinker? I was a gulper, and it's *my* story. Now, I've turned this mess into a message. I hope you're still with me. Stay tuned as we dive deeper into my journey together! The next chapter is the main reason for my move to Washington, DC. It will move the story forward, but first, I take a dive into my past to explore my feelings about my mother, growing up, as well as my thoughts about becoming a new mom. I enjoyed revisiting my childhood; it was hard to stop writing about my passion for nostalgia. It's written from my thirty-two-year-old perspective and a rewrite from my current viewpoint. First, take a look at my playlist; it includes some of my favorite oldies but goodies from 1994 to 1999.

Jewels Playlist
Scan the QR code to listen to the playlist.

If Your Girl Only Knew—Aaliyah
Softly, Softly—Sweetback
Femininity—Eric Bonet
Keep Tryin—Groove Theory
Count the Days—Prince
Slow Wine—TTT
No More Rain—A. Stone
You Make Me Wanna—Usher
50 Candles—BTM
Breakdown—MC
Stroke You U—Changing Faces
Pony—Ginuwine
My Body—LSG
Candy Rain—Soul 4 Real
Come Inside—Intro
This Lil Game We Play—Subway
Be Happy—MJB
Downtown—SWV
Don't Say Goodnight—The Isley Brothers
In My Bed—Dru Hill
Love Song—Glenn Jones
Freek'n You—Jodeci
Feenin—Jodeci

NoNDicCuaL

Ex-Factor—Lauryn Hill
No Guarantees—Joe and Chico DeBarge
Sumthin' Sumthin'—Maxwell
You Will Rise—Sweetback
Call Tyrone—EB
Breaking My Heart—Mint Condition
Brown Sugar—D'Angelo
When A Women's Fed Up—RK
Let's Get Down—TTT
No Scrubs—TLC
Honey—MC
I've Been Waiting—Glenn Jones
Whose Is It—Melvin Riley
The Sweetest Thing—Lauryn Hill
Can U Get With It—Usher
I Got a thang for ya—Lo Key
Nice and Slow—Usher
You're Always On my Mind—SWV
Like This and Like That—Monica
Last Two Dollars—JT
Don't Leave Me Girl—Blackstreet
You—Jesse Powell
Is It Over—Jesse Powell
T-shirt and Panties—Adina Howard
True to Myself—E. Benet
Virgin—Chico DeBarge
Hopeless—DF
Something In the Past—One Way
The Roof—MC

Creep-TLC
I've Been a Fool—Miles Jaye
Special Kind of Fool—Basic Black
Don't Be a Fool—Loose Ends
Don't Be Afraid—Aaron Hall

Albums

R Kelly—Twelve Play Album and the debut album
Jodeci—the first 3 albums
Mary J Blige—the first 3 albums
Maxwell—the first 2 albums
Erykah Badu—debut album
SWV—the first 3 albums
Brian McKnight—95 and 97 albums
Joe—the first 3 albums
Chico Debarge—the first two albums
Eric Benet—the first 2 albums
Glenn Jones—Here I Am album
Melvin Riley—debut solo album

Babyface—Never Keeping Secrets

A Mother's Love

(part I)

The most solitary and unconscious love relationship anyone can ever have in their lifetime is the love that exists between a mother and her children. It is the single foundation upon which a child emulates every other relationship after that initial dedication to unconditional love. This bond is the primary and unique emotional connection to love and, literally, the first deep, intimate experience a child has in their life. Mothers receive impervious, unconditional love from their children. Through the eyes of a child, there is no wrong way to assess the authenticity, suitability, or judgment of how their mother should raise or cherish them. It is a bond that remains forever significant, regardless of the circumstances. Children come into this world as uncontaminated, vacant slates, and a mother's responsibility is to show them how to analyze this world, as well as how to interpret love, humanity, and common sense. So deeply ingrained in their children's subconscious minds, mothers become the owners of the voice of reason. It is essential to reinforce the respectable attributes and distinctions connected to them. Be mindful of the most significant job you have as a mother because, ultimately, children grow up. The evidence of a solid foundation will be clear through their accomplishments, behavior, and choices... and yes, there will be a report card one day.

Woah... I'm good. Y'all might mess around and think I'm intelligent. (Insert laughter here.)

January 1999

So, I was back at home with Mom, but there was an uneasy feeling associated with that decision. I couldn't quite put my finger on it, so I ignored it and did it anyway. I didn't have a choice then. At seven months pregnant, I didn't have time for self-indulgent pride. It was a blessing that I could turn to my family. I returned to my old room, but Mom had turned it into a computer/TV room, removing all resemblance of me. My self-painted pink and mauve-colored walls, resembling a Pepto-Bismol bottle, were now a tedious, somber eggshell white. Cold laminate wood floors replaced my plush off-white carpet. Stripped clean were all hints of my personality in that room. Who was I to grumble? I hadn't lived in her house for eighteen months. What did I expect? My identity, as I had known it, was disappearing into oblivion at hyper-speed. There was nothing I could do about that, but try to accept it, and I think that's called the cost of growing up.

Mom was very nice to me when I moved back home. A little too nice, which made my antennas go up, predicting the other shoe to drop, fall off a cliff, and ignite the avalanche I knew would come! The only question was: when? She would bury me underneath fresh allegations of being unworthy, ungrateful, and accused of taking advantage of her loan shark kindness. In other words, it was too much like right for it to be truly genuine. I knew I was on borrowed time. I could feel the clock ticking just below the thin layer of niceties. Just like the crocodile who swallowed the clock in *Peter Pan*.

For now, I would try to enjoy her alleged earnest attempt at feeling excited about having her baby back home. Not to be obviously cynical, but I knew we would be back to fighting like we always did over inconsequential issues that only made sense to her: my selfish, non-empathic demeanor, and my narcissistic ways of being consumed with my own pending circumstances. Well, now that just would not cut it for her. Far be it for my nurturer to recognize things were going to be different. I was pregnant. I was going to have a baby of my own and I could not continue to give her all my attention, as I had done for most of my life. It was wishful thinking, but I was optimistic that my circumstances would soften her up a little. I was praying my stay would be brief. Little did I know I would get what I prayed for.

It was Super Bowl Sunday, January 31, 1999, and I wasn't in the mood to attend the party to which I had received an invite. It felt like my baby's head was right between my thighs. You know, the mucus plug—thick mucus that covers the opening of your cervix during pregnancy? Well, my girlfriend, Yolanda, told me about it during our many "having a baby" conversations. It happened! It showed up that Friday while I was out with Dimiel, sharing a Coke and conversation at a hole-in-the-wall off I-170 and Natural Bridge. I discovered it on one of my frequent trips to pee. I didn't give it much thought. However, on that Super Bowl Sunday, I was lying on the couch, watching the game when my pager went off, and it was him—the sperm donor, or at least that's what I thought. The phone number on the pager was the old number for the apartment we once shared. I returned the call. The girl—his side chick—answered the phone. I was so shocked that I hung up. I couldn't believe it, so I checked the number, hoping I had dialed the wrong number, but I hadn't. I didn't bother to call back. I had only been gone two-and-a-half weeks, and he had already moved her in. I cried myself to sleep, praying and telling God I couldn't take it anymore; I was tired of being pregnant, tired of my heart aching, and all the stress I was under.

At six o'clock Monday morning, my alarm clock went off, and my water broke. The baby was coming eight weeks too early. I screamed for Mom and said to God, "No, not this early!" Mom and Grandma rushed me to the emergency room at St. John's Mercy Hospital. I was so scared and I kept asking myself, "What have I done? She is too early." The doctors tried to stop the labor. It worked for about fifteen hours. Everyone was around me early on. Once the excitement died down, everyone went home with promises of returning in the morning, and I was alone. Everybody had somewhere else to be. During this time, I reflected on my relationship with Mom, taking a trip down memory lane. Could I be good enough? Was this the part where I would understand Mom and what she went through to raise me? I reached one conclusion: she did the best she could with who she was.

I love Mom with every fiber of my being. She brought me into the world with the help of my granny and my nanny (great-grandmother). They raised me to be a respectable, responsible, productive, and independent young lady, but I have serious insecurity, self-esteem, and self-worth issues too. I come from a long line of beautiful, feminine, strong, sweet, independent, elegant, courageous, loving, humble, God-fearing angels. The true divas! I celebrate my feminine legacy and honor them with my existence and good work in the world. Hopefully, I will pass these jewels on to my precious daughter. This was my prayer.

I am a little angry about my childhood, though. Can I be a brat for a minute? I did not live like the characters portrayed on TV. Mom took me through so many life-altering changes and my father robbed me of my innocent thoughts. They didn't allow me to live in a child's place. Where is that place for a child anyway? My child's place was a bout of scary, twisted, violent memories and secrets. With each word I write, I think about what my family will think of me for bringing up old stuff, but I didn't get to choose my parents. I didn't have a say in my childhood. For that matter, they didn't choose me either, but damn, I'm grown now! I need to write it down so I don't have to carry it around with me anymore. Right here is where I will leave it. My physical wounds didn't exist long enough for some telling signs of what would become my emotional baggage.

I can hear the intro to The Emotions, "Best of My Love," in the background as I begin this story. Just like most daughters, Mom was my idol growing up. My earliest recollection of her was the infamous scent of Estee Lauder perfume, the smell of her white, full-length leather coat with silver snaps down the front, and Wrigley's Spearmint gum. She was always going somewhere, ping-ponging from her bedroom to the bathroom, getting her look for the evening just right. Then, she would whisk me off to my great-grandmother's for the evening. Sitting in a dimly lit room, watching *Bonanza*, *The Waltons*, *Gunsmoke*, *Barnaby Jones*, *Mannix*, *Columbo*, *Kojak*, *McCloud*, *The Rockford Files*, *Quincy*, and *Baretta*, just to name a few. Finally, the local news bored me to death. The room smelled of Half and Half pipe tobacco, kerosene from the space heater, and scratchy wool blankets. My great-grandparents' bathroom always smelled of Ivory soap and Efferdent or Listerine. Ah, the good ol' days. I must say it must have been great to have a built-in babysitter; my Nanny was the best. I called my great-grandmother Nanny because I couldn't pronounce Granny when I was young.

It brought me immense joy to see Mommy's face. She was the only one I wanted to see before I went to sleep and the first one I wanted to see in the morning when she woke me up. I wonder if my daughter feels the same way about me...

When I was young, I loved thumbing through her photo albums, and she had volumes and volumes. Now I know where I got my love for capturing moments in four-by-six photos. I loved stacking them up in chronological order and interpreting what was going on when they were taking the pictures. It would entertain me for hours. She loved taking pictures, and that was no secret. I studied every one of them, wondering if, when I grew up, I would even be half as beautiful as she was to me. Mom's face—and mostly her feet—appeared in *Seventeen* and *Ebony* ads for Baker's Shoes in the early seventies. I didn't understand what modeling was then; I guessed it had something to do with her face in square boxes on picture paper, sometimes nine, twelve, and twenty-four. The more pictures, the smaller the image. She would dress in beautiful clothes she didn't own because they still had the tags on them. As I got older, I learned the correct term—contact sheets. I often wonder why she quit. I remember asking, but I don't remember her exact words. Something about not being tall enough, but it never answered why she didn't pursue print work. The camera loved her face. I believe it had something to do with the whole casting couch stuff—something about an incident in Chicago. I don't remember the details. She really didn't talk about it; otherwise, I could regurgitate every detail. Mom was good to me when I was little.

She was a busybody who loved sports—volleyball, bike-riding, hiking, softball—and sometimes she took me with her. She had lots of girlfriends, was a real social butterfly, and was always going out to parties. When she would take the time to read me a bedtime story, she always did it with expression. Her voice sounded like an established actress reading lines from a script, making the story come to life. Funny, I always thought bedtime stories were supposed to make you sleepy, but I would be wide awake by "The end." I guess I enjoyed our time together so much I didn't want to go to sleep and didn't want it to end. When she would let me, I loved playing with her hair, which smelled of her favorite perfume. Her hair differed from mine. It naturally laid flat without using brushes and grease. It was incredibly soft, shiny, straight, and long, and always smelled good. I was happy being an only child. I had her love exclusively, and I couldn't imagine sharing her affection with another sibling—or a man, for that matter. Mom was my hero. She was a warrior, and she didn't take any shit from any man in her life, excluding both of our fathers—the first man she loved, her father, and my father, the first man she chose to love.

My first memory of Mom's fire was her defending herself at the hands of a man. When I was about two or three, Mom took me with her to her then-boyfriend James's apartment. He lived on the east side. I never liked him. There was something off about his aura. I guess kids know. Anyway, I heard them argue about something. I heard a scuffle, and then a fight ensued. He hit her in the eye. Mom lost it and hit him in the head with a cheap 1970s gold Buddha statue. She cracked open the back of his skull and broke the statue. She thought she had killed him. The song "Love Won't Let Me Wait" by Major Harris was playing on the radio. I thought the lady moaning in ecstasy was sad and crying, so I started crying too. It got quiet, so I went looking for Mom. I walked toward the living room to see what had happened. I felt a lot of fear as I got closer. That's when I saw the blood on the linoleum floor. The blood had soaked into the pattern. A wall separated the living room from the opening of the kitchen. Mom had told me to go back into the bedroom as she had him bent over the kitchen sink, washing the blood from his head. He survived, but the relationship ended. I never liked him anyway. Every time I hear "Love Won't Let Me Wait," I am reminded of that incident. What a memory for a kid!

Mom told me I was two years old the last time she left my father. Dad was Mr. Playa Playa. They were young when they got married. Mom was nineteen, and Dad was twenty-one. Dad got a job on the assembly line working for Chrysler. His big brother worked there and got him hired. Mom got a job as a doctor's assistant for Dr. Randolph at the Kings Highway Medical Building at the intersection of Kings Highway and Natural Bridge. Dad didn't have a clue how much of a good wife and mother to his child he had. He was sleeping with other broads he met at the lounge. He always chose trifling chicks who were one step up from hookers. One time, after Mom got the phone number changed for the third time, one of Dad's women showed up at the front door with a gun pointed at her. The woman was ordering Mom to leave "her man" alone. After Dad persuaded the woman to leave, with violent force, of course, an argument ensued between my parents. Dad put his hands on Mom. Once the smoke cleared and her eye was throbbing, she threatened that if he went to sleep, he would never wake up. Dad must have believed her because he stayed up all night. Little did he know, Mom had loaded the shotgun and placed it underneath the bed, waiting for him to fall asleep. When a woman's fed up, there ain't nothing you can do about it. The official story about why she left was to keep from killing him. The next day, while he was working at Chrysler, which used to be on the corner of Natural Bridge and Goodfellow, she packed all our belongings and we moved back home with her mother.

I loved living with my grandmother and Uncle Donnie. I enjoyed Saturday mornings, waking up early to watch cartoons while I ate cereal. The cereal was simple then. I loved Cheerios, Frosted Flakes, Sugar Smacks, and Corn Pops. I was a seventies baby, so the cartoons of that time were the bomb! Heck, they made movies out of most of them. *Scooby-Doo*, *Fat Albert*, *Speed Buggy*, and *Josie and the Pussycats* were my jams. I can't leave out *Super Friends*, *Dastardly & Muttley*, *Shazam*, and *Isis*. It was the only time I had control of the television. Cartoons were usually over by noon, and then I was off to whatever adventure I could dream up. Sometimes, I would watch some old movies on KPLR Channel 11. My favorites were Bing Crosby's and Bob Hope's "Road to…" series, "My Friend Erma" movies, films starring Doris Day, Gidget, Dean Martin, Jerry Lewis, Abbott and Costello, and the silly antics of The Three Stooges. It was a great time for watching TV, and I miss those days.

A Mother's Love (Part I)

Mom wasn't hurting for companionship, and she kept a gang of suitors. Once, she was even dating a prince. She bragged about the fur coat and diamond jewelry he had bought for her. He asked her to marry him, but he could have more than one wife, so she told him no. We stayed in our family home for five years until she met her second husband, Wayne, in 1977. He was a special education instructor by day and a deejay by night. He was slightly younger than Mom, but their birthdays were on the same day. Ummm... That should have been a sign. He was nice to me; sometimes he would take me to work with him. I would entertain the kids he taught. He had two little sisters around my age, so he made sure that they were around, and that made me happy. I was an only child, and it gave me someone to play with. He was always kind and soft-spoken. After they got married, we moved to the Central West End to Maryland Gardens apartments behind the St. Louis Cathedral (where Pope St. John visited in 1999). I had many loving memories of living there, such as going to the pool for the first time, having a bathroom of my own, and getting my hair corn-rolled for the first time by my Aunt Valerie, Uncle Donnie's wife. Uncle Donnie was my mother's younger brother. Man, I was—and still am—tender-headed, but I loved the way it felt afterward. I loved going trick-or-treating at the beautiful mansions across the street from the apartments. I cleaned up! I had candy for weeks. My mom was always having friends over to play games: Bid Whist, Backgammon, and Dominoes. Of course, I had to stay out of the way, so I was in my mom's room because she had a TV in her bedroom. I liked that part. As kids do, I found any excuse to leave the room and check out the grown-ups having fun.

I have fond memories of the things we did together while we were there, like the first time we made a cake. It was a simple Stir and Frost cake, but it was so good. We laughed, made a mess, and we would always fight over the last piece. I remember my Christmas that year. Mostly, I remember all of my presents. I got a real record player that closed up like a suitcase, a greatest R and B hits of 1978 record, an Easy-Bake Oven, Play-Doh Fuzzy Pumper Barber and Beauty Shop, Superstar Barbie, Fashion Photo Barbie, a Black Suntan Christie, a Black Tiffany Taylor doll, and a Black life-size baby doll almost as tall as me. They didn't work out—the adults, that is. They argued a lot, and the marriage ended before the first anniversary. We moved back to the family home on Page, which was literally down the street and around the corner. It was a bittersweet return, but it was home. The familiar creak of the floorboards, the smell of my grandmother's cooking traveling through the house, and the warmth of family made everything feel a little better.

Our lives changed soon after Mom successfully graduated from the training school in Bloomington, Illinois, to be a claims adjuster for a major insurance company. She landed her first well-paying job. Primarily held by white men, she was the first Black woman hired for this position in 1978 from the Midwest. So, in 1979, she left the nest again, but for the first time independently. We bounced from three different apartments. The first place was in Laclede Town. We had to move because a drug dealer had moved in next door, and the addicts were mistaking our apartment for his. The second place was a two-family flat on Ashland Avenue, and we stayed on the second floor. We spent Christmas of 1979 there. I got a thirteen-inch black-and-white

TV, an orange and white typewriter, a "Rapper's Delight" single, an *Off the Wall* album by Michael Jackson on vinyl, and Barbies. I knew I wanted to be an author even back then. We probably would have stayed there if the nosy landlord, Mrs. Roberts, who occupied the first floor of the two-family flat, hadn't been found snooping in our house while we were gone. She almost got two-pieced, but I guess Mom thought better of herself than to hit an old lady.

Our last place, just before the life-changing move, brought us to Overland, Missouri. We moved there right after school was let out for the summer. It was a first-floor, front-corner, two-bedroom, and one-bath apartment. It had windows in every room! As I think about it now, living on the first floor was the worst place security-wise for a single woman with a child to be—too many points of entry. Life was good there. Mom was thriving in her new position, but she faced a lot of harassment from the jealous men on the job. They would threaten and say inappropriate things to her. She started to fear for her safety, but she hung in there for a while.

We went shopping every payday. We would hit Northland and River Roads Shopping Center, or Ventures and JCPenney. I love shopping; it was one of my favorite things to do with her. I made some friends in the apartments. The one I remember the most was a girl named Lisa. She was a beautiful mixed girl, but that's not why I remember her. I remember her because I got my tonsils taken out that summer. She had hers removed before I did, and she gave me the 411 on what was going to happen from a child's point of view. It made me less nervous, and I was thankful for that. Eating ice cream and popsicles was a great idea until it wasn't. I wanted *real* food! The one positive outcome was that it helped me overcome my thumb-sucking habit. It hurt too much to suck my thumb while my throat was healing, so I had to give up my best friend.

It was the summer of 1980, My favorite past-time was roller skating, I would practice my made-up routines on the smooth flat sidewalk area in front of my apartment to Peaches and Herb's "Shake Your Groove Thing," and some of my other favorite disco tunes at the time. Sometimes I would be by myself and sometimes a friend would show up.

Since I was ten years old, I could stay at home by myself while Mom went to work. It was a great summer, and Mom and Dad were actually getting along. I spent a lot of time at Dad's house, hanging out with my cousins, along with going back and forth to Big Momma's house—my father's mother. There was nothing more fun than my family cookouts. Since I was an only child, it was nice to be around family, kids to play with, music always playing, good food and joyful laughter. There was a cookout every weekend at Big Momma's house, or so I thought because I wasn't actually there every weekend.

Up to this point, I attended the same school in the city close to my family home with my grandmother, Mom's mother. However, when we moved to Overland, it meant I would attend a new school. I didn't know at the time, but it would be the first of many new schools. It was exciting to start a new school. I got to ride the yellow bus. It was the first time for me; instead of walking to school like I had all the years before in the city. Before this, the only time I was on a yellow bus was on school field trips. I had become a latchkey kid—a child who is at home without adult supervision for some part of the day, especially after school, until my mom returned from work.

I liked my independence, but I missed coming home to Nanny, my great-grandmother, having a hot dog or my favorite peanut butter and jelly sandwich ready, and most of all, not being alone. The pressure of not losing the house key around my neck or missing the bus was on my mind every day. Mom threatened me daily along with, "You bet not go outside or let anyone in my house while I'm at work!" I wanted no part of Mom's belt.

My dad suggested I take band. He gave me the clarinet, an instrument he never returned to Sumner High School. He also borrowed a trumpet and a flute. Imagine a world where schools issued musical instruments. He was musically inclined. He loved to play "Feels So Good" by Chuck Mangione on his trumpet. Watching him play is one of my best memories. That thought leads me to another memory; the music store, McMurray's, was in Overland, practically around the corner from our apartments. It was where I bought my first reeds and pads for my clarinet. It was also my first time ever in a music store. I had never been so close to electric guitars, complete professional drum sets, and keyboards, except in church, but not close enough to touch. The instruments were all shiny and the store had that new smell. They sparkled under the lights, and the whole place smelled like new toys. I knew I'd be back one day because I was going to be a star that was my dream. The new school was okay, but I missed my old friends from Stevens. It was weird starting over. The Ritenour school district was predominantly white. This was the first time I had gone to school with white kids. I lived within the city limits of St. Louis, where it was predominantly black. The only experience

I had with white folks was on television. *The Brady Bunch* was my favorite show, which was shown in syndication on Channel 30. Back in the day, before cable, we only had VHF/UHF channels: Channel 2 (ABC), Channel 4 (CBS), Channel 5 (NBC), Channel 11 (KPLR), and Channel 30 (KDNL).

I signed up to be a safety patrol during my lunch period. I was so proud to wear the orange sash and silver metal badge at lunch. See, it worked out because I hadn't really made any new friends outside of the kids at the apartments and I didn't have any classes with them.

Whelp, in late October 1980, Mom got a brilliant idea. Let's move to Alaska! Yup, good ole gold rush mining, pipeline laying, cold as fuck Alaska! Mom had fallen in love with her then-boyfriend, Jacob. She quit her good-paying job, sold her paid-off car—a 1976 Ford Cougar—and packed us up to go to the coldest place in the nation. My family pleaded with her to leave me in Saint Louis until she got settled, which was code for "if it doesn't work out," but she wouldn't hear of it. Least of all, I didn't get a say. We were off on our new adventure. She had already made an earlier trip to Alaska, so on our ride from Anchorage airport to our new home, she was giving me a window tour, pointing out all the obvious things, like the mountains. They were hard to miss and natural damage like "the bowl" a huge crater left over from the 1964 earthquake. It was a 9.2-magnitude quake. I had never seen anything so enormous in my life. The mountains seemed to go on and on. It was cold, with snow on the ground. I mean, of course, it was—it was frickin' Alaska!

We finally made it to the house on Lionheart Drive, an L-shaped duplex. We lived on the shorter side of the building. It was wide, shotgun style, but new. There were picture windows in the living room and the eat-in area. There was a large fireplace in the center of the stone wall with a mantle the length of the wall. It smelled of hickory even when there wasn't a fire. The ledge at the bottom of the fireplace stuck out just far enough to be my stage for future pretend shows I would give to my audience of dolls.

My room also had a huge picture window and a nice-sized walk-in closet. My full-size bed frame was solid wood with an air mattress, which was cool. I had never slept on an air mattress before. I mean, minus the occasional bangs to my elbows and knees up against the solid wood frame, thanks to my wild child sleeping habits, I liked sleeping on it.

Our neighbors were a Black couple with two daughters: Sonya, who was a year younger than me, and her little sister, Nancy, who was three years younger. So there, in a neat little package, Mom thought she had worked out all the checked boxes, making the initial shock easier. It was quite an experience. I was one of three Black kids in my fifth-grade class. Jeff and Cornelius were the other two. Jeff favored a young Michael Jackson with his signature afro. We lived across the street from the school. If I had to say something nice about it, I lived in the most beautiful Grizzly Adams-type of place in the world, full of beautiful bike/hiking trails.

My elementary school, Wonder Park, was an ultramodern education. It exposed me to the first Apple computer, gymnastics, ice skating, instrumental music, reading books by Judy Blume and Beverly Cleary, and my new then-pastime of *Archie* comic books. This is where I developed my love for reading, the escape away from my troubled and confused existence. I joined the chess club, band, and gymnastics team at school. My first crush was a white boy named Cory. Among the new things I encountered were sled riding and ice skating. I won first-place track ribbons for the fifty and one-hundred-yard dash—my very first. Imagine that—a Black kid running track in frickin' Alaska.

There was a roller-skating rink I went to on the weekend with my friend, Tammy, who was in my class. It seemed like all roller-skating rinks looked the same, so I would pretend that it was Skate King, the popular skating rink at home in St. Louis. They mostly played white music, so I got exposed to Billy Joel's "It's Still Rock and Roll to Me," Queen's "Another One Bites the Dust," Pink Floyd's "Another Brick in the Wall," and Hall and Oates' "Kiss On My List." When I hear these oldies but goodies, I think of being trapped against my will in Alaska (insert laughter here). Anyway, Tammy wore these glasses with large lenses that made her eyes look huge, but when she took them off, she was a beautiful blond-haired, blue-eyed girl with a Black girl's butt. We never discussed race beyond the obvious. She was my friend, and I was hers. It was that simple. She introduced me to *Archie* comic books. Every time I'm in the grocery store and see one, I think fondly of Tammy.

The first time I learned about my puberty was when I got pulled to the side by a female teacher to let me know I needed to wear a training bra because my buds were noticeable. How embarrassing... Even now, when I think about it! I still remember the trip to JCPenney to get the training bras with Mom. It was white padded with a small pink rose in the center. It smelled clean, like a department store clean with a hint of fresh popcorn scent. Some department store clothes have a certain smell you can only get there. Some of you will know what I'm talking about.

A Mother's Love (Part I)

Mr. Muhar, my fifth-grade teacher, signed our class up to do a dance (the hustle/slide) to "Celebration" by Kool & the Gang and "Take Your Time (Do It Right)" by the S.O.S. Band for a school program. But I was the best dancer in the class, so I was front and center. I tried to make the best of it as only an eleven-year-old could. I was so homesick, and the feeling wouldn't go away. This was my first experience of what depression felt like. I found The O'Jays' greatest hits on a cassette tape in Jacob's collection. I played it every time I took a bath. It always took me home mentally. By the time "Family Reunion" was playing, I could smell the barbecue and hear Dad's family talking loudly with their joyful laughter. The music took me where I wanted to be, and that's when I realized just how important music was to me in my life. It would always connect me to whatever moment I wanted to relive. My personal happy time machine.

There was one incident that, to this day, I still feel was so unnecessary. So, look, I was getting my hair pressed out, and I made the statement, "Now my hair will be straight like the white girls at school."

Mom slapped me. "Don't ever let me hear you say that again!"

She offered no other explanation. It made no sense then, and it still doesn't! Getting slapped in the face for no good reason was hard to take. I get the sentiment behind it now, but to an eleven-year-old, it was just abuse. All I wanted to do was fit in, not become white. Mom would become notorious for jumping to the wrong conclusions. There were so many ways she could have handled it better, but I used to get my butt beat for trivial things all the time up to that point.

Okay, let's talk about something else, of course, there weren't any Black radio stations in Alaska, except on weekends. The DJ would start the segment with Tom Browne's "Thigh High." It was there I heard "Don't Stop the Music" by Yarbrough & Peoples for the first time. These songs remind me of Alaska. They played all the goodies of the time: Shalamar, The Whispers, Switch, Earth, Wind & Fire, Kool & the Gang—all the greats. I loved Saturdays because we could get *Soul Train* on the cable channel WGN in Chicago. Oh, yes, cable was a thing way back. I especially loved the Black commercials. Posner sponsored the show with the "Positively Beautiful" song by one of my favorite vocalists, Natalie Cole (RIH), and Carefree Curl, "Carefree, Carefree, Carefree, Carefree, Carefree Curl."

I was trying to adapt to the culture shock. No, I didn't live in an igloo, though I did take a ride on a dog sled. I went to school and came home in the dark during the coldest time of the year. I saw the northern lights ,called the Aurora Borealis, the equivalent of the Fourth of July, without the boom. Every kid owned a snow suit and winter moon boots. However, I actually wore shorts in June 1981. We fished in the Russian River, where I caught my very first fish. It was hooligan fish we caught with nets instead of fishing poles. Mom caught a huge three-foot-long female King Salmon, the largest catch of the day. I can still smell the OFF! (bug repellent). We had such a good time. I didn't feel a change coming. I guess I had tuned out the adult business.

Then there it was, all at once. The slap echoed throughout the house. It was so loud it sounded like a gunshot in my mind. Mom slapped Jacob during an argument. I didn't even hear them arguing, just the slap. I was practicing my clarinet in my room. Then I heard the front door slam. So, I came out of my room. Mom was sitting on the sofa, quietly crying and wiping away her tears. I sat down beside her, not really knowing what to do.

A Mother's Love (Part I)

She hugged me as she cried harder. I hated hearing her cry. I felt helpless. I didn't know how to fix it, so I gently patted her on the back. For whatever reason, she felt we needed to leave the house to get away from Jacob. I don't remember how we got there, but I do remember being in the neighborhood 7-Eleven around the corner from our house. It's where I bought my first Paper Mate Erase Mate and Trapper Keeper. I was so proud to have popular school supplies. Mom used the pay phone outside as I looked at the school supply's new inventory. I wondered who she was calling because we really didn't know anyone in Alaska. I now know she was talking to a representative of a women's shelter who picked us up at the 7-Eleven—a women's shelter for battered women.

    I was very confused because Mom was not a battered woman, and she was taking a bed from someone who was battered. She didn't explain to me why she felt we needed to be there, sleeping in a strange place with strangers. I felt the bottom drop out of my entire life. Everything that held my life together at that point was gone. I no longer felt secure with her because she couldn't keep me safe. I desperately wanted Dad or my grandmother to rescue me. I could not trust her with me, and I didn't know how to respect her decisions anymore. I didn't know how to articulate my feelings about being so alone.

    With all my might, I wanted to be back home in St. Louis, where I felt protected. I remember reading the book I brought, *Ramona the Brave* by Beverly Cleary, until I fell asleep in the bunk bed they provided for us. It was my first time sleeping in a bunk bed. It reminded me of *The Brady Bunch*. If it wasn't so sad, I might have liked sleeping in the bunk bed. Thank God we were only there one night. Jacob came and got us the next morning.

Mom had discovered he was fooling around at work. I guess he talked her into coming back home, but they didn't work it out, and just like that, we were on a plane back to St. Louis, Missouri. The day we left, it was seventy-five degrees in Anchorage, and I had on shorts—in Alaska!

I was so happy to be going home, my prayers were answered. I missed everybody and everything I knew. I tried not to show my excitement too much on our long trip back on the TWA flight because I knew Mom was nursing a heartache. She cried the whole trip back as she smoked a pack of cigarettes. In 1981, you could smoke on airplanes. I couldn't wait to get off that plane. America was not in a good place. We were in the middle of a recession, thanks to Reagan. "The Message" by Grandmaster Flash & The Furious Five said it best: "Don't push me, 'cause I'm close to the edge. I'm trying not to lose my head," echoed by the polarized unemployed and the poor in the nation. She couldn't get her old job back. She couldn't find a new job because of the recession. Good old Reaganomics was *damaging for the economy because, while it primarily enhanced growth and recovery, it eventually had more negative effects than positive* and mostly affected the Black community.

I wondered what our lives would have been like if we had never gone to Alaska. Wow, what a difference nine months made. It felt like an eternity, a prison sentence. Would she have been laid off anyway during the recession? Or would she have flourished right through it? Would we have eventually bought a home and had roots? Who would I be without Alaska? Because there would have never been what happened next. If I had the chance to choose whether we went to Alaska with all that I know, would I have chosen to stay in St. Louis back in 1980? Yes, without hesitation! But reality won. I was forced to leave my foundation, even though we needed our family. Who knows what difference it would have made if I were there in St. Louis? Unfortunately, I was robbed of that unknown experience.

The recession hit the Midwest twice as hard because it was the main source of the auto industry. My dad was a foreman at Chrysler, and they laid him off. His second wife, Gloria, had left him, and he was alone in his house. My dad had become a heavy drinker, so I didn't have a real coherent relationship with him before I left. He would talk crazy when he was drunk. One minute, he loved Mom; the next, he was bad-mouthing her because she took me away from him. I learned how to tune him out. He had spurts of sobriety, but he was mean when he wasn't drinking, so I didn't want to interact with him. That's the past, I remember, but I did want to see him when I got home. I mean, he was Dad, after all.

One of the first things I wanted to do was go over to Big Momma's house. She was the nucleus of the family where everyone gathered. My father's side of the family was loud, happy beer drinkers who loved to get together on the weekends. It was a big family—eleven living sisters and brothers and a lot of cousins. It felt so good to be in their presence again, but I still felt like an outsider because I wasn't around them all the time. I missed out on a lot of events. Big Momma always made sure to make me feel special because, openly, I was her favorite. There was a bit of jealousy among the cousins.

I was close to Mellie, my cousin, who is three years older, and our fathers were brothers. She lived on the same street as Dad. After her mom got remarried to Dad's neighbor, Mr. Irvin,

I stayed at her house in U City most of the summer. I kissed my first boy, Nigel Tutton. Well, it wasn't a real kiss. It was a peck on the lips. Nevertheless, the deed was done. I was officially a fast girl. I can still smell his curl activator, and I can even hear Stacy Lattisaw singing, "Love On a Two-Way Street." Mellie was like an older sister to me. I learned a lot of teenage girlie stuff from her. Her stepfather had two kids. We were all around the same age. Her house was *the* hangout spot in the neighborhood. I had so much fun hanging out with Mellie in U City that summer of 1981.

Mom wasn't able to find a job in St. Louis. I don't think she tried hard enough. She was talking to her cousin, Gilda, who lived in Texas, about how there were a lot of jobs there, so she took another chance—to move to Houston, Texas, right before my first day of sixth grade.

Mom left me with my grandparents for the school year while she got things set up in Houston. My grandmother was an operating room technician at Missouri Baptist Hospital. She was a hardworking, God-fearing woman who lived on the 1st level of the 2 family flat we owned. and kept a quiet, pristine household. My great-grandparents lived upstairs. During my time with her, I attended all church activities: Sunday school, youth choir, and Bible study. It would not have been so bad if she hadn't made all my dresses, cleaned Mom's old dresses complete with petticoats from the basement, and made me wear them to church. The children at church quietly made fun of me. I probably would have made fun of myself, too. I had two long pigtails and greasy bangs that she created by mixing Ultra Sheen hair grease with warm water, brushed through with a hard black and white bristle brush, and rolled up tight on a black foam roller. Set for ten minutes, and voilà! Instant damp, springy, shiny, curly, greasy bangs.

One of my fondest memories is of her buying me my first pair of pumps and stockings for Easter that year. I felt so grown-up wearing a half-slip with lace on the bottom. She bought me my first pair of kit pumps and skin-tone stockings at Bakers in Northwest Plaza. I loved going shopping with her. Man, she could *really* shop.

I started sixth grade at Stevens Middle School. I was still playing the clarinet; I joined the Girl Scouts, a dance troupe, and was a cheerleader for the basketball team. The school used to be kindergarten through eighth grade, where I had attended kindergarten to fourth grade, and it had converted over to a middle school, sixth to eighth grades, while I was in Alaska. I even had a little boyfriend named Djuan, who played the saxophone in the school band. He looked like a cute Herbie Hancock's little brother.

My grandmother and I grew close during this time. We played cards and board games. She taught me how to sew, tend to her garden, make peach fried pies, and ice cream, and she let me talk to boys on the phone. At twelve, I was at that awkward age where I still loved my Barbie dolls but knew I was getting too old to continue. So, I kept my doll-playing on the down-low. My ride-or-die since kindergarten, Rene, confessed she still played with hers, too. Whew, at least I wasn't the only one holding onto childhood a little longer.

When I got back from Alaska, Rene and I picked up right where we left off. We were on the phone constantly and practically lived at each other's houses. I missed her so much while I was away. We had been inseparable from kindergarten through the fourth grade, and she was my best friend. There's one story I always tell about us. Once, our classmate Stephanie decided to play 'mean girl' and told everyone not to play with Rene. Naturally, I wasn't having any of that nonsense and played with Rene anyway. Stephanie, in all her petty glory, told everyone not to play with me either. Rene was about to follow that ridiculous rule until I pointed out how stupid it was. Here I was, standing up for her, and she was about to leave me hanging! We laughed about that for years, but I never let her forget it. I've always hated bullies and cliques, and I wasn't about to start following the crowd. Even as a kid, I held my own.

Rene kept me updated on all our old classmates, and we were excited to be going to the same school for sixth grade, even though we didn't end up in the same class. The school year was full of activities for me. I joined the dance group; we performed in front of the school. I hadn't been on that stage since Miss Cooney's second-grade Spring Day performance, where we had to dance with the boys. I had to dance with Steven Green. Yuck!

Back to sixth grade, our dance group performed a dance to "Mama Used to Say" by Junior and "Let's Get Physical" by Olivia Newton-John. It was a big deal that I was in the Annie Malone Parade with my school. A bit of St. Louis history: the Annie Malone Parade has been a Black tradition since 1910, when the first May Day Parade was held. It is the second-largest Black parade in the country. I always wanted to be a part of it and finally got my chance. The path of the parade started at Kings Highway; it came straight down Page and turned left at Newstead, right before my block. My dad, grandmother, cousin Ronnie, Great Aunt Jerry, and Nanny and Hobo (great-grandparents) were there in the crowd. Mom missed it because she was in Houston. It was a big moment for me. I was so happy to be shaking my red and white pom-poms down my street, just like I had dreamed of when I was small.

    I couldn't wait to tell Mom all about it. I communicated a lot with Mom before she came back and got me. She would write me letters and call all the time, even though back in the day, it cost an arm and a leg to make long-distance phone calls. Mom got a job at the Houston Police Department, as a 911 emergency phone operator, was one of the test markets picked for the pilot program that kick-started the three-digit dialing that exists today. She had to learn how to speak Spanish. She was excited about that, too. Once school let out for the summer, Mom came back to get me to start this "brand-new life in Houston," quoting from a letter she wrote me. I had missed her. I was excited about being with her, even if it meant leaving St. Louis behind…again. I would miss my grandmothers, my friends, and the security of being around my family. I had a great year. Little did I know it would never be the same. If I had known that then, maybe I would have appreciated it more.

    That summer, before Mom came to pick me up, one incident happened that would change me forever. My neighbor, Mr. Larry, had moved next door where Ameena, my beloved childhood best friend, used to live. Every time I hear "Sukiyaki" by A Taste of Honey, Natalie Cole's first album, Donna Summer's hits, or Sister Sledge's number one song, "We Are Family," I am reminded of my time with her. The song that captures the time is "I Wish" by

Stevie Wonder. I think of my very first best friend, Ameena. She was the older sister I wished I had. Her younger sister, Khalilah, and I fought all the time. She changed my world into a happy place. Blowing bubbles, playing Double Dutch, rubber band rope, playing jacks, making pom-poms out of newspaper, and building a fort under the back porch. She always came up with fun stuff for us to do.

We lived on a busy city street with four lanes of traffic. Only the older kids could go to the corner store because they had to cross the street to get there. I had to place my order with my cousin, Ronnie, or Ameena. My favorite candy was Now and Later—watermelon, cherry, or apple flavor—sunflower seeds, penny candy, hot pickles, and a bag of Funyuns or BBQ potato chips. She was my play mama. Do you remember this? It may be just a St. Louis thing. There was a gang of us kids on the street. We played games like "That's My Car," "Rock Teacher," "Devil and the Pitchfork," "Ol' Stinky Momma," and "What Time is It, Ol' Witch?" Do you remember putting your foot in to decide who was "it?" You would start with "bubble gum, bubble gum in a dish" or "I had a booger that tastes like sugar." The last foot in would be "it." A very democratic thing to do. Maybe that was a St. Louis thing, too. We played board games like "Sorry," "Trouble," and "Twister." She read stories to us. I knew every nuance of her face; I loved her so hard.

I had the biggest crush on Ameena's dad. She was in my life from the age of three to ten. Her mom was a seamstress who made amazing Black Raggedy Ann and Andy stuffed cloth dolls. I loved them so much. She made them for me for my birthday one year. I loved the whole family. The moment their mobile home pulled out of the driveway, I felt a sense of loss like I had never felt before. I never quite got over it. Hell, I even missed ol' big-head Khalilah. I would have given anything to have them back. The street was never the same. It broke my heart when they moved away.

I hated the sicko who moved into their home and tried to devour such happy memories. He was always very nice to me. He said nothing out of line to me at first. That's why what he did was so shocking, because it came out of left field. He had a lot of kids and was always doing fun stuff with us. He had a young son, about three years old, who was so cute and looked just like him. As a matter of fact, all his children looked like him. The genes were strong on his side of the family. His wife looked very young to be with him, my grandmother would comment.

One day, he asked me to babysit for him. I was excited when my grandmom said I could, because I was so eager to go back inside that house. I hadn't been inside there for three years. I rang the doorbell. It was that kind of doorbell that you had to turn to the side for it to chime. I didn't wait long before he let me in. Surprisingly, everything was as I remembered. The white vinyl built-in couch was still there, and the wall of framed pictures with famous Black people, such as Malcolm X, Martin Luther King, Jr., and Charles Drew, a Black surgeon and researcher who organized America's first large-scale blood bank and trained a generation of Black physicians at Howard University. Drew was born in Washington, DC, on June 3, 1904. There were many others on the wall, but that one stuck out because he died not being able to use the invention that he created. On the opposite wall was a built-in wall unit with a TV.

As I took in the scene, my mind replayed some of the happy memories in that room with my beloved Ameena as he made small talk. I asked him what I needed to do for little Larry while he was gone. He didn't seem like he was leaving. He did something weird. He laid on the living room floor and asked me to get down on the floor with him and the baby. I thought it was a strange request, but I did it anyway. We played with little Larry for a while. Then, out of the blue, he asked me to get on top of him.

I asked him, "What did you say?" I was hoping his explanation would be something innocent. My mind was racing. At first, I didn't understand the meaning of his words, but I was feeling very uncomfortable. I said, "No." Then I told him I was leaving. I didn't wait for his answer and quickly headed for the front door and left. As I jogged back home, I felt safe after I closed my front door and locked it behind me. I wondered what I had said or done to make him think that what he was asking me to do was okay. I thought he was cute for a grown-up, but I never said or did anything to lead him on. I felt sick.

Later that day, when my grandmother and I were in the basement, hanging laundry, she asked me how the babysitting went. I got the courage to tell her what really happened.

It was shocking when she asked me, "What did you do?"
What did I do? I mumbled something under my breath.
She heard it. "What did you say?"
I didn't answer.
She asked me again more intensely, but I said, "Nothing."
She became aggressive. "What did you say?"
"Nothing," I repeated.

A Mother's Love (Part I)

She grabbed me and wrapped her hands around my throat. "What did you say?"

I couldn't speak with her hands around my neck. I was floundering in the white sheets hanging from the clotheslines. As I gasped for air, I put my hands over hers and tried to loosen her grip. She realized I couldn't breathe and released me. We argued about it—if you want to call it that. It was the first one ever, and I told her I was going to tell Mom. There was silence as I tried to get my breath. I held a grudge against her for a long time. That incident forever changed our relationship. I didn't share it with Mom until we were safe in Houston, and she called my grandmother and went off. I didn't feel good about that part, but Mom validated me. She gave me what I needed to put it behind me. I never thought about Mr. Larry again. I buried my feelings of being violated so I could keep my inner joy and continue to be a child.

It was a long eighteen-hour road trip to Houston in an old station wagon with no air conditioning that my grandfather it to my mother in his will, with only country music on the radio for ninety percent of the trip. If "Are we there yet?" were a person, this was it. I had asked that question a million times. Finally, we pulled up to the apartments. The two-bedroom we lived in at Gasmer Apartments, next to Westbury High School on the southwest side of Houston, was small. I had a bedroom and a vanity of my own in the Jack-and-Jill-style bathroom. So, I thought it was cool. Mom had partially furnished our apartment. I had a bed and dresser, and so did she. We had an ugly black pleather sleeper sofa with terrible spring support in the living room/dining room combo. Mom brought her record collection and a stereo system, which sat on a cheap white plastic stand—a put-it-together-yourself job. We didn't have a kitchen table yet. The TV rested on the floor, but it had cable, which was included in the rent. In that apartment, I became acquainted with Donnie 'Pretty Eyes' Simpson, who hosted *Video Soul* on BET. It was a two-hour video show that showcased music videos by Black artists.

I went to my first flea market. Mom was dying for wicker tables to go with the couch. The flea market sold wicker furniture and knock-off designer clothes. The eighties were the decade of excess for the ridiculously overpriced name-brand clothing. So, the flea market offered Jordache, Calvin Klein, Chic, and Sergio Valente jean knockoffs along with Polo and Izod shirts. I bought a few, and I was happy to have them as long as nobody ever found out where I got them. There were two pairs of shoes you had to have; a pair of loafers and white Keds, also known as "white girls."

Mom was determined to get a dining room set she saw at Target. So, on one of our Saturday adventures, we traveled over Loop 610, which looked more like a roller coaster than a highway because it was so high in the air and it scared me. I held my breath and prayed we didn't fall off in an accident driving next to eighteen-wheelers. We made it to Target to pick up the dining room table and chairs. It came in a big box, and we struggled to carry it up the stairs to our second-floor apartment. Mom and I spent a couple of hours putting the set together with the half-wit directions that came along with it. That was the first time she treated me like a person with an opinion, trusted, and not just a little kid. I was proud I had done most of the work on the dinette set. Even without instructions, I figured out all the parts that went together. I was proud of myself. I felt useful, and that made me feel worthy.

After everything had settled down, Mom talked me into going swimming at the pool in the apartments. A lot of kids my age lived in our complex, and I made friends fast. Tina, who was originally from London and had a Southern ethnic dialect, was the first friend I made. We met at the pool, and she introduced me to all the other kids in the complex. She had a crush on a Black boy who lived in our complex named Arthur. This was my first experience with diversity in its simplest form. We were inseparable. Mom invited her to come with us to Galveston Beach. It was the first time I had ever been on a beach or seen palm trees. Of course, it wasn't like in the movies—I didn't see any surfers, and the water wasn't blue. It was dirty gray, but it was fun, just the same.

By the end of the summer of 1982, I had befriended four more girls around my age: Patrice and Denise Johnson, implants from Chicago, and Mimi and Nyweli. Ironically, we were all attending the same school in the same grade. We all walked to school together and "Ain't Nobody" by Chaka Khan would pop on the radio at the same time every morning as I crawled out of bed, as the alarm clock rang out with the local radio station giving the station's call letters, just as the full melody began. "Majic 102!" the morning on-air personality would say. Back home, we had Majic 108. It was my first day at a new school—Johnston Middle School. Thrilled at the thought of entering middle school, I was twelve years old, almost a teenager, and boy-crazy. Mom drove me to school the first day in the busted-ass station wagon. I wanted her to drop me off at the corner, but she insisted on the front as the Brady Bunch station wagon sputtered and had the nerve to backfire as she drove off. I pretended it wasn't my car as I dashed away quickly to the school's front door. She picked me up, too. Oh, the horror!

I would nurse my first heartache, and his name was Blain Lea, the eighth grader. It started great; we talked on the phone every night. Prince's album *1999* had just come out. "International Lover" was our song. We were more like phone buddies than boyfriend and girlfriend. I was supposed to meet him by the bleachers for a kiss one morning, but I chickened out. He broke up with me. Such is life.

I kept busy being in the band, talking on the phone, and playing outside when I could because Mom worked from 1:00 p.m. to 10:00 p.m. When I was inside and not watching TV, I would often pull out Mom's records and sing along, pretending I was performing in front of a large audience. My dream was to become a singer worldwide like my idol, Stacy Lattisaw. My favorites from Mom's stash were The Emotions. She had all the great albums like Earth, Wind & Fire, Natalie Cole's "Inseparable," The Commodores, Al Jarreau's "Breakin' Away," and she had Luther Vandross, "Forever, For Always, For Love" on an 8-track.

Stalking my new crush, John Beal, from a safe distance in the hall way and lunch room, I was settling in nicely. I didn't miss home in Houston as much as I did in Alaska. It was nice to have friends that looked like me. I was playing my clarinet so well that I was in the second chair. I remember practicing "Freeze Frame" by the J. Geils Band and "We Got the Beat" by The Go-Go's in class. Rachel was the first chair, and we became friends quickly.

I was cool with the popular girls in seventh grade, as we had all our classes together. The girl's face that pops up in my mind is

A Mother's Love (Part I)

Shelley Roberson. She was pretty, with long hair that was always done as if she had just left the salon. It smelled of TCB oil sheen. I know that because I had the pleasure of sitting behind her in class. We had all our classes together except band. She wore reddish-purple lipstick, and eyeliner. She always wore designer clothes and expensive sneakers. She was a cheerleader and smart, with a bright smile, and she had the prettiest handwriting.

She was nice to me. She didn't treat me like I was invisible. She gave me a chance. I was always joking with her and her clan. I kept her laughing so she wouldn't notice my imperfections like the jeans I had sewn up myself to make skinny-leg jeans—they were in style in the eighties—the knock-off flea market Izod polos, or the hand-me-down loafers that were two sizes too big I got from my grandmother. She stood for all the things you wanted to be in middle and high school. I think that's why I still remember her. I admired her. She wasn't a mean girl; she didn't make fun of or talk down to folks who had less than her. It was refreshing.

I wasn't friends with the cool kids, but it wouldn't have been awkward if I sat with them. I just ate lunch with my friends: Patrice, Kysla, Carmen, and Rachel—no pressure there. I didn't have to be something I wasn't. I wished Mom had the money so I could have been a cheerleader, but it wasn't in the cards for me.

Johnston Middle School was pretty diverse. I also had a nice white friend in an English class named Michele. She had a haircut like Joan Jett—the "I Love Rock and Roll" and "Love Is a Battlefield" girl. It was nice to relate to different people.

Then there was Michelle, a pretend friend who was a foe. Your typical school bully. She didn't take your lunch, but she was always starting some mess. She looked like Evil-Lyn's offspring with a busted Jheri curl. I got on her radar because of the very brief relationship with Blain Lea, who was a football player and very popular. Texas was all about football. There were mini-stadiums all over the city, and most of the schools had decent football facilities on campus. Our middle school even had an Olympic-size pool. Anyway, I steered clear of bad Michelle. She made it hard because she was a busybody, always in other folks' business, and I had one class with her. She lived in the Piccadilly apartments across the street from mine, and sometimes she would walk to school with us, something I hated but tolerated.

There were several good-looking guys in our school: Blain Lea, Glenn Iris, and John Beal. Bad Michelle had a big crush on John Beal, but of course, he never gave her the time of day. That didn't stop her from being in his face every chance she got, though. I managed to stay off her shit list, as she would say.

My school picture was the worst. They made us take it after gym class. Who does that? The Houston humidity killed my first-ever permed hair, so I called myself adding a headband, thinking it would make it better. I was sadly mistaken. It was a gigantic failure, but I survived it. To this day, Mom blackmails me with that picture.

At the end of the year, we had a school dance in the lunchroom during the last two periods. What I remember most was all the kids going crazy when the deejay played "Atomic Dog" by George Clinton. They played DMSR (Dance, Music, Sex, Romance), "Little Red Corvette," "1999," and "777-9311" by Prince, "The Walk" by The Time, "Nasty Girls" by Vanity 6, "Popcorn Love", "Candy Girl" by New Edition, "I'm Just So Freaky" and "You and I" by O'Bryan. I was a dancing fool with my friends; I was making

A Mother's Love (Part I)

all my best impressions of the dances I saw on *Soul Train*. I must have been cute that day because I got to dance with John Beal! It made my day! I was looking forward to going back to Johnston for eighth grade, but it was not to be. We would move again.

We stayed in Houston for four of my formative years. We moved three times, and I went to four different schools around the areas of the city. 1983 was the starting year for fully integrated music, after the birth of MTV in 1981. Friday Night Videos premiered on NBC that summer of 1983. Most of my music idols were grown-ups, and the music I liked was race-free. I loved Janet Jackson as much as I loved Madonna, Cyndi Lauper, or Billy Idol, as much as Michael Jackson and Prince. Hall and Oates, Shalamar, Chicago, The Deele, Dreamboy, DeBarge, Go West—hell, even Van Halen and Billy Joel. We had options to explore our expression of music. Run-DMC made rap music popular first because of the MTV exposure. Kurtis Blow was out there doing his thing too, because they played his hits "The Breaks" and "Playing Basketball," during the basketball and football games. "The Message" by Grandmaster Flash & The Furious Five was also recognized before the debut of Run-DMC. I liked that you weren't limited to one single from an album. The radio deejays had the freedom to play any song they wished, and some of the songs would become local favorites. One song that comes to mind is Zapp's "Do You Really Want an Answer," but that's unheard of nowadays. Nowadays, radio DJs mostly play what's popular, so they don't get the chance to push unpromoted random singles from an album. Okay, enough of the music history lesson, back to the regularly scheduled program. The second move was to Hiram Clarke in the summer of 1983 on Grapevine Street off

White Heather. We left the apartments right after school ended for the summer. It was just when I was getting comfortable… nope, time to go; we moved again. My best friend, Patrice, we called her Tricey (tree-cee). She moved too. Her mom, who was a nurse, had bought a house in Brentwood—not far from where I moved, so that was the only bright spot.

So, let me start with this: I don't like to talk about Mom's personal business unless it intersects with mine. I don't know why we had to move. Mom was dating George. He was not cute in any shape, form, or fashion. He looked like a busted Bama version of Rollo from *Sanford and Son*, mini afro included. He was a small and skinny man, with yellow teeth, and his eyes stayed cherry red. He was a self-described entrepreneur; he had a cleaning/janitorial business with one employee—himself. He drove an old, rusting Datsun 260Z. I don't remember their courtship while we were at the apartment, if one existed. The next thing I knew, we were moving into his house.

The inside looked better than the outer appearance. It looked like it was well past a fresh paint job. It used to be white, and it looked like someone rubbed the paint off its edges on its brick and wood frame. The shrubs that lined the front underneath the windows on each side were badly in need of attention. The two-car garage door was off its hinges on one side, so it sunk in, leaving an annoying gap.

It was a three-bedroom, two-bath, single-family home, with a nice big backyard on a quiet street. I had a large bedroom with a huge closet and two big picture windows. This was the biggest space I had ever had. I had room to practice my made-up dance routines. I had a huge mirror that hung over my closet door where I could watch myself practice. I would play my records and sing into my hairbrush, pretending I was singing in front of an audience.

The layout of our house was an open floor plan. The front door opened into the living room, and straight ahead flowed to the dining area, leading out to a patio. The kitchen was to your right—a small galley with a bar paralleling the length of the appliances. It reminded me of a takeout counter more than a breakfast bar. The walls in the dining area had that awful brown wood paneling, and the kitchen had an awful *Brady Bunch* green flower-colored wallpaper with pea-green appliances. There was a washer and dryer in the garage. We never parked inside, but the space was open if we wanted to. No more going to the hot laundromat, spending half the day listening to Ms. Pacman's and Space Invaders' theme music over and over, over and over. It was the most miserable task ever, but it was over. There was a God!

The three bedrooms were on the left side of the house. When you entered the hallway and turned the corner from the living room, you would find the main bathroom on your left. Across the hall on the right was the third bedroom. My bedroom was next to the third bedroom on the right, directly across from Mom's room at the end of the hall on the left. She had a master bathroom in her room. All the bedrooms were carpeted. The rest of the house had linoleum floors.

This was the first time we had lived with a man since Jacob. The one positive thing I can say about George—well, I can say a few things. He wasn't a bad dude. He loved to cook; he was very good at it. He made the best barbecue ever, just the way I like it, well-seasoned and with no sauce—I model my own after his style to this day. He had a good heart. He wasn't a pervert, and he put up with Mom. I always thought he was kind of slow, but now that I'm an adult, I realize he was just high most of the time.

Mom enrolled me in Dick Dowling Middle School for eighth grade, which was a far, far cry from Johnston. It looked like it was well past its better days. The school was divided into three sections. Students had to walk outside to get to each of the buildings and they had shacks or temporaries, as they called them, but more like permanent ones because they had been there for a while. The one common thing was the popular girls dressed in designer clothes. Their hair was always done, and makeup was on their little eighth-grade faces. Once again, I was in starting-over mode. I made some new friends. I was in the band. There were a lot of cute boys at the school, so I was in heaven. It was a realistic feeling of being grounded, so I reveled in the idea of just being able to be a teenager.

I had to turn this into a 2-part chapter. This is a great place to pause. Everything changes after this point, including the music. So, part one playlist has all of my younger childhood songs and it includes some of my favorite disco tunes. Enjoy!

A Mother's Love Playlist (Part I)

Scan the QR code to listen to the playlist.

Love Light in Flight — Stevie Wonder
Give Me the Night — George Benson

A Mother's Love (Part I)

I Call Your Name — Switch
Back Down Memory Lane — Minnie Ripperton
I'll Be Around — The Spinners
Cry Together – The O'Jays
Don't Ask My Neighbors — The Emotions
Happy — Rick James
Feel the Fire — Peabo Bryson
Promise Me — Luther Vandross
Two Hearts — Stephanie Mills & Teddy Pendergrass
Back Together Again — Roberta Flack & Donny Hathaway
Love Come Down — Evelyn "Champagne" King
Can't Hide Love — Earth, Wind & Fire
Just to Be Close to You — The Commodores
I Don't Want to Be the Last — Shalamar
Free — Denise Williams
Me for You — The Emotions
I Can't Say No — Natalie Cole
Candy Girl — New Edition
You and I — O'Bryan
Atomic Dog — George Clinton
Send for Me — Atlantic Starr
I Like It — DeBarge
Ain't Nobody — Chaka Khan
777-9311 — The Time
If Only You Knew — Patti LaBelle
I've Loved You Somewhere Before — Stacy Lattisaw
Tell Me If You Still Care — The S.O.S. Band

NoNDicCuaL

Heartbreak Hotel — The Jacksons
Going to Have Funky Good Time – James Brown
A House Is Not a Home — LV
Lollipop Luv — BL
I Will Survive—Gloria Gaynor
Get Down Tonight—KC and the Sunshine Band
Never Can Say Goodbye—Gloria Gaylor
Boogie Oogie Oogie—A Taste of Honey
Rock Your Baby--George McCrae
Love Machine –The Miracles
Dancing Machine – The Jackson 5
Kung Fu Fighting – Carl Douglas
How Deep is Your Love – The Bee Gees
A'int Gone Bump No More –Joe Tex
Funky Town – Lipps Inc.
Get off -- Foxy
Last Dance—Donna Summers
Rock With You —Michael Jackson
Young Hearts Run Free—Candi Staton
Float On – The Floaters
Mary Jane – Rick James

Albums

Al Jarreau
George Benson
Earth, Wind & Fire

A Mother's Love (Part I)

Kool & the Gang
Emotions
Natalie Cole
Ohio Players
P-Funk
George Duke
Commodores
Luther Vandross
Shalamar
DeBarge
Switch
Cameo
The Dramatics
The Manhattans
The Stylistics
The Ojay's
The Spinners
GQ
Teena Marie
Teddy Pendergrass
Barry White
Curtis Mayfield
Isaac Hayes
Stevie Wonder
Chaka Khan
The Jones Girls

A Mother's Love

(part II)

Living in Hiram Clark in 1983 was the first time in a while we lived in a house that had a semblance of stability, so I would try to enjoy it.

My street was full of kids my age, some younger and some older. I met Michelle first. She lived next door to me; we were the same age, and she attended Dowling, so I had someone to walk to school with. Her mom would drop us off at school if we were ready to go when she was. "Sunshine" by the Clarke Sisters would play on the radio every morning on our way. Mom couldn't take me because she had to be at work early. Michelle introduced me to Cindy, who would become my new best friend.

Cindy lived across the street on the corner from me. We were the same age, but she was a whole one month and three days older than me. I always like to point that out, as if that makes a hill of beans of a difference. She knew the gossip about everyone in the neighborhood; it was a wealth of knowledge that was better than welcoming the neighborhood cookies and very helpful when it came to who to stay the hell away from. I could tell the adults in her life were a heavy influence on her. She was regurgitating what she heard secondhand. You could tell it wasn't in the jargon of what kids would say.

She was a talker! Just like me! She was different from all the other girls I had met before. She was so sweet, kind, inclusive, and smart. She knew answers to stuff I would never think of asking. She had the perfect Black girl shape: nice round booty, shapely legs, and a handful of boobs. She was the epitome of a Southern belle, such a well-mannered young lady. Don't get it twisted. She was a spitfire. She would give you the shirt off her back if you needed it but may choke you out with it if she thought you deserved it. She had braces and wore glasses just like me—the glasses part, not the braces. I inherited my grandfather's gap between my front teeth. I would have loved the braces to close the Grand Canyon between my front teeth, but of course, like most things, we couldn't afford it. We both were blind as bats (even though Cindy would correct me and say bats aren't blind) and silently protested against our own interests, meaning we only wore our glasses in school. Anyway, she loved Prince, and I loved Michael Jackson, and she was also just as boy-crazy as I was. She didn't go to school with me. She was bused to Lamar Middle School.

Her mother was a high school teacher, and her father was a chemical engineer for a major company. Her parents were recently divorced. Cindy's and my backgrounds couldn't have been more different. We both loved music—that was our first connection—among hundreds of like interests. We stuck to each other like glue. I started going to her church, New Faith Baptist, which was very close to Wieners (a clothing store), before they erected the new building right in front of the old one. I joined the church, the youth choir, and attended a youth Bible study with her. We were always together. We were on the phone or hanging outside at her house.

The Christmas of 1983 was coming. I had made a list of things I wanted; my mother was doing well at her job, so in my mind, I was going to get my heart's desire. I asked for a stereo system, which was a record player and a tape player with speakers. My list included The Deele, Shalamar, Dreamboy, Midnight Star, New Edition, and DeBarge records. I was so excited I couldn't wait for Christmas Day. Welp, I got the stereo, but Mom couldn't find all the records I wanted, so she bought Gladys Knight and the Pips and Lionel Richie. Go ahead and laugh. It's funny now, but it wasn't a total loss. I got New Edition, Midnight Star, and The Deele. Don't sleep. Gladys' song, "You're Number One (In My Book)" became one of my favorite jams. Cindy got the DeBarge and Shalamar albums, so I borrowed them so I could tape/dub them.

I want to note right here some very iconic, history-making things that happened while I was in this house. The beautiful Vanessa Williams won Miss America, becoming the first Black woman ever to do it. I remember arguing with Mom, saying I knew she was Black because I saw her knees; they were darker than those of the white contestants. We didn't have cable in this house, just rabbit ears, so we had terrible reception, but I could still see her knees, and I knew she was one of us. I was so proud. Michael Jackson, whom I was in love with, won eight Grammys that year in February 1984. It was his memorable moonwalking, glitter glove, and socks performance. I screamed my little thirteen-year-old head off as I watched him moonwalk across the stage and into my heart.

A Mother's Love (Part II)

Then came the devastating loss of Marvin Gaye on April Fool's Day that year. My friend Tricey called me and said those awful words, "Did you hear Marvin Gaye is dead?" I thought she was playing a trick on me because it was April Fool's, so I hung up on her. The radio was on, and the announcer repeated what she said. It hurt, and I couldn't figure out why. I mean, I didn't know him personally, but it still felt like he was a part of my family. His music was a part of my history. Just as one icon was gone, new ones were emerging. Madonna had hits like "Lucky Star" and "Holiday," and "Glamorous Life" by Sheila E, a Prince protégée, was also a summer jam. Run-DMC released their iconic first rap album, and Prince released "Purple Rain." One of my favorite summer jams of all time is "Hey DJ" by The World's Famous Supreme Team.

Cindy and I graduated from eighth grade in 1984. We were excited to go to high school in the fall and had the best summer together that year. *Purple Rain*, *Back to the Future*, and *Breakin'* were among many movies that came out. We saw all of them at the Shamrock movie theater. We talked our moms into letting us go to Astro World, an amusement park like Six Flags in the center of the city, to see The Deele (which was Babyface's group before he went solo), Zapp with Roger Troutman (RIP), and The Gap Band (long before Charlie Wilson went solo) in concert. Back then, it was less than twenty bucks to get in. We enjoyed all the groups' performances as we stood on a field of mud, thanks to Houston's summer rain that day. We both had mud up to our calves and we ruined our shoes. But we would do it all again because we were standing in the front row of the stage, screaming our heads off. We boasted that we had the best spot, we were not moving, not even to pee.

Then came the biggest party at the beginning of the summer at the Archery House in Hermann Park. Heck yeah, we were going! Cindy's mom drove us to the party in her old, but still regal rose-colored Cadillac. Her mom was fussing the whole way; it was her M.O. I tuned her out so I couldn't tell what the infraction was about this time. I pretended to listen to the gospel music. With my chin resting in my palm, I hummed along to the songs that played on the car radio as I gazed out of the window. She was constantly getting on Cindy about something; this time it was why she wasn't worthy of going to the party. She threatened to turn the car around because she hadn't cleaned the house to her standards. Man, we couldn't get there fast enough. She was barely driving the speed limit. She said she would come back to pick us up at midnight, and we had better be outside waiting for her, or else. We said, "Yes, ma'am," and jumped out of the car before she could start on another tangent.

After we paid to get in, we beelined to the restroom to put on makeup. Remember the days when you burned the tip of the eyeliner to make it soft? Yeah, we did that and added a coat of borrowed lipstick from my mother's stash. Anyway, when we came out, there was a commotion. A couple of guys were breakdancing on the dance floor as the crowd assembled around them. "Hobo Scratch" by McLaren and then "Hey DJ" by The World's Famous Supreme Team were blasting over the speakers of the hall.

The hall had a very tall, beautiful wooden architectural ceiling, like the kind you would see in a museum. There were a lot of strobe-colored lights dancing off the walls, the floor, and the ceiling. The ambiance was perfect for this dance. This was where I met my first love. He was one of the two breakdancing on the dance floor, looking like a cross between Shabba Doo RIP (from the *Breakin'* movies) and Howard Hewitt (the lead singer from Shalamar). I lost my little fourteen-year-old heart.

In the corner of the room, right below the stage, sat a piano with its matching bench. The DJ had set up on the stage, spinning tracks and getting the crowd moving. Cindy and I claimed it as we watched the kids dance and mingle. I had a great seat to watch him dance. Apparently, he saw me staring and smiling because he came over with his friend, and they introduced themselves: Francis, aka Fresh Fran, and Phillip. I don't remember much about our initial introduction, other than we all ended up sharing the piano bench and talking. Cindy and Phillip seemed to hit it off. Fran was very popular with the girls, as they continued to come by to say hi. I know why; he was so fine! That smile, his face, his eyes, his hair, those lips! I didn't let on that I had just died and gone to heaven in his hazel eyes. I acted as if it was no big deal. I was arrogant with my Aries spirit, thinking I was cute, too.

I was kind of tall at five-foot-six and super skinny. Mom called me "Boney," but I hated that term. My skin was kissed by the Houston sun, so I had a caramel complexion; thanks to the Texas humidity, my hair bore these black, shiny, springy curls with the help of Soft Sheen. My hair looked like I had a Jheri curl, minus the drippy mess. It was naturally curly. I had the nerve to still roll it up in sponge rollers for maximum curl, just like my grandmother taught me. I had my father's thick eyebrows, Mom's almond-shaped eyes, and the ugly gap between my front teeth, which I hated; but I gave myself an eight-plus on cuteness.

During our initial conversation, I found out Fran was two years older than me and lived in the Third Ward. I had never heard of that place, but now I know it was in the city limits of Houston, and I lived on the other side of town in Hiram Clarke. As young teenagers with no access to a car, it was going to be difficult for us to see each other.

Back to the party. The deejay played Cindy's and my favorite song, "30 Days" by Run-DMC. We started dancing in our seats and singing along, so they asked us to dance. What a coincidence; it was Fran's favorite song, too. The crowd went wild, rapping along to every word. We danced together to a few more fast songs: "Stick Em" by the Fat Boys, "Friends" by Whodini, and "Jam on It" by Newcleus.

Then a slow song came on. I started walking off the dance floor and back to the piano bench when Fran grabbed my hand and said, "Where are you going? Aren't you going to slow dance with me?"

"Of course, I thought you never ask," I said, my voice a cocktail of excitement and nerves. We danced to "Slow Jam" by Midnight Star. My stomach fluttered with wild butterflies, and I couldn't bring myself to meet his gaze. But he, ever so gently, coaxed my chin upward, and there I was—drowning in the cutest pair of eyes I'd ever seen. My cheeks, I know were beet red, and I prayed he didn't notice. His scent was a mix of fresh cologne and pure charm, wrapping around me as his arms secured my waist. I looped my arms around his neck, and just like that, we were floating. The lights spun a hypnotic web, and I could've sworn a smoke machine was adding to the illusion because we were dancing on cloud nine.

He whispered in my ear, "You are so pretty," and then he kissed my earlobe and stuck his tongue in my ear. It tickled me, so I laughed. He laughed too and said, "Why are you laughing? I'm trying to get my Mack on!"

"Oh, is that what that was?" I said sarcastically. "I'm sorry; I'm ticklish." I was genuinely apologizing while laughing. He was a great dancer all around. We were slow-dancing and singing all over the dance floor.

I felt like the belle of the ball, his choice; making me the envy of every eye in the room. We were lost in our own world until the clock caught my eye—12:03 a.m.! Panic hit me like a wave. I nudged Cindy, who was dancing beside me, and pointed at the clock. Our eyes locked in mutual alarm, and we bolted from the dance floor, leaving our dates confused without exchanging numbers. Glancing back, I mouthed a silent "Sorry," our Cinderella moment cut short by the stroke of midnight.

Why is it that when you are just getting into the party, you always have to leave? Curfews suck! We were jogging down the sidewalk. Cindy's mom had just gotten out of the car and closed the door, with big pink rollers in her hair, an orange terrycloth house robe, and fluffy red house slippers. She looked like life's greatest embarrassing moment. We met her on the curb before she could shame us. Tragedy averted.

Cindy and I were on a mission—Operation: Get Fran and Phillip's Digits. Cindy was the mastermind; the social butterfly with a phone book that could rival the white pages. She worked the phone like the teenager she was, and word on the street was our mystery boys might go to St. Mary's dance in the Third Ward that coming Friday. It was a long shot, and the Third Ward might as well have been in another time zone for us. But Cindy's network? It was vast. One of her friends was our inside girl, she was going and just like that, Fran's number was in our hands. I was shocked—it actually worked!

Come Saturday, I was rehearsing my script like I was up for an Oscar. The butterflies in my belly were doing the cha-cha as I dialed his number. Ring, ring, and then, "Hello?" An older voice, greeted me. It was showtime, and I was live on air. I choked back my fear and pushed out, "Hello, ma'am. May I speak to Fran?"

When she called him to the phone, he asked, "Who is it?" Then I was greeted with, "Why did you guys run out?" We laughed; I explained the curfew thing, and we talked like old friends. It amazed me that he remembered us and was so easygoing, as though we had already known each other forever. While we were on the phone, I was watching *Soul Train*, my Saturday ritual. Teena Marie was performing "Out on a Limb."

The summer of 1984 was all about those long calls that stretched into the night, turning me into his local long-distance love. I was smitten—head over heels, and every other cliché you can think of. If I wasn't burning up the line with Cindy, I was deep in conversation with him, sometimes all four of us tangled up in a three-way call that was the 1980s version of a group chat. He was my personal DJ, spinning tracks that would become the soundtrack to our summer romance. Run-DMC's beats were our backdrop, with "Wake Up" and "Sucker M.C.s," he was teaching me the ABCs of hip-hop. And Eddie Murphy? He had his first comedy album, and he played it while we were on the phone. His jokes had us rolling, bonding over belly laughs and punchlines. Fran was always mixing records, scratching on records like "Why

A Mother's Love (Part II)

Is it Fresh" and "What is a DJ if He Can't Scratch." In a time when every dude fancied himself a rapper, a DJ, or a breakdancer, he was no different—Bronx-born, with that New York swag, even out in Houston.

That summer, we were living in a bubble made of vinyl records and laughter, a world where the music never stopped, and neither did my heart. I had never met anyone who talked as much as I did or loved music as much as I did. The only time we didn't talk that summer was when he went back to New York, the Bronx, to visit family. Even then, he called me and even wrote me a letter with his school picture. He had the most beautiful handwriting for a guy. He sprayed the letter with Polo cologne, and I kept it under my pillow. I was in love!

With the ringing of the morning warning bell, summer officially ended, and there I was, stepping into the halls of James Madison High as a fresh-faced freshman. I had dreams of "FAME," about dancing on tables and life-changing episodes, but reality handed me a schedule and a locker combo. I felt like a fool for buying into TV magic, but hey, we live and learn. Despite the new school, I wasn't flying solo—I had my middle school crew in tow. And you'd best believe I was talking about my summer fling. Fran's picture? Only the VIPs got a peek. His letter? Shared with only a precious few. Just as I was finding my footing in this high school maze, the first big game was on the horizon: Madison vs. Yates. I was all in. The hype was real, the radio station pumping up the game, and that's when I heard "The Show" by Doug E. Fresh for the 1st time.

So, there we were, Cindy and I gearing up for the showdown of the year—Madison vs. Yates. And it wasn't just about football; it was about laying eyes on Fran since our summer romance. I was extra cute. Cindy's Aunt DeeDee, bless her, played chauffeur to my very first football game. Madison's band was cute, doing their thing, but Yates? Child, they came to slay! Dropping beats like "Five Minutes of Funk" and "Friends," they had the crowd losing their minds like they were giving away free money.

We found Aunt DeeDee a cozy spot in the stands, then Cindy and I set off on our mission. The stadium was packed tighter than a weave on prom night, but we had eyes like hawks. We spotted our summer flings by the snack bar, and my stomach was doing the wobble with nerves. They spotted us, and it was all smiles and hugs. They hooked us up with popcorn and cokes, and we spent the game chatting it up, walking around like we owned the place. We walked back to where his aunt was sitting in the bleachers, and he introduced me to her. She was a beautiful woman and looked exactly like he described her. We barely knew who won because we were walking and talking with Fran and Phillip the whole time. All the girls from my class saw me with him, so they knew I wasn't lying about him. I didn't care; I was happy to hold his hand and hear his voice in person, even if I acted otherwise. The game was over too soon, we gave our goodbye hugs and we both disappeared in the crowd to find our rides home.

Fall is my favorite season. It sweeps in crisp air, pumpkin spice, and that Texas high school football craze. Down here, football isn't just a game; it's a religion, and the high school stadiums? These "arenas" put some college fields to shame, and we're talking 1980s grandeur. The marching bands? Baby, they didn't just march; they strutted and brought the house down with every step and note. The choreography was off the chain, and the energy. It was electric, contagious, a live wire of school spirit. And there's me, wondering why my clarinet's gathering dust when I could've been out there, part of the band, the spectacle. I could've been making those halftime shows even more legendary. But hey, we all have our paths, and mine just took a detour.

The school year began with no hint of change, but a change was the one thing I could count on. Just when I was getting used to the walk home from Madison, Mom informed me we were moving again. This time, we were moving to the Third Ward—close to where Fran lived. I couldn't believe it! I couldn't wait to tell Fran. Then flash, the sadness hit me all at once: I wouldn't be close to my best friend anymore, simply running across the street to start our next adventure. But we vowed to continue to do what we do; we would just have to be more creative.

Before we moved in, Mom took me to our new home; she wanted to show me our new place. She couldn't stop talking about this barbecue spot that wasn't far from where we were moving to. Who did I see leaving out of the same place as we drove up? Fran! Bonus! I got to see him again, and Mom finally got to meet him. It was quick but memorable. I ran to him, gave him the biggest hug, then I introduced him to Mom. They exchanged greetings. It was the 1980s. He was actually walking with his huge ghetto blaster in one hand and carry-out barbecue in the other. After we said our goodbyes, we got settled back in the car. Mom made a remark about Fran.

She said, "Oh, yeah, he's cute, but he's gonna get fat." It came out of left field, just like most things with her. (Shaking my head.)

Anyway, we moved a mile away from him, and I would attend the same high school: Jack Yates. The night before I was to start my first day at the new school, reluctantly, Fran had something he needed to tell me. I had to force it out of him. Finally, he said it: he had a new girlfriend. He met her at a back-to-school party. He explained he didn't believe we could ever be a couple because of the distance. He was right. I lived in Hiram Clarke, and he was in the Third Ward. There wasn't any way for us teenagers to see each other, but now my move to the Third Ward complicated the situation. He still wanted to be my friend; his feelings were split. He insisted on talking to me every night before bed like we had been doing since we met. He promised to show me around school, eat lunch with me, introduce me to people, and walk me home. The insulting part was that he told his girlfriend I was his cousin. I was so devastated. I cried into my pillow all night. I was starting a new school with a broken heart.

After I got registered and Mom kissed me goodbye, whose face did I see as I left the administrative office? Fran! The butterflies in my stomach let me know they were still there. I couldn't say anything when I saw him, but he said, "Let me see your schedule." He then noticed my eyes were puffy from crying. He hugged me, grabbed my hand, and led me to my next class. I tried to protest, but he wouldn't hear it. He said he would wait for me after class because we had the same lunch. He kept all his promises; he never left me alone and actually tried to keep other guys from trying to talk to me. Imagine that? See, I don't think he remembered how cute I was. He had only seen my face twice: the night we met and the football game. There I was, throwing it in his face every single day. I can't say I really blamed him. I mean, it wasn't like we had a real in-person relationship. But it *was* a relationship with feelings. Our encounters were only phone calls. If I had never moved to the Third Ward, we would have probably naturally faded away anyway. I didn't get to nurse my heartache because we still talked every single night until my curfew. He was there every day to eat lunch with me. He introduced me to people. I almost forgot that there was a girlfriend until one day after school. He was carrying her books with his arm around her neck and walking her home. My heart was crushed, and I remembered my place.

In my neighborhood, two girls on my street went to Jack Yates. I walked to school with Tammi and Mary. Mary was older, and Tammi was in the same grade, but we didn't have any classes together. Tammi lived a few houses down from me, and Mary lived across the street. We didn't have any real connections other than walking to school, so there wasn't a friendship. The songs that commemorated this time were "Jungle Love" and "If the Kid Can't Make You Come" by The Time because they were blaring inside Mary's house every time Tammi and I rang the doorbell to have her walk to school with us.

The house we lived in was old, like back home. It was a block away from the historically Black affluent part of the Third Ward, and I lived on Rosedale St. The big house we lived in was chopped up into sections. We were on the second floor. After you climbed the stairs, you walked through the front door into tall ceilings, hardwood floors in the living room with floor-to-ceiling windows, and a faux fireplace. A French-style door was my bedroom door, leading to what should have been an enclosed porch, but it was my room.

My new bedroom was a far cry from the last two places. It was a porch with a lot of windows—six of them, three on each of the two walls—and the third wall was a sealed door that led to Mom's room. Mom covered the windows and French door with really nice bohemian wood shades, and I put my Michael

Jackson poster up to cover the door leading to her room. It was large enough for my full-sized bed, dresser, and two-tier entertainment stand. There was no closet, so I had to stick my shoes under my bed. It was not like I had a lot anyway. As always, I just went with the flow.

The next room off the living room was Mom's bedroom. You had to walk through her room to get to the kitchen and bathroom, which was the next room to the right. To the left was a butler's pantry in the hallway of the bathroom.. The kitchen was a huge space but void of cabinets except over the sink. The refrigerator was a few feet from the gas stove. It just looked like someone had arbitrarily placed them randomly, not uniformly side by side like you would normally see. It was in serious need of renovation.

There were windows in each corner and a breakfast bar. There was also space to fit a small washer and dryer that Mom bought with her JCPenney card. When the dryer was running, the house smelled like a laundromat; the aroma of Tide and Downy was everywhere. I still love that smell, even though my allergies didn't.

Mom and George had broken up, and the house went into foreclosure, so I guess that was the reason for our move. Also, Mom had a new male friend. He was very attractive; that was new for her. She really liked him; I could tell because she took lots of pictures of him. I was happy for her. She deserved to be happy. He looked like he was Puerto Rican and Black. Just fine! I was proud of Mom. He was a police officer; I believe he helped her find our new place. I remember he picked me up a couple of times from school; he had a cool red sports car—a 1984 Pontiac Fiero. It was very cool getting picked up in a shiny red sports car in front of my friends and, of course, saving me a walk.

Starting at a new school wasn't all gloomy. I made new friends and reconnected with some old ones from Johnston Middle School, like Kysla and Natalie. It turned out better than I had expected. There were a lot of cute guys at Yates, so I was in cute-boy heaven. There was a fall dance at the infamous St. Mary's, where I got Fran's number that started this relationship. Ironically, I lived two blocks from the church.

Fran asked me to go with him. He came over to my house to walk me to the dance. This was a big deal. I couldn't believe we were having a real date, and we would be seen together. I forgot for a moment that he had a girlfriend who was conveniently out of the picture that day. I don't remember the reason why; it didn't matter at the time.

He rang the doorbell, alerting the butterflies that started to dance inside me. Once I saw him standing in the doorway, they calmed down a little. Mom answered the door as I was coming down the stairs behind her. We greeted each other with a hug.

Mom said, "Bring my baby back the same way you got her."

He half-chuckled. "Yes, ma'am." We were off.

As we walked to the church, we bantered about our day. He was always animated and comical as he gave the details. I always loved the way he told a story. As we arrived at the church doors, there was a sign that read: THE DANCE IS CANCELED. It didn't give a reason why, but we decided to stay on the playground at the church for a while before going back home. This was where I had my first real kiss with tongue. Firecrackers and bombs bursting in the air happened. It gave me tingles all over my body. I don't even know if I had my eyes closed. I didn't know where to put my arms or hands. It was so unexpected because there was no warning or build-up as I had seen in the movies.

It was also the first time I ever experienced an erection. It was uncomfortable as it pressed up against me, so I backed up to see what it was. I thought it was a big wad of money in his pocket. He laughed at my naivety and the embarrassment on my red face. I pressed my fingers against it, trying to prove my point. Oh, what it was like to be young. So embarrassing! (Shaking my head.)

The incident didn't help us remain friends. He still had that damn girlfriend, but I knew he loved me, or at least that's how I felt, and he always said he did. It was a twisted situation. One time we argued about it. I hung up on him. He called me back, asking me to turn on the radio. He had dedicated a song on the radio to me: "I Promise I Do" by Dreamboy. He got back in my good graces with that one. So, the saga continued.

As I said, there were a lot of cute boys at Yates. Charles comes to mind. I don't remember how I met him; we didn't have classes together. But we did have the same lunch. He was so damn pretty he looked like El DeBarge spat him out. Instead of a tail in the back, he had one big curl. Then there was Fred, the baseball player who let me wear his letterman's jacket. But I didn't like either of them as much as I adored Fran. The rest of the year was good. Mom was thriving in her new job; she left the police department for a better opportunity. I got everything I asked for Christmas: clothes and shoes. I was so happy about what I got—especially the double belt, the black lace gloves like Madonna, and new jeans, shirts, and shoes.

Mom let me spend the weekend during the Christmas break with Cindy at her father's house. We had so much fun just being around each other like the old days. We went to the Galleria Mall and the movies.

A Mother's Love (Part II)

New Years Eve, Mom and I spent it at her cousin Gilda's house. She had lamb and ham for dinner. I had never had lamb before; it reminded me of the time I had moose steaks in Alaska. I didn't like that either. Gilda turned on HBO while we ate. This was when I was introduced to Ms. Whoopi Goldberg and her HBO one-woman show special, *Direct From Broadway*. I didn't get all of her jokes at my young age, but I fell in love with her that night. The thing that resonated with me was her skit about long luxurious hair as she put a white towel on her head, play-acting that it was her hair while pretending to be a child. I laughed until my stomach ached. I could relate to it because I had done the same thing as a small kid.

1985 slid in without issue. At the start of the year, Mom's boyfriend, Don, unexpectedly came through with Purple Rain tickets in January 1985—the best concert ever! I think he had to work at the event; that's how I got in. I didn't care. I was so happy I was finally getting to see my favorite artist, Prince, in person. I didn't even care that I had nosebleed seats. I didn't sit down anyway; I was too busy dancing the whole time. Did I mention it was the best concert ever? I can still see him singing "Purple Rain," swaying his arms back and forth to the music. I told Cindy all about my surprise tickets. She had tickets for the next night's show. I couldn't wait to hear about her experience.

The next day, I didn't hear from Cindy, but I didn't think anything of it. I figured she got back too late to call me. Out of nowhere, she showed up at my school, and she found me in the lunchroom. I was shocked to see her. I shared my lunch with her as she explained what had happened. It was a long story.

Here it is in a nutshell: Her mom put her out of the car after an argument, then pulled off and left her in the parking lot, intending to teach her a lesson, but she didn't come back. Cindy befriended some college girls from TSU at the 7-Eleven while she was desperately calling her mom on the pay phone, to no avail. They felt sympathetic to her predicament, took her back to their school, and let her spend the night in their dorm room at Texas Southern University. I lived a few blocks from the university. That morning, she walked to Yates, which was down the street.

I couldn't believe her mom did that to her; Cindy and I were both worried about what would happen next. I did my best to calm her down. I was happy to have my best friend with me, but not under these circumstances. Phillip hung out with her until the end of school, and then we all met up and walked back to my house. Of course, Mom was surprised to see Cindy. She explained her story to Mom. Mom called her mom, begging her not to beat the living crap out of her, and thank God it worked out. We drove her home. On the way, Mom gave Cindy a speech about how it was hard for single moms trying to raise girls alone. I'm sure that was cold comfort to someone who had been abandoned at night by her mom.

Speaking of moms acting poorly, the turn in my relationship with my mother happened during an incident at the Valentine's Day party I attended. It was back in Hiram Clarke, in my old neighborhood. Jackie was Cindy's friend, but we became friends too because her boyfriend, Frank, and Fran knew each other. Fran was supposed to come with Frank. Jackie's grandma had given her a birthday party at her house, and I was excited to see Cindy, but when I got there, she wasn't there. So, I walked across the street to Cindy's house to find out why she wasn't there. As it turns out, she was still being punished for the Purple Rain incident and couldn't go. Disappointed, I returned to the party. It was lame, except for Frank. I had someone to talk to about my favorite subject: Fran.

I remember going to the restroom and catching my face in the mirror; it was the first time I thought I was attractive to myself. So, what happened next was incredible. The party was over. I was supposed to get a ride home with Jackie's cousin or uncle. I don't remember who was driving. The car was very full, and I was told to get out. I didn't understand why, but I complied. Then two of Jackie's friends who were at the party started a fight with me. Jackie was nowhere to be found, oddly. I was fighting one of the girls—I was winning. Then the other girl jumped on my back and knocked me down. While I was down, one of the girls kicked me in the temple.

The next thing I knew, Frank was picking me up off the ground, telling me we had to run because the grandmother was going to get a gun. This didn't even seem real to me. I thought I was dreaming, but instant panic overwhelmed me. Frank and I started running. We ended up fleeing to the Stop and Go, where I used the phone to call Mom to come and get us. I had a few scratches; my temple was sore, but other than that, I was fine. Mom wanted me to press charges against the girls; I just wanted to forget it ever happened and for the nightmares to stop. Mom wasn't satisfied with my answer. Of course, she called Jackie's grandmother to find out what had happened. I'm not sure why she expected them to tell her the truth after she pulled a gun out. They told her I was drinking and flirting with Frank. Mom used what they told her to answer why I didn't want to press charges.

So, let's unpack this. First of all, Mom should *know* her only child. They were lying on me! I had never done a socially bad thing in my life! I didn't drink. I was *fourteen*! Where would I have gotten alcohol from, if not from that house? If I were drunk, why not call Mom? If I were flirting with Frank, I could see addressing that, but Jackie knew I was there because I thought Fran was coming. As a grown woman looking back, I can see how, from a distance, it could have appeared as flirting, especially when she had two trolls—her friends—putting that in her ear. Anyone who had spent half a second listening to our conversation would have known that I wouldn't shut up about Fran. I guess Frank didn't like Jackie as much as she liked him. But Jackie knew how crazy I was about Fran. I don't know why she would believe them. I did not have an interest in Frank, only our mutual connection to Fran. So, Mom took their word over mine and grounded me for three months. Not only did I get my ass kicked, but I was grounded for it. No talking on the phone or going anywhere for THREE MONTHS.

Mom wasn't satisfied with just punishing me. There was rage coming from somewhere. One day, I was taking a nap after school and she woke me up, whipping me with an extension cord because I hadn't taken the trash out yet. See, it was different this time. I refused to cry. I was tired of her cruelty and refused to shed one tear for her. Well, that just enraged her more, so she grabbed me by my throat and dragged me up the wall. My feet were dangling, and I saw my life flash before my eyes.

I guess she must have felt some kind of way about it. She left the house—whereabouts unknown. This was the second time. What was it with the women in my family choking me? There was a separate phone line that Mom didn't know about. I used it to call Fran. I was crying hysterically. He calmed me down. I told him I wanted to run away because I was tired of my mother's shit.

He offered a logical response. "Where are you going to go? What will you do for money?"

He talked to me until I calmed down. I had never had anyone care about me like that, validating my feelings and making me feel better about my circumstances. I will always be grateful to Fran for keeping me from making a bad decision.

I served every day of that three-month sentence. Mom didn't let me off for good behavior either. I used the time to write a fictional story about my friends and me meeting Michael Jackson and Prince. I called it "CanNatKeyCat". It was made up of the first three letters of my friends' and my names. I also wrote some raps, a few dozen songs, and a lot of poems. I recorded them on my tape recorder. I kept my mind busy. I actually enjoyed going to school during that time; it was my only source of communication and interaction for three months.

Finally, the summer came; I was off punishment, and Cindy could finally spend the weekend with me. I had entered a lip sync contest. It was a promo for the Video Jukebox Network "The Box"—a TV channel where viewers requested videos via telephone for a fee. I actually got a call back. They called me in to audition. I was so excited. I chose the song "Shame" by The Motels to be different, and it worked. The date of the audition just happened to be the weekend Cindy came. Cindy and I rode the downtown bus to the eighty-four-floor building to the Video Jukebox Network office. I thought this was my chance. They videotaped the auditions. I looked directly at the camera and gave it my all. The Box representatives were very impressed with my audition. They said I was a natural. I'm guessing they said that to everyone, but I thought I did great! Cindy said I was good. I was sure I was going to make it to the finals. On the way back, we stopped by Fran's house. The downtown bus rode right by his house, so we jumped off. It just so happened that Phillip was there, and they were breakdancing on the front balcony of his house with Run-DMC blaring, bouncing off the buildings. My butterflies were on full-time. Cindy and Phillip hadn't seen each other since the Prince incident. We separated into couples—Cindy and Phillip on the porch, and Fran and I stepped inside the doorway of his house. It was kissy-kissy time. His breath tasted like the Coca-Cola he was drinking, and he was trying to get me to come upstairs with him. Well, that wasn't happening—at least not that time. We didn't stay there long; I was nervous Mom would drive by and catch us, so we left and walked back to my house from Fran's. Cindy and I talked about what we did all the way home, like the giddy teenagers we were.

Remember the contest I auditioned for? Well, I won a spot as a finalist to perform at the Astrodome before the Astros baseball game. I lip-synced "Shame" by The Motels. I was so nervous, but I pushed through and gave it my all. It was the largest audience I had ever performed in front of. It must have been 8 to ten thousand folks in the stands. Can you imagine? I caught my face on the enormous jumbo screen. The crowd gave me a huge applause after my performance. I will never forget it. I won second place, and the girl who won first place lip-synced "Saving All My Love" by Whitney Houston. It was a really big deal for me. I am still proud of that moment; I promised myself; it was the first of many to come.

A Mother's Love (Part II)

I spent the summer riding my bike; I got it from our landlord for Christmas. He was such a nice person. He was in love with my mom, but like a sister, not romantically. Read between the lines there. Anyway, sometimes I rode bikes with my friend Vincent, who had graduated that year. He lived in one of the historical homes a block from me on Rosedale. He would come and get me to ride our bikes. One time, we rode to the McGregor Park neighborhood.

Another time, we stopped by his friend Kirk's house. He was so cute. He always had this mischievous grin on his face. We knocked on the door, but he wasn't home. So, then we stopped at Tyrone's house. I had a huge crush on him. I even took a picture with him in front of the Jack Yates lion cage. I still have that picture. He was so damn fine. He was there. I wished we had stayed longer, but he had to leave—something about his girlfriend.

I would sneak out and ride my bike over to Fran's house twice that summer. It was on my second visit to his bedroom that we made it to second base. We were listening to records, talking about nothing. I was sitting on the edge of his bed when he kissed me. He gently leaned me back on his bed as we continued to kiss. He raised my shirt over my chest, exposing my white bra. He pulled my bra up over my breasts, exposing them. He started to caress and kiss my erect nipples.

My mind was spinning. I wanted him to stop, but I couldn't say anything because I liked him, and I didn't want him to think that I didn't. So, I started crying out of nowhere. It was too much. I wanted him to stop because I couldn't handle it. I was having flashbacks of things that happened to me as a child that I wasn't really ready to deal with. Fran was confused.

Honestly, so was I. I didn't understand why I was feeling so dirty. I really liked him. But I couldn't stop the images of being violated from popping into my mind. I tried to explain it without going all in, and he picked up on that. Fran was always the perfect comforter. He put me back together, my bra and shirt back in place, and kissed me on my forehead. He held me until I calmed down.

So let me stop here and explain. I had the incident with Mr. Larry I told you about, but it wasn't my first encounter with being sexually assaulted. There was a time when I was younger, about four or five, when an older cousin sexually assaulted me while I was at Big Momma's house. He was sleeping next to me, along with other cousins. He put his hands in my underwear. I tried to pretend I was asleep. I tried to close my legs tighter to get his hand out. He tried to put his penis between my legs, but it was limp, so it didn't work. I tried to turn away from him, but he still tried to put it in my butt. I was so afraid, I wrapped myself in the covers like a mummy so he couldn't go any further. It worked, but I was never the same. The trauma is real to me, even today as I write these words. All of that rushed back to me at that moment with Fran. I was with someone I liked, but I couldn't get the nightmare of those events out of my head. I felt dirty, and I didn't want to be touched that way. Sex was filthy to me. The damage had been done, and I hadn't even lived my life. I thought, in my young mind, my broken thoughts, it was all I was good for—pleasing men. I don't like talking about this. Moving on…

Prince released the *Around the World in a Day* album in the summer of 1985. I had become a die-hard fan like Cindy. I had a lot of his music and analyzed all the words and innuendos. The Time, Vanity 6 (I didn't like the new girl), The Family, Sheila E,

Jesse Johnson, and Alexander O'Neal. The whole Purple Family intrigued me. "Screams of Passion" by The Family, "Erotic City," "17 Days" by Prince, and "Affection" by Tamara and the Seen were just some of the tunes that came out that year. I fell in love with some new groups; Lisa Lisa and Cult Jam's "I Wonder if I Take You Home" was *the* new summer jam. Ready for the World's "Oh Sheila," Cherrelle's "I Didn't Mean to Turn You On," Alexander O'Neal's "If You Were Here Tonight," Force MDs' "Tender Love," and Full Force's "Alice, I Want You Just for Me" were some of the hits on the radio.

All the new rap groups that ushered in the summer of 1985, like Whodini, Doug E. Fresh, UTFO, and Roxanne Shanté, were popping on the airwaves. I went to my first rap concert at Astro World. I was with Cindy. Of course, we met Fran and Phillip there. It was the 1985 Fresh Fest. We saw Kurtis Blow, Run-D.M.C., The Fat Boys, Whodini, Boogie Boys…classic! Not to mention, we also saw New Edition, who also performed at Astro World that summer. Epic! It was one of the best summers for Black music. As always, the summer ended, and it was back to the grind: school.

I started tenth grade at the same high school, Jack Yates. This is a feat worth mentioning because I had changed schools every year for the past five years. I signed up for drama class with Mrs. Sheldon. She also ran the debate club, and I joined. She was an amazing teacher. She taught us pronunciation and how to speak with diction.

I made two new friends at the beginning of the year. They were both juniors. Robin, whom I met in the drama class, lived on Rosedale, a couple of blocks from me. I finally had a real friend to walk to school with and chat about our personal soap operas. She lived with her aunt; she introduced me to a dish called gumbo during one of my many visits. Yum! They were originally from Lake Charles, Louisiana.

The second one was Ramonda, who took pictures for the school yearbook. She was a really good photographer. She also had a side gig taking pictures of the students for $1. I was originally friends with her sister, Amanda, who was in the same grade as me, too, and we had most of our classes together. I met Ramonda through her sister, and we became friends.

The school was having a talent show, so I created a dance group with Robin and Ramonda called Protégé. I made our costumes. We performed a dance to "Love Bizarre" by Sheila E. Ramonda, who favored Sheila E, had the same hairstyle, played the drums, and even tossed her drumsticks up and caught them in our performance, just like Sheila E did in the video. We stayed after school every day to practice until the day of the talent show. I loved staying after school and practicing on the stage because it reminded me of my favorite TV show, "FAME."

The night of the talent show, we were so nervous because there would be butts in the seats when we performed. We did an amazing job. We were awesome. When we heard our group called for first place, we lost our minds, and so did the audience. We won! I couldn't believe it. I guess I could because we had worked so hard to get it just right.

Hyped off the momentum of our very first win, we heard that Jones High School was having a talent show, so we entered it. It was Cindy's school, and I got to see my best friend. We won second place. The guys that won were a whole band, electric guitar included. They performed "Oh Sheila" by Ready for the World. They were good, and they deserved it.

I spent a lot of time after school practicing for the upcoming debate. Mrs. Sheldon took the debate team to other schools to debate and perform poems. I had to perform "And Still I Rise" and "Phenomenal Woman" by Dr. Maya Angelou, and I was so nervous. I had the words in front of me, and I still stumbled over a few words, but I won second place. Not bad for my first time, but I was still disappointed in myself for not winning first place. Our team won first place in all the other debates. Jack Yates was a force to be reckoned with.

Speaking of winning, there was the biggest Madison and Yates game of the year, which was a must-attend because it was for the state championship, and Yates won. I came to the game with Robin, but I ended up leaving with Fran to get a ride home, because I couldn't find her when the game was over. He offered to take me home. His aunt drove us. He jumped into the backseat with me. We held hands the whole trip home. He whispered in my ear, "I still love you," and kissed my earlobe just like he did the first time we met at the Archery House. The butterflies were still there for him. Rene and Angela's "You Don't Have to Cry" was playing on the radio. Of course, whenever I hear it, I think of that sweet moment I never wanted to end. It would be the last time we were ever that close. He was still with his girlfriend.

I was breaking free from the emotional hold Fran had on me. I started genuinely liking other guys, my interests shifted, and I had new things to focus on. This brings me to Natalie Johnson. I knew her from Johnston Middle School. Now we were at Yates, and we had a class together. Our friendship became tighter because she stayed after school, too. She was in the choir, and played the piano for them. We talked on the phone all the time. She wore all the latest fashions, she even had the Michael

Jackson "Beat It" jacket, Madonna's black lace glove, belt, and studded boots. She looked like an implant from Hollywood with the clothes she wore. She was a preacher's daughter, where she learned how to play the piano and the organ. She stayed in a beautiful home in the McGregor Park neighborhood.

Mom let me spend the night at her house one time. I remember going to the Galleria Mall with her that weekend. She wanted to buy me stuff, but I turned her down gently. I liked her for her; she didn't need to buy my friendship. I loved hanging out with her. I wished I could have done it more. We wrote two songs and recorded them on a little tape player, and I got a copy.

All the things I was involved in, I was oblivious to what was going on with Mom for a change. She got a new job, but it was short-lived. She tried to go back to the Houston Police Department, but they weren't hiring for her old job at the time. We weren't eligible for unemployment, so we had to rely on my grandmother for help.

I didn't realize how really broke we were. I mean, eating beans and rice with sausage every single day wasn't a sign to me. I finally got that it was serious when Mom sent me to the grocery store to buy a loaf of bread with a food stamp. FOOD STAMP! *That's for poor people!* I thought. I pleaded with Mom, with tears in my eyes, to find a real dollar, four quarters, ten dimes, twenty nickels, or any combination, but please don't make me go to the store with that. She found a "real" dollar. I exhaled. Humiliation avoided.

The two block walk to the grocery store was always pleasant. Two vintage 1968 convertible Mustangs sat in the driveway at the corner of Rosedale Street and Live Oak. I always passed them on my way. One day, I will buy myself one, I thought.

A Mother's Love (Part II)

The Christmas of 1985 was the sweetest, and the most broke we had ever been. Utilizing the money our family sent, we got each other one gift we really wanted. Mom got me Lee Press On Nails, and I got Mom Luther Vandross' *The Night I Fell In Love* album. Under our pitiful Charlie Brown Christmas tree, we couldn't wait until morning, so we opened our gifts at midnight, and we created a tradition from that Christmas until the present.

A new year—1986—and I was dealt another blow. Mom still could not find another job. We were out of money and my grandmother finally convinced her to move back home. I had no desire to go back to St. Louis. I wasn't ready for this change. I knew Mom didn't want to go back defeated again either, but we had no choice. I had grown tired of packing, moving, changing, and uprooting. I loved the little teenage existence I had created in Texas; I was finally settling into my identity. It would be a bittersweet homecoming.

My established life, my sense of stability, and all my friends—reluctantly, I had to leave it all behind. The day I left, Cindy gave me a teddy bear. Fran gave me his chain with the F charm, and I hugged them both so tight, not wanting to let either of them go. This scene reminded me of *The Wizard of Oz*. I cried all the way back to St. Louis—the entire eighteen hours! I think the teddy bear had a big, round, permanent tear stain by the time we made it back to St. Louis. I played "Tender Love" on my tape player all the way home. I was once again shuffled back into obscurity and the unknown. It was like moving to a new place I had never been. I had amnesia because I couldn't remember anything of substance, just buildings, faces, and the feelings of déjà vu. Starting over hurts.

Back to February 1, 1999

My labor pains had become overwhelming, even with my high threshold for pain. I hit the nurse button for the fourth and final time to tell her I needed to push. I felt like I needed to go potty really badly. The nurse attempted to use the crank (that's what I call it). I quickly put my hands between my legs and told her the baby's head was right there. She listened to me, did a physical exam, and informed me I was fully dilated. That's when she called my doctor, who had just delivered his third baby that night and was on his way home, to return to the delivery room. By the time they finally administered the good drugs, my doctor was there, and so was the sperm donor. He made it just in time to hold my hand and to watch his baby girl make her debut in the world. It only took three pushes, and my baby diva was born.

Alexa was born on February 2, 1999, Groundhog Day. It took a minute before they held her up to show her to me. She should have been crying, as I'd seen in the movies, but that wasn't happening. It seemed like forever. Finally, the doctor announced, "Here is your baby girl." She still hadn't made a sound when they handed her to the nurse, who took her to the warming station. Once there, she took one look at me and screamed. I laughed, cried, and finally exhaled a sigh of relief. She was four pounds, four ounces, and eighteen inches long. The reason it took them so long to hold her up was that the umbilical cord was wrapped around her neck four times. They were concerned she may have been deprived of oxygen, but by the grace and mercy of God, the only thing wrong with her was that she was early. She was fully developed and entered the world with a full head of hair. She didn't have any booty cheeks. She had to remain in the hospital until she met certain conditions: she could maintain her body temperature, suckle, and breathe on her own. In 1999, it was no longer a condition for preemies to gain weight. The order of preemie survival is Black female, white female, Black male, and white male. She remained in the hospital for two weeks. They released me from the hospital on a Friday, and I went back to work that following Monday. I know what you are thinking, but I had to. I had just started a new job as a circuit designer for a long-distance company, and I was not yet eligible for maternity leave. They were kind enough to give me a week of vacation early, and I needed the money. I don't have to tell you that the sperm donor acted as if it were someone else's responsibility to take care of his baby.

I decided to breastfeed. Okay, it was more like the hospital coerced me into it—emotional blackmail! So, I went back and forth to the hospital three to four times a day for those two weeks. I never even got a chance to have a baby shower, so my co-workers surprised me with more gifts than I deserved. It wasn't for me now, was it? I became humble, so appreciative of the kindness of others—more than I had ever been in my life—and I did a lot of crying. Mom had purchased two packs of no-name baby wipes from a dollar store. In her defense, the baby was two months early, so maybe she didn't have time to buy her only grandchild anything at that point.

Mom was going through something. I guess it was because she couldn't accept being a grandmother, so she didn't participate in helping me early on. I don't know the right answer, but she didn't make any bottles, change any diapers, or barely hold the baby. If I asked her to watch her while I went to the store for diapers or milk, she would call me on the phone, claiming I was taking too long—I must have made other stops. I wasn't adjusting very well to crazy baby hours. I was feeling the baby blues at those 2:00 a.m. feedings. When she woke up crying, hell, I cried right back! I was blessed that my grandmother watched her while I went to work. I loved my grandmother for it; she was excellent with my angel. I could not have supported her the way she did.

Well, the shit hit the fan later, just as I suspected—the niceness had run its course. It was a petty argument about the gas bill, giving her a perm, and baby bottles left on the counter in the bathroom that escalated to blows. Please understand that I would never hit Mom, but I had to keep her from attacking me. Here's what happened: I had just put my baby to bed. Do you know how precious the moments are when your baby finally goes to sleep?

Mom had gone out that night to a party with the girls. She returned around one in the morning. I had just put the baby to sleep, finally! Mom came into my bedroom, where I was getting ready to sleep. She wanted to talk. I could tell she was tipsy because her tone was amped up. So, I asked that we take it to another room because I didn't want us to wake the baby. She said she didn't give a damn about that; this was her house, and she could talk in any room she wanted. I asked her to lower her voice before she woke the baby. Needless to say, trying to reason with a person, when they've had too much to drink was pointless. So, I ushered her out of the room, closed the door behind me, and, I will admit, I was pissed off that I had to do it that way.

I don't remember the word-for-word, blow-by-blow account of what happened, but it went something like this: I don't remember what made her charge at me, but when she connected her blow, like a female, she grabbed my hair. I grabbed her wrists to keep her from hitting me again. We scuffled from the hallway into the bathroom across from the bedroom. I just wanted her to let go of my hair. I was five-foot-six, one hundred eighty pounds, and Mom was five-foot-four, only weighing a buck-o-five dripping wet, if that. I forced her to the ground—more like I fell to the ground on top of her. I aimed her away from the tub so she wouldn't hit her head on the way down. I guess she felt vulnerable at that moment. I had fallen on top of her. That's when she dealt the blow to my heart. She said that I deserved to be molested as a child. I must have liked it because I never told her, and that I was a whore, a slut. I always wanted every man she ever had, including my father. I had always been jealous of her. I always used her, and she hated me.

 Her words hit me harder than any physical blow I had ever experienced in my life. It felt like what I would imagine stab wounds would feel like. I could have never imagined that Mom thought that way about me. It was like a dream—a terrible nightmare. I got off her and threw myself against the wall in the hall, collapsing in pain. Her words rang in my ears so stridently that I didn't hear my baby screaming in fear. Mom passed me in the hall and opened the door to the bedroom where my baby was screaming in her bed.

 My motherly instinct kicked in, and I jetted behind her just as she was picking up my infant. I screamed at her, "Don't you touch my baby, you bitch!"

 I grabbed my baby from her arms. I couldn't believe that word escaped from my lips. I never thought of Mom that way. I was sorry as soon as I said it. I couldn't comprehend what was going on at that moment, but I ran downstairs to my grandmother's bedroom, sat in her rocker, and sobbed with the baby in my arms. My grandmother took her from me and settled her down. When the baby had finally calmed down, she laid her on the bed and focused on me. I sobbed uncontrollably as she put her hand on my head. "Put it in God's hands," she told me, advising me to go get my things and my baby's and stay with her.

My mother's words still haunt me to this day. For the life of me, I can't understand why a mother would wish such horrible things on her own child. I could never fathom saying or feeling that way about my own child. I wondered what I did to make her feel that way. I was ashamed of how others in my family viewed Mom in a bad light. I always tried to protect her from ridicule, defending her even when I knew she was wrong. I wouldn't let anyone talk badly about her in my presence. If apples don't fall too far from the tree, then I fear for my own sanity."

I knew I needed to find peace and make amends with her, but how do you do that? My grandmother says I have to be the bigger person. I say, bigger with a suit of armor and a shield protecting my heart from her sword of pain. I told myself I would never let anyone change me because they chose to be less than me. At some point, her attempts to get under my skin failed to make contact. I was over it. Miserable people want to make other people miserable. I learned how to cut her off from accessing my feelings.

I promised my grandmother I wouldn't burden her for long. Of course, she said I didn't need to leave, and we were not a burden. I found a place, but it wouldn't be ready for another two weeks. It was May 1999. I was so excited about this place. It was a cute little two-bedroom bungalow off Page and North and South.

A Mother's Love (Part II)

It needed some work done, but the landlord promised he would have it completed by Memorial Day weekend. I even went to the house to paint the living room. It just was not meant to be. I walked in on the day I was to move in, and the bathroom was still sitting in the kitchen; literally, the toilet and the tub were sitting on the kitchen floor. To make matters even worse, I found out that the owner of the house had run away with the deposit I had given him, never to be heard from again.

I moved temporarily to my great aunt's house, who was my grandmother's sister and Ronnie's mom. She was having surgery and needed someone to watch her house while she was in the hospital. I was happy to have the peace and quiet. She never asked me for a dime; she only wanted me to get on my feet. Two weeks later, when she came home from the hospital, she offered to let me move into the basement to give me more privacy. I appreciated the offer, but I wanted to get a place of my own. I was at a loss regarding what to do next. I moved back in with my grandmother while I figured it out. It actually felt good to be back home.

On the Fourth of July holiday weekend, my cousin, Mellie, and her family, who lived in DC, came for a visit. I hadn't seen her in two years. I was very excited to see her, her husband, and the girls. My cousin and I got caught up. I told her all the things that had been going on with me up to that point. After listening to my story, she asked me if I would consider moving to Washington, D.C. I thought about it for a moment. Hell, what did I have to lose? We talked more about it; she said she would love to have some family with her in DC. She told me to email her my resume on Tuesday after they returned home, and I agreed. I had the greatest time with them that weekend, more excitement than I had experienced before the baby arrived. The girls fell in love with my angel. When it came time to say goodbye, I was going to miss their company. After we hugged, Mellie made me promise to email her my resume. I did.

Tuesday morning, as I drove to work, I thought about the idea of moving away from home. It frightened me. I had never been on my own before. I thought about Mom when we moved to Houston, Texas, and how we ended up coming back home after four years of struggling, and how it didn't work out. I did not want the same thing to happen to me. However, this would be a little different because I would have some family there. I trusted my cousin. I knew she would be there to help in any way she could. What the hay? It couldn't hurt to send my resume. If she couldn't find me a job, at least I kept my promise, right?

My first task when I walked into the office, after greeting my co-workers, was to email my resume to my cousin. She called me to confirm she had received it. She told me she would post it on a popular employment board online called Monster. We would wait and see what kind of bites I would get. Just for kicks, I researched online to see what kind of salary they were paying for the type of work I was doing, the cost of living, and what kind of money I would be looking at for renting a place. The thought of leaving all this sorrow behind me and moving forward to start fresh sounded more like the plan.

I owed my angel the best life I could provide for her. It was my duty as a mother to try. I was going to take my grandmother's advice. I put it in God's hands. If it were meant to be, it would happen. I couldn't believe it; I received several offers and little did I know that Washington, DC, in 1999, was hot with telecommunications jobs. I don't even remember accepting the offer, but the consultant gave me two weeks to report to my new position.

The salary was twice what I was making; my mind swung with all kinds of thoughts. I called my cousin and told her I had gotten a job. She was overjoyed and surprised it happened so fast. She was going to fly home to help me drive back to DC. I would have to leave my baby here until I got settled. The thought of leaving her for a second scared me, let alone for a few months until I got us a place.

I had to break the news to my family. I could hear them now. Half would be happy for me, and the other half would be negative about it. I made up my mind I was going to take a chance. I could always come back home, if you want to call it that. Being a mother now, I can only imagine how Mom felt. Now I get it. People judge you by your all-encompassing decisions.

I would never sell my paid-off car, quit my good-paying job, and move my child to an isolated place with no family for the love of a man who did not put a ring on my finger without even the promise of marriage. I know what it's like. I believe it was my history that gave me the courage to leave a bad relationship when it was impossible to continue.

I know what it's truly like to be in love, to surrender to thankless selflessness. To willingly give every part of my soul away to see the smile that God made just for me. I am honored to be a part of my daughter's life. It's God's love I see when I look at her, and I am in love with my child more every day. My song for her is "Queen of My Heart" by DeBarge. That's how I feel about my angel. I'm sure Mom at some point felt this way about me, maybe ages one through twelve. Yup, I'm sure she did; in some parallel world, she still loves me wholly, even the bad parts—whatever they are to her.

I have never let these feelings out before, but now I have come to accept her and love her for the good in her. She raised me. The worst fate in life is being without your mother's love. I felt I had been dealt such a fate. It is truly the loneliest feeling in the world.

I wrote Mom a letter and left it in her mail slot the night I moved to D.C.

> Mom,
>
> *I'm sorry it has turned out the way it did. I'm sad that you haven't embraced being a grandmother yet, but I know you will come around. I know you didn't mean the awful things you said to me. I forgive you for what you said. You are in pain over things that don't concern me. I love you. You are all I have. I hope you can resolve those things. Life is beautiful. You only have to look at Poo and know she is here to show us that beauty. I love you with all my heart. If you need anything, I will always be here for you. I will* never *abandon you. However, I do hold you accountable for the hurt and pain you have caused me. So, I will not take the second step to make amends. This is the first step. I will leave it up to you. I can't fix what's wrong inside of you. I only pray God will take the pain away and allow you to move past it, so you can start to love without conviction. I love you unconditionally, no matter the situation. I just can't deal with you right now. I must let it go. I truly love you, Mom.*

I want to say that you only have one mom. Regardless of our history, she will always be the one who gave you life and looked after you. There is honor and respect due. You can look over your whole life, and it will lead you back to the beginning. No matter what you do, you cannot escape it. Until you forgive, let the past go, and realize none of that stuff matters.

Your life will never be complete. My lesson here isn't new; it's cliché. You only have one mother and never wait to say "I love you" because one day you may not have the opportunity.

In a scene from the movie *Imitation of Life*, the daughter was grabbing at her mother's coffin, screaming, "I love you, Momma," but it was too late! The point is to find a way! I don't want to be that girl. Don't be afraid; feel good about your love, even if it's not returned the way you want it to be. Never let the book close without giving it your best because you don't want to regret it. I LOVE YOU, MOM!

I will never give up on my relationship with Mom. It hurts, but I will always try. It's the unconditional love that will drive me forever. We shared a heartbeat. She is my first love, and we've got time in this. My mom always supported all my crazy ideas, all the things I wanted to try when I was growing up, even when she didn't agree. I want to mention some cool stuff we did together, like all the concerts and plays I attended with her: The Ohio Players, Parliament, *The Wiz* (with Stephanie Mills), Maze (several times), Patti Labelle (*Your Arms Are Too Short to Box with God*), Jesse Johnson, and Earth, Wind & Fire. All the albums she bought, played, sang along to, danced to, and showed me how to dance to them. She introduced me to my best friend: Music. They are on my playlist. She is the original deejay to the soundtrack of my early life. I owe her everything, and I am thankful to have her as my mom. It has been quite a ride.

Speaking of rides, the drive to Maryland took a long fourteen hours. I had a lot of "Are We There Yet?" moments. I was tired and hungover from the small farewell party my friends threw for me. My cousin was driving, so I drifted off to sleep.

Here is part two of my beloved playlist for "A Mother's Love."

A Mother's Love Playlist (Part II)
Scan the QR code to listen to the playlist.

Glamorous Life — Sheila E

I Promise I Love You — Dreamboy

Tender Love — Force MDs

I Wonder If I Take You Home — Lisa Lisa and Cult Jamm

Outstanding — The Gap Band

Slow Jam — Midnight Starr

Sunshine — Alexander O'Neal

Real Love — Lakeside

Spending Time — Bobby Brown

Jungle Love — The Time

Rocket 2 U — The Jets

Somebody Else's Guy — Jocelyn Brown

Only Human — Jeffrey Osbourne

You Don't Have to Cry — Rene and Angela

Can You Help Me — Jesse Johnson

A Mother's Love (Part II)

Too Lonely to Be Alone — Kwick
Love's Train — Con Funk Shun
Anticipation — Bar-Kays
Angel — Anita Baker
Out on a Limb — Teena Marie
Sunshine — Alexander O'Neal
Real Love — Lakeside
Hangin' Downtown -- Cameo
Computer Love — Zapp
Saturday Love — Cherelle
Affection — Tamara and the Seen
Cool It Now — New Edition
Just My Luck—The Deele
Yearning for Your Love—The Gap Band
Love Light in Flight—Stevie Wonder

Albums

Cameo
Prince
The Time
TaMara and the Seen
Jesse Johnson
The Deele
The Gap Band
The Family

NoNDicCuaL

DreamBoy
Michael Jackson
New Edition
Bobby Brown
SOS Band
Alexander O'Neal
The Whispers
Janet Jackson
The Dazz Band
Rene and Angela
Jody Watley
Howard Hewitt

Dreamin'

Sigmund Freud's dream theory suggests that when you can't work things out and find closure to accept reality, your subconscious takes over. My former relationship haunted me throughout my time with the sperm donor. I'm not sure if this theory works for everyone, but for me, one thing is certain: this subject is still unresolved. I broke up with Dimiel to date the sperm donor. Immediately, I knew it was a mistake, but I stayed in that bad situation. I was too busy trying to make it work because he convinced me I was the problem. However, I could never really close the book on my chapter with Dimiel. I couldn't stand living with the "what ifs." So, I worked it out in the only place I could at the time—in my dreams.

When the show's intro music started, the audience stood and applauded as the host entered the stage. Then the crowd hushed as the host began to speak.

HOST: Thank you. Thank you. Please be seated. Today's show is about reuniting old lost loves. Our first guest is Lex. She says life has never been the same since she broke up with Dimiel, and through it all, she would like to ask him for a second chance. Hi, Lex. Welcome to the show. Please tell us why you want to reunite with Dimiel.

Lex: Well, I met Dimiel when we were seniors in high school, and we dated for about six years. He was my very first love. I spent more time with his family during that time than I did with my own. I even had a key to his family's home. We had our young, immature problems, but I believe they were things we could work out. I feel like we can start over. I just want a second chance with Dimiel. I still love him.

HOST: Lex, I don't understand. He sounds like a really great guy. Why in the world did you break up with him?

Lex: He is a great guy. I have regretted my decision to break up with him every day…but we were young! He liked to spend most of his time with his friends. I wanted to get serious and take our relationship to the next level, but he wasn't ready, so I compensated by hanging out with my girls and pursuing my dreams. Again, we were young. I wasn't very good at communicating my needs, so we fought constantly.

HOST: Lex, tell us how you guys met.

Lex: I saw Dimiel at the movies during the Friday premiere of Eddie Murphy's *Raw*. I was actually on a date with someone else when I noticed a group of cute guys on my way out after the movie ended. He was with a group of his friends, sitting in the first row. I knew one of the guys he was with, so I spoke to him and made a mental note to reach out later to get Dimiel's phone number. I called him after I got his number from a mutual friend. We talked forever! It reminded me of the first conversation I had with Fran (my first puppy love)—it was so easygoing. We started dating in my senior year of high school. I went to St. Louis VAP Magnet School, a visual and performing arts school, just like in the movie *Fame*. I was determined to be an entertainer—singer, dancer, songwriter, book writer, model, and actress, just to name a few. We had only been dating for a few months, so I didn't ask him to go to my prom. My thought at the time was that if we didn't work out, I didn't want to have any evidence of it. I was so vain back then. So, I went with my girlfriends, and I was crowned prom queen. It was the first time I had ever won anything. I had the whole world in front of me, and I was going to do it all. He called me his little superstar, but deep down, he didn't really believe in my dreams. That was a real thorn in the relationship.

HOST: Wow, that's serious. Tell us what you mean when you say he didn't support your dreams.

Lex: I don't think Dimiel ever really believed I'd make it. I mean, he came to all the beauty contests I entered, but he hated seeing me in bikinis and other guys gawking at me. He protested constantly about it. He would joke about me being too skinny. He thought he was being funny, but I don't think he ever understood how much his words hurt me. Looking cute in a two-piece wasn't really my passion. It was just one way to get noticed. I love music. I used modeling to network; I was able to meet people with music studios, some in their mother's basements, and I spent a lot of time at those studios cutting demos. I even recorded a couple of songs at Oliver Sain's studio—an American saxophonist, songwriter, bandleader, drummer, and record producer. He was an important figure in the development of rhythm and blues music, and I was excited and honored to work with him on a song. Dimiel never really got into it. If I'm being honest, he didn't think I could sing; he called me average. He was right! I wasn't Patti LaBelle, but I could do better than hold a tune. Plus, I had a lot of heart, a look, creativity, and ambition, and most of all, I believed in my dreams. I was way more than just average; I was a complete package. I would have been completely content if I had been a one-hit wonder. After all my efforts, I think I was worthy of that.

January 1986...

I arrived in St. Louis from Houston on the same weekend as the first Dr. Martin Luther King, Jr. Day holiday celebration. I didn't really have time to process the last forty-eight hours of my life. I was just in Houston, and now I was back in St. Louis. My head was still wavering. The pain of leaving Houston was so great that I didn't understand how to deal with this move back. My family was so happy to see me, but I just couldn't make myself feel the same. That made me feel guilty and selfish. It was devastating. I resented being back, but I knew I was safe and secure from poverty and homelessness...so that was a plus. I just buried it and tried to make the best of it. I mean, I was home with the family I loved, so how could that be a bad thing?

I had to get registered for high school. I thought I could go to Sumner like my mom and dad, but the city had rezoned, so I was going to Vashon. Back in the day, the school had a bad reputation. It was so bad that some boys literally chased me out of school on my first day. Thank God my mother was waiting to pick me up. I jumped in the car before they caught up to me.

It scared the crap out of me. Out of breath and crying, I told Mom that if I had to go to that school, I wasn't going to school at all. She found a way to get me into Sumner, a celebrated historic Black high school founded in 1875. It was the first all-Black high school in the Midwest, and it was a better school.

I settled in quickly. I joined the drama club just in time for the Black History program. I performed "And Still I Rise" by my favorite poet, Dr. Maya Angelou. I remember being on that stage, looking out at the crowd. The theater was huge; it even had a balcony. All those people! I forgot the next line as I stood there for about five seconds while my anxiety started and the sweat broke across my brow and the back of my neck. But I didn't totally panic. The haters would have loved that. Thank God it came back to me, and I finished the poem. To the onlookers, it looked as if I did it on purpose to give the poem more effect. Embarrassed, I bowed and left the stage with a quick walk. Looking at the hardwood floors as I exited the stage, I just knew I blew it until I heard the crowd cheering for me as I got beyond the curtains. The teachers shooed me and made me go back out to bow again. It was a moment I will never forget—the words of the poem were really my life at the time, and still, I rose. It was my confirmation that my dreams were possible.

My new best friend, Lynn, who was a year older, felt like the sister I never had. We met in the drama club at Sumner. We struck up a conversation and never looked back. She had a warm, radiant smile, a laugh that was both endearing and delightfully annoying, and a goofiness that was simply infectious. Always the life of the party, she had a knack for making everyone laugh. We could easily pass for family, sharing a small gap between our front teeth and a striking resemblance. Lynn's signature look was two cornrow braids parted down the center, sometimes with bangs, sometimes without. Our mutual love for Prince was the first of many connections. We spent the rest of the year practically living at each other's houses. Lynn lived on Norwood Ave, just off St. Louis Ave, in a charming neighborhood with homes reminiscent of U. City. I adored her home. Her divorced dad even dated my single mom for a while. Lynn had two brothers: Ty, who was in my class, and Cee, a high school senior. She made my transition from Houston easier, and we have been friends ever since.

Back in the eighties, I found teenagers to be less mature than Houston kids. I must admit, though, missing my old friends made me very biased. Also, I thought the St. Louis kids weren't as serious about being famous as I was. The real deal of it was that dismissing them was my way of coping with my feelings of inadequacy and disconnection. Actually, they were as serious as I was. I just hadn't found my tribe yet. I was the answer to one of these things that didn't belong. There was a lot of diversity in Houston. The kids there didn't sweat the texture of hair, skin color, or race. To be fair, back then, St. Louis only had two prominent races: Black and White. It was the Midwest, and that's just how it was. People questioned anything that didn't fall in line, and unfortunately, I fell into that category. My hair was different. It was naturally curly. I didn't have a Jheri curl, and I didn't have a perm. I didn't dress the way a St. Louis teenager dressed, so people stared at me. I came back home with a Texas Southern accent, which I quickly changed back to the St. Louis dialect so people wouldn't laugh. I didn't want that attention. I just wanted to go back to being me and around people who knew me. I was tired of explaining myself; that I wasn't mixed with anything other than Black, but people still questioned it. Even though I had spent much of my life in St. Louis, I still felt like a stranger when I got back. What I experienced in my travels made me different, but it also made me interesting. I didn't comprehend that back then.

Music was the one thing that was a constant in my life. It knew me and held all my happy thoughts. It was the connection holding the fragmented pieces of my history together, and I clung to it for dear life. Music would allow me to revisit all the good times whenever I needed it, just like an old friend who would come to visit or a new one who knew exactly what I was going through.

One thing that happened that made me the happiest person in the world was when I got my front teeth bonded. I was so happy to be rid of the gap. I had to teach myself to smile with my teeth because I wasn't comfortable with it before. For the first time in my life, I felt whole. I was attractive to myself. When I was little, before I got my teeth fixed, I used to put tissue in the gap between my teeth to see how I would look if they were together, and I wished it were real. It was a dream come true—I had done a lot of work to fulfill my dream after I returned; the pieces fit together like a puzzle. I bravely entered the local staple, the Judy Best International Model of the Year contest, at sixteen. I think I placed sixteenth. Not bad for my first time. I didn't know what I was doing (giggling to myself). My first photoshoot was with Carl Bruce, a famous local photographer (RIP). He saw me at the Judy Best modeling contest and gave me his card. He took pictures of the contest. It was the first time I had ever seen myself in professional pictures, different and beautiful. I didn't even recognize my own face. My first professional photo shoot with Mr. Carl was at Union Station. I couldn't believe it was actually happening, but it was happening, and it was incredible and exciting.

I also met the wonderful, dynamic, brilliant Phillip Dennis at the Judy Best contest. He asked me to join his show, *Star 80* at the Chase Park Plaza, hosted by Don Clark. The concept of the show was that teenagers produced it, both in front of and behind the camera. Our shows aired on the local access cable channel. I think Phil was the equivalent of a camp counselor or a favorite teacher with no bad tendencies. He was purely all about the kids, so it was easy to stay focused on the goal. I thank God for him for allowing me and others to live our dreams. Side note: he is a beloved judge in St. Louis these days.

I had a lot of plates turning at the same time at such a young age, but I enjoyed every minute of it. I did a lot of fashion shows with the Robert Toliver Group at Harris-Stowe. I joined the group with my cousin. Let me tell you about the time I started a new dance group in St. Louis with Lynn and her friend, Angela. We called ourselves Protégé, just like my old crew in Houston. We practiced at my house all the time, and let me tell you, we were fierce! We entered our first talent show with the local chapter of Jack and Jill, dancing to Janet Jackson's "What Have You Done For Me Lately." And guess what? We won! We were on cloud nine, but sadly, that was our first and last performance together. But the story doesn't end there. I was asked to perform solo at my old high school, Sumner, for a Christmas program. And you know I had to bring back Janet Jackson's "What Have You Done For Me Lately" to the stage. The applause was deafening, and I felt like a superstar returning to my roots. Sumner showed me so much love, and it was a moment I'll never forget. Janet Jackson, girl, you have my heart forever! She was my idol. I still hope to meet her. I would watch her music videos over and over, making sure to imitate her dance routines perfectly. I was asked to perform at a local festival with Sonny Metcalfe, who saw my performance at Sumner. He worked with talented kids in the neighborhood and gave them outlets to be productive in the summer. He is still doing it—bless his presence and concern for the kids.

I joined a band called The Young after I saw them perform at one of our *Star 80* shows; they were performing "Love You Down" by Ready for the World. I couldn't believe how great they sounded; the music was pitch-perfect. They were all in high school, and I wanted to be a part of it. Luckily, I got in the band because the former girl quit, and I replaced her. Finally, I had a place to record my voice and create music with the band leader, Carlos, but he insisted on being called Christian. I did my first-ever singing performance during a taping of our show *Star 80* with the band. I performed "Looking for a New Love" by Jody Watley, and I sang the background vocals for "Have You Ever Loved Somebody" by Freddie Jackson. I got through it without messing up the words. I was a nervous wreck, but I did it, and I was so proud of myself.

Carlos had a studio in his mom's basement, complete with instruments and a singing booth. I was in heaven. I never thought I would hear my voice recorded to music. Here I was doing it! I loved writing lyrics to the music Carlos—um, I mean, Christian—came up with, and I thought we made a perfect match. We would spend hours making music. We were both heavily influenced by Prince, so the library of songs mostly had a Prince sound to them. *Sign O' The Times* had just come out. I listened to it for the first time with him in his basement studio with those loudspeakers. "If I Was Your Girlfriend," "The Ballad of Dorothy Parker," "Starfish and Coffee," and "Adore" stand out in my mind. I thought it was a sign that I was really gonna make it!

Meeting stars in St. Louis was easy once you knew the right people. Back in the early days, it was a small circle that controlled the entertainment that came to town, and that was the radio stations. If you could get cool with local radio on-air personalities, then you're in, baby. I met Tony Washington, a radio personality, while on the set of the *Star 80* show. He replaced Don Clark as host. We moved from the beautiful ballroom at the Chase Park Plaza to the nightclub, The Wiz, in Alton, Illinois. We filmed the show on Sunday afternoons at the club because we were all minors. If I needed tickets to a concert or wanted to get backstage, I'd call Tony first. If that didn't work, I'd improvise and become resourceful. I met quite a few artists: Tony Terry, Kid from Kid 'n Play, Salt-N-Pepa, Aaron Hall, Bobby Brown, Alfonso Ribeiro, Angela Winbush, and Phil Perry, just off the top of my head.

In 1987, I met a new recording artist at Motown Records and a sibling of the famous musical group at Hudson's Embassy Records and Tapes. He was in town to promote his new single. The record store was up the street from my house on Page Boulevard. I couldn't believe my luck. My friend, Lyla, came along. She went to Visual and Performing Arts High School with me. She was a senior, and I was a junior. Side note: I auditioned for V.A.P. (Visual and Performing Arts) and was accepted in my junior year. Yes, it was just like *Fame*, my favorite TV show. We had history and theater together and became good friends.

Okay, back to the story. I knew someone in his entourage, Keith, from the fashion shows we did together with the Harris-Stowe modeling group. Keith got us in. He introduced us. I couldn't believe it! I was meeting him in the flesh! I had just watched him on *Soul Train* and *Video Soul*. Now he was here, standing in front of me. He was so beautiful, but I played it cool. He asked me if I wanted his autograph. I told him he should have asked for mine. He laughed at that, telling me I was sassy, and he liked it. He invited us to go to a club on the east side (East St. Louis) where he was going to be performing. We hung around talking after the meet and greet at the record store. He gave us a ride in his limo back to my house. Lyla and I played it really cool until we got out of the limo, walked to my house, watched the limo pull off, and closed the front door. Then we screamed our teenage heads off so much that Mom thought something had happened to us. She ran out of the bedroom, asking, "What happened!?" When we told her we had met him, she said, "Girl, don't be scaring me like that," and we all just laughed.

We needed to meet him at the hotel where he was staying, so we could go together to the club. I got my cousin/brother, Ronnie, to convince my mom to let us go to "a party." He dropped us off at the hotel and told us we would need to find our way back home. He was interested in me. We went to the club in the limo. We danced together all night, or at least that's how it happened in my seventeen-year-old mind. We all left the club together and went back to the hotel. His hairdresser kept playing this new single, "As We Lay," by Shirley Murdock, in the limo. Every time I hear it now, I am instantly returned to that once-in-a-lifetime moment, forever captured in the song's melody. Once we arrived at the hotel, he and I hung back in the limo for a moment. We talked for a bit, and then he kissed me. I saw sprinkles, fireworks, and stars. Did I say unicorns and rainbows? I just remember his lips being so soft, like pillows; I was in a trance. Then he asked me to come up to his hotel room just as his people were grabbing him out of the limo, and they disappeared inside the hotel. Lyla jumped back in the limo, where I was still floating on the love cloud. She snapped me out of it, asking what we were going to do. The limo driver intervened, saying he had girls our age, and he was not letting us out to go to the room. He locked the limo doors, and he was going to take us back home. He did! We didn't protest at all. Besides, I was past my curfew, and we knew it was the best decision. See, back in the day, grown-ups intervened. We were their business, and they looked out for us, and I thank God for that. I called his hotel room once I could sneak on the phone, and I talked to him all night until he fell asleep. Ironically, I saw him again ten years later. Like I said, St. Louis is small, so you can get to the stars if you know the right people. He came through to promote his 1997 CD. I ran into him at a downtown club on Washington Boulevard. Believe it or not, he remembered me. We talked for a while and laughed about that night. Perfect ending.

Back to my early pursuit of becoming famous. I found out that I was connected to Fred "Rerun" Berry on my father's side. He was family. He knew my whole family, and my cousin Vernon was his best friend. They grew up together and maintained their friendship throughout the years. I thought, I am going to Hollywood! I got his phone number and called him up. He talked to my mom and told her I would be safe with him, so I got on a flight. I couldn't believe my luck! I daydreamed about meeting all my favorite stars. I was so excited I couldn't sleep. It didn't even bother me to be on a plane by myself for the first time, and it was a long five hours from Missouri to Los Angeles. I imagined Freddy living in a beautiful mansion with a pool and a butler. I was going to be picked up in a limo. It was going to be champagne wishes and caviar dreams… the Lifestyles of the Rich and Famous, or that's what I envisioned.

I told Cindy all about it. What a coincidence that she was going to be in Los Angeles at the same time. Bonus! Her mom had moved there to teach school. I went to Hollywood in the summer of 1987. Back in the day, you could go up to the gate to meet your party. So, there was a small reunion at LAX Airport. Cindy and I screamed when we saw each other, ran to each other, hugged, and jumped up and down like we were contestants on *The Price Is Right*. It was the second time we had seen each other since I left Houston back in 1986. (I will share the first time with you in a later chapter.) Then I saw Freddy. Of course, he was signing autographs. He wanted to get out of the airport with the quickness. I didn't even realize that Cindy and I were running our mouths a mile a minute while I waited for my luggage on the carousel. I don't remember if we hung out later that day, but Cindy and I said goodbye inside the airport.

Now, this is where the harsh reality of life awakened the fantasy in my head.

My visit to Los Angeles was right after the big scandal over his contract with *What's Happening Now*. He asked for more money, and they told him no. So, he quit, or he was fired. In either case, he was no longer working on the show. So, as I was looking for the bomb ride that I just knew he was rolling in, he pointed to a white utility van. I said, "Oh, this you?" I thought he was kidding until he pulled out the keys. M'kay, no limo; alright, alright. I mean, that was okay. Everybody has a moment. I was sure the crib was going to be fly, right? I mean, he was on the show for what, three to four years? He had been an original on *Soul Train*. He appeared on *Saturday Night Live* and guest-starred on several TV shows. I thought he just had to have a badass crib.

Freddy was just as you saw him on TV. His voice was the same—still jovial, and his laugh was the same, just less animated. But I picked up on the sadness as he explained his pending divorce from his wife, and that was why he was living in a trailer home. Yes, a trailer home! I did not know how to take it. I thought he was kidding. I had just met him, so I didn't know where his joke meter was. We were somewhere off Crenshaw—I remember seeing the street name. To his credit, it wasn't just any old trailer park. This one was full of beautiful urban art and murals everywhere—art pieces made from green and brown beer bottles, and rocks lining the sidewalk had carved faces. I think there was a famous Motown mural that Diana Ross came to see in person. At least that was the story he told me. There was also an article written about this place. I remember seeing it in *Ebony* or *Jet*.

Freddy's trailer was very large. It looked like a silver pill from the outside. In the center of the trailer, there was the front door. So, when you walked in, you were facing a small dinette set. There were two twin-size beds to the right. On your left were the kitchenette and a tiny bathroom with a shower. He didn't tell my mom he was living like that because if he did, she would have never let me go. Anyhoo, he was a great host. He was trying to pitch a new pilot with some young white guy. I do not remember his name. He scheduled meetings with Paramount Studios. I was actually on the lot where they made movies! I thought I had died and gone to heaven. We went to Eddie Murphy's office trailer, which was on the lot, but he wasn't there. As we were walking back to the van in the parking lot, I met Arsenio Hall. He was chatting up some girl. Freddy introduced me to him, and true to my confident teenage spirit, I said, "You will see me again!" I was always a little overly confident in my youth. I'm not even sure I believed it, but it came out of my mouth. I got to walk down the famous Hollywood Boulevard. I went to Fredricks of Hollywood, Grauman's Chinese Theatre, and the Walk of Stars. I bought a map of the stars' homes, and we toured Beverly Hills. The streets looked so normal, like neighborhoods in Brentwood or Clayton, Missouri—St. Louis's county-rich neighborhoods. He told me we were in an older part of Beverly Hills. It was fun looking at the stars' houses.

I wanted to go to *Soul Train* because he could have gotten me in; he was an original dancer after all. Unfortunately, I came on the wrong week when they weren't filming. He took me to a club in Anaheim. Although I was underage, they let me in; I only drank Shirley Temples. I met some Solid Gold dancers... that was crazy. We went to Venice Beach, and unlike Houston, the water was blue, just like on TV. It was just like you see in the movies—people singing or dancing for money, roller skating with boom boxes, bike riding, skateboarding, and people surfing. I bought an acid-washed blue jean jacket just like Janet Jackson's in the "Pleasure Principle" video in a shop on the strip. He took me to A&M Records. I met the owner, who was really nice. I saw the studio booth where Janet Jackson recorded "Diamonds" and the room where all the stars, like Michael Jackson, recorded "We Are the World." I couldn't believe it! I was in awe of this town. Freddy introduced me to his friend. I don't remember his name, but he must have lived close by. I believed it was on the same lot because I don't remember riding in a car to get there. He promised me he'd take me to meet a very famous music producer, an old friend of his. But it didn't work out. He was out of town, so that was my luck. I wonder what would have happened if I had gotten that opportunity. I didn't have a demo on me. I probably would have sung a cappella. I have thought about that missed opportunity for years. Freddy was the real deal—a diamond in the rough-and-tumble world of fame. Our nightly chats were a throwback to childhood sleepovers, complete with twin beds and midnight talks. My spot by the window became the backdrop to his storytelling—all while "Wildflower" by New Birth spun its melodic tale on the radio. Freddy broke down the song's essence, reminiscing about a girl he knew who embodied its spirit. As the night wore on, "Olivia" by The Whispers crooned through the static, and Freddy extracted a pinky promise from me—to stay in school and steer clear of the boys. We chuckled, our laughter mingling with the music. In that moment, Freddy shredded his global superstar skin, revealing the man beneath—a man of flesh, bone, and heartfelt tales. He exposed stardom, teaching me to see beyond the glitter to the human core. Now, whenever those tunes play on the quiet storm, they carry me back to those twin beds, to the wisdom imparted without pretense. Those nights were my Hollywood fairytale. Seeing Freddy, not at his peak, but in his humanity, was a reality check wrapped in a velvet ribbon—a cautionary whisper not to get swept up in the razzle-dazzle, for the fall from grace is a steep one.

Dreamin'

When I returned to St. Louis, I got my first professional modeling portfolio when I was seventeen. The owner of a graphic design studio, where my mother used to work, paid for it. He did ad work for a major beer company in town. He said I had a unique, exotic look. A self-described, unapologetic dirty old man, he had a disturbing crush on me. Seventeen will get you twenty. I kept him at bay by threatening to tell my mom and his wife. He was a perv, but he wasn't crazy. He encouraged me to pursue print work modeling because I wasn't tall enough for the runway, but I couldn't do any beer ads until I was twenty-one. He promised there would be an ad with my name on it once I turned twenty-one. He kept his promise, and I got a poster and two separate beer promo ads. After my high school graduation, I worked all summer on my demo and sent it out to record labels. The cassette tape sleeves had addresses and phone numbers for record labels.

One day, my dream came true when I auditioned for a new girl group with a well-known music producer. The audition was in California, and he flew my mom and me out. It started out great. We got picked up from the airport in a limo. It was my second time being in one. The first time was my father's funeral. I thought this was it! The music producer introduced me to B. He was an incredible songwriter, and I hung out with him in the studio. Impressed that I could write lyrics to songs on the fly, he called a famous new jack swing male artist and a famous agent as a dare to prove he knew them. They both said they couldn't wait to meet me in Los Angeles. It was an absolute dream, and I couldn't believe this was happening. Regrettably, it turned out to be a casting couch situation. It was a scene straight out of a cautionary tale—the kind my grandmother would've clicked her teeth at. There I was, green and hopeful, thinking I was stepping onto a path of dreams. But the reality was a far cry from the star-studded journey I'd imagined. I was still a virgin, saving myself for the right guy, and that was Dimiel. I didn't flirt with the producer, nor did I give him any energy like that. Besides, I didn't find him attractive at all. Please, he couldn't spark a fire if he were a match. But there was that moment, a warning I brushed off like lint on my jacket—he crossed a line in the studio office, and I froze. He grabbed my breast while I was on the phone. I didn't know what to do. I felt stupid and tried to disappear in the moment. I pretended it didn't happen, not wanting to stir the pot, all while my dreams hung in the balance. Unfortunately, he wasn't trying to take no for an answer. He took me by surprise and attacked me after a studio session. We walked into his house, and it was very dark. As I was trying to find the light switch on the wall, he grabbed me, dragged me, threw me on the bed, and jumped on top of me. Now, he was about the same height and weight as me, and he wasn't just going to take it. He underestimated me, or he thought I was going to give in. Something clicked in me. He was unsuccessful in trying to pry my legs apart. I took karate for a year as a child; my mom dated the instructor because he was cute. Anyway, I kneed him in the dick and tossed him over my head with my legs. He landed in a heap on the other side of the bed as I ran out. I hid in the bathroom and locked the door. The front door creaked open, and in came the familiar sounds of shopping bags and laughter—my mom, his girlfriend, and her mother. Their timing was divine. I was a whirlwind of emotions—a cocktail of relief and turmoil. I had outrun him, the man who thought he could take what wasn't his to claim. My heart was pounding, but my spirit? Unbroken. He was quite the performer, masking his pain with a tale of a pulled muscle. I knew better. I had left my mark—a reminder that I was no one's prey. The thought of telling my mother? It crossed my mind, but the image of her unleashing a St. Louis-style ass beating held me back. We were far from home, and California bail money wasn't in our budget. There I was, still wondering if I'd made the cut for the group.

It's funny, isn't it? The shock of betrayal can leave you questioning even the most obvious truths. But let me be clear—I didn't let that moment define me. I wasn't about to hand over my dreams to someone so undeserving of them. I was never his victim.

Now, let's hit the pause button for a second. In this era of the Me-Too Movement, I'm not looking to stir up old ghosts. I've found peace. My mental scars have turned to wisdom. I pray that I was the last and only chapter of his misdeeds, that he learned his lesson well. This book, my story, is not a one-trick pony. It's a symphony of triumphs, big and small. So, with that said, let's dive back into the melody of my life.

Back in the comfort of home, Dimiel took me to dinner at a fancy restaurant in Clayton. He presented me with a promise ring, a glinting diamond that symbolizes love and a key—our names etched together on a keyring. My excitement overshadowed the drama of California, but the echoes of that ordeal lingered in my dreams. I kept the secret close, not even whispering it to my mother. The nightmares were persistent visitors, reminders of a chapter I wished to close. Therapy might have been a wise choice, but it wasn't an option. In those days, showing vulnerability wasn't an option for Black folks—we wore resilience like armor. So, I pushed it down and filed it away as just another mile on my road to the stars. Then there was the girl from the audition, shining from the TV screen on *Video Soul*. A twinge of 'what if' tugged at me—I could have been there, sharing that spotlight. But with the fame came the memory of violation, a reminder of the price I refused to pay. I wondered about her journey, if she had faced the same crossroads, made different decisions. I finally found the courage to tell Dimiel about what had happened to me in Sacramento. He didn't hit me with, "I told you so." He was very empathetic, only concerned with my well-being.

Surprisingly, Dimiel and I became closer because of the incident, but I didn't stop pursuing my dreams. I had a lot of different options to move away and further my career. I could have moved to Los Angeles with my friend, Jacks, or Atlanta with Mia, or ended up in New York City with my friend, Kas, who was living with an up-and-coming hip-hop producer. I had no desire to starve or go anywhere with no money or options to get it. After the incident in California, I was no longer naïve about the fact that some people in the industry were just bad and sick. I needed to play it safer, and if I'm being honest, a small part of me was not ready to leave Dimiel or face another episode of the cruel part of the music industry I was so eager to be a part of.

It was 1989. Magic 108 announced a new beauty contest that had come to town. The top prize was a new Suzuki Samurai. A famous Jackson was supposed to appear and perform. I was excited, so I entered it. To qualify, I had to sell a certain number of tickets. I didn't sell enough, so I talked to the organizer of the contest. He offered me a way to work it off. I think it was stuffing envelopes or something like that. It was in his hotel room, but I didn't go alone. I went with my best friend, Cindy. Perfect timing. She came to town to visit me for spring break. I would find out later that he wasn't looking for an honest way to work it off. I did what was asked so I could participate. But some girls slept with the organizer, thinking that would give them a leg up. I am happy Cindy was there for me, and I followed the voice of caution. First of all, he was ugly and older, and I didn't want to know him like that. I was in love with Dimiel, and that was never an option for me. Every cute girl I knew in St. Louis, and even the ones I didn't know, had entered this contest. My whole family attended the event; even this comedian (before he was famous and still living in Berkeley, Missouri) was there in my camp because he and my cousin were in comedy together in the early days. They performed on Tuesdays at the Funny Bone in Westport on amateur night. I won third place; my family lost it, and they flipped over a table. Leave it to my family to cause a dramatic scene, embarrassing me. Of course, they thought I should have won, but the winner was good, and she deserved it. It was a great experience, and I networked. Incidentally, the organizer ran away with the money, the entertainment was canceled, and the winner never got her car. Ha! You gotta love this industry.

Despite my luck, I still had the beauty contest bug, so in 1991, I entered the Miss King Cobra pageant. I had been waiting to participate since I was sixteen. The famous local photographer, Carl Bruce, took me to my first one. The girls were so beautiful. It was a St. Louis thing because the headquarters were located there. In my mind, it was like a Miss America pageant, only with the most gorgeous Black girls I'd ever seen. I wanted to do it when I was of age. You had to be twenty-one, and I would be twenty-one before the contest. It was in April 1991, and I really cut it close because my birthday was in April.

It was hosted by the morning show radio personalities of Majic 108. A few of the girls from the previous contest were in this one. I made some new friends. I was the jokester. I didn't take it as seriously as some of the others, so I kept them laughing all night. Dimiel helped himself to the open bar. He was a lot tipsy and a little handsy. So much for the photographer he was supposed to be that night. Good thing I had other family members there so I could have the event memorialized. A very famous member of a Motown male singing group was a judge. I didn't win the $1,000 prize or the chance to do a poster. I think I won third place. I sucked when it came to my question. I had rehearsed it, but not good enough. When it was time to answer, I was distracted by Dimiel's behavior, so I was tripping all over my tongue. I blew it! But I had a great time; I got all pretty, and people noticed me. I did some networking and made some lifelong friends, so it was worth it.

I may have been more upset about losing if I hadn't ended up doing two beer ads that year, worth more than $3,000. It was the most money I had ever made in my life for a few hours of work. I did a photo shoot with a photographer who saw me in the contest, and she sold my photos. My photos were used twice in *Black Pages* without my permission, but it was free publicity, and you can't beat that. I attended the Magic 108 anniversary jam at the Ritz-Carlton in 1992 or 1993. My picture was featured in an article in *The St. Louis American*, taken by Maurice Meredith about the event. I did some networking at the event and met a music producer named Justin. We hooked up. I went to his studio, and he gave me a few songs to put melody and lyrics to. We recorded it, but I could never get back in the studio after the second session.

In 1995, the opportunity to do a poster for a beer ad finally happened. I got a whole poster for a Bud Ice ad with just me on it. I am still proud of it. In 1995, I did my final beauty contest and entered the Miss Colt 45 contest. I won second place to my friend, Kathy. I was done with the horse and pony show, prancing around, showing my ass.

I hosted a local cable access TV show for a cable company. It was called *The Cable Connection*, and I penned the slogan, "Where you get the hookup?" I filmed five twenty-minute shows plus commercials. I really thought I'd go places with it. I should have put together a demo tape of the shows and sent it to BET or something, but I wasn't thinking like that. I no longer had people around me who were motivating my dreams. They had all moved away. The energy was gone, and it was whack! I wanted to be like Oprah. She was my idol. My dreams eventually just slipped into oblivion.

Back to the show...

HOST: Wow, girl, you were really into making your dreams happen. What were some of the good things you did with Dimiel?

Lex: One time, Dimiel's mom treated us to a free trip to New Orleans. It was my first time there, and we had a ball. On my twenty-first birthday, he and a friend spent all day putting a brand-new boom system in my little 1989 Dodge Colt while I watched from the window. Finally, we went to the Dub Club, a reggae club on Laclede's Landing, to celebrate my twenty-first birthday. There were beautiful birthdays when I would celebrate with his parents and grandparents. We spent the Christmas holidays around the fireplace at his house exchanging gifts. I loved the weekends I spent at his house watching Blockbuster movies and eating Imo's pizza or Pasta House carryout. His parents were amazing. I loved his mom. She always treated me like I belonged. I felt included, and my voice had value with her. It was a real escape away from the BS back on Page. I found major peaceful solitude, loving hugs, and my favorite frozen dinners. It was home for me. I really miss it, and I probably always will.

The weekend before the Rodney King verdict in 1992, Dimiel and I were in Atlanta for Freaknik separately. We ended up leaving together because my two girlfriends got hit by a car when a driver took off in a crowd full of unsuspecting partygoers in the parking lot of a local nightclub near the amusement park in Stone Mountain. I didn't get hit by the car, but I hit my head on the curb of a median, banged up my knees, and sprained my ankle while trying to get out of the way. I spent the entire night in Grady Hospital Emergency, where I had to call my friends' parents and explain what had happened to their daughters. I thank God everyone pulled through the ordeal. Dimiel had to drive me home from Atlanta. I sprained my right ankle. He took care of everything; it was a chance to see a glimpse of the mature man I knew he could be.

By 1994, our relationship had just become old; it lacked romance. Not from a lack of trying. One time, we stayed at a fantasy suite hotel in Clayton called Cheshire Inn for Valentine's Day. All the rooms had themes, waterbeds, and hot tubs. Dimiel was a good provider. I knew he would take care of home. He just loved hanging with the boys more than he liked hanging with me, and they always seemed to come first with him. It left a lot of time for me to go out with my girls, and the opportunity to meet other guys was there.

Nothing was ever serious—just something to do when he wasn't available, and I needed my ego stroked. He was overly critical about anything I wanted to do; he called me a dreamer. My self-esteem was shot. It didn't stop me from pursuing my dreams. It only made me work harder at my goal. It also caused me to resent him a little. I went out more and more. Eventually, I met someone who gave me the attention I was seeking. He validated all the things I thought were important at the time, and he was just a friend to vent to at first.

He said all the right things I wanted to hear—everything Dimiel neglected to say. I fell for it, and I called it quits with Dimiel.

HOST: Okay. I understand that Dimiel didn't take that lying down. He tried to win you back. Tell us about that.

Lex: Well, our relationship was at an end, but neither of us wanted to call it quits. There was so much time invested in the relationship. He was my first love and my first everything. As much as I loved Dimiel, I knew he was nowhere near the maturity I had reached after six years of play and pretending. I was tired of trying to make him love me the way I deserved and move forward to the next phase of our relationship. After I called him and told him it was over, first came the flowers at work. I thought, Damn, I didn't get roses on Valentine's Day, my birthday, or just because. It was a little too late for that. I have to give it to him; he made one hell of an effort after the fact. Later came the "Baby, can't we work it out?" phone calls at two a.m. after hanging out with the boys. His final attempt? He came up with the idea to take me on a shopping spree in Atlanta. It wasn't the idea of shopping in Atlanta that enticed me. I wanted to be sure I was making the right decision to end it. Our love deserved to be sure that it was over. It was an eight-hour ride. I figured it would give us some time to talk through some of our issues. It was worth trying.

Behind the wheel, it was my show now, and Dimiel was out like a light. So, I dialed up the tunes—Anita's soulful serenades, Aaliyah's fresh beats, and Zhane's harmonies were my co-pilots as the miles rolled by. We hit ATL in style, cruising into Buckhead with the swagger of a music video, and the Ritz-Carlton rolled out the red carpet just for us.

Our room was our castle, but the mall was calling—Dimiel, with his traveler's checks, was on a mission to spoil me rotten. He showered me with the kind of luxury that had me feeling like royalty. Later that evening, we hit Club 112, where Dimiel's two-left-feet shuffle was the cutest thing..

Back at the Ritz, with Dimiel riding high on spirits, he was all about that bedroom romance. But I wasn't having it—not tonight, not with my heart tangled up elsewhere. So, I pulled the classic 'not tonight, babe' line, and bless those double beds, they saved the day. Dimiel, bless his tipsy soul, crashed hard, leaving me to my thoughts and the Atlanta skyline.

The next day, we visited Union Station, soaking in the hustle and the history. Dinner was at Hooters—yeah, that Hooters, where the wings are hot and the vibe's chill. Then it was back to our temporary castle to slip into our club gear. The night was young, and so were we, bouncing from club to club. Then, back to the hotel, we were both tipsy, and we stayed up talking all night, reminiscing over the past. We cried, and we laughed. When we finally went to sleep, it was daylight outside. He took me shopping again one last time before we left for home. He was feeling generous again, splurging on a shopping spree that felt like a farewell tour. And there he was—a side of him peeking through that I'd never seen—no more games, no more fear of losing what we had.

Men, they're a riddle wrapped in a mystery, and my heart was already solving another puzzle. My affections were with someone else. I really felt sorry for him. I didn't want to break his heart. I needed to move on to figure out if this new thing was what I wanted, and I owed it to myself to find out.

HOST: Well, Lex, it seems as if you made the best decision. You met the man of your dreams. What changed your mind now?

Lex: Oh, that's easy. The man of my dreams turned out to be the worst hellish nightmare of my life. I dealt with that ridiculous mess for four years. Dimiel didn't leave my side. He stayed in my life through it all. We are the best of friends now; we are stronger now than we ever were together. This speaks volumes to me. I just want the chance to try again. I really hate I put him through all that. I know how that feels now. Karma always collects. My song that explains my feelings for him is "Always Be My Baby" by Mariah Carey.

HOST: Wow, that's a good song. He sounds like a wonderful person. Are you ready to see Dimiel again? Are you ready to ask for another chance?

Lex: Yes, I am very ready!

HOST: Okay, Dimiel, come on out.

AUDIENCE: Cheers and applause.

HOST: Welcome, Dimiel, to the show. Do you know why Lex has asked you to join the show?

Dimiel: No, not really.

HOST: Dimiel, do you remember your relationship with Lex?

Dimiel: Of course, I do. She was my first love.

AUDIENCE: Awwwwww!

HOST: Okay, Lex, it's time to tell him why you brought him here.

Lex: Okay, Dimiel, we have been through a lot together and separately, but we have maintained a loving relationship over the years. I would like to have a second chance with you. I am ready to try us again and want to know if you are open to it.

HOST: Okay, Dimiel, Lex has put it out there. What do you have to say?

Dimiel: Lex, you know I love you, and I always will. But we have changed. I always thought of you as my one and only. I never thought you'd have a baby by another man. I love the baby… that's not it. I just don't think I can get past it.

Lex: C'mon, Dimiel. I didn't get pregnant until four years after we broke up. You have two kids by two different women. The first baby you had was by a friend of mine, and we hadn't been apart for a year.

AUDIENCE: Booooooo!

Lex: What a nightmare she turned out to be. I told you that girl was crazy as hell. Your second baby's mother didn't work out, either. I'm not saying let's get married tomorrow. I'm only asking if you would be open to the possibility of us trying again.

Dimiel: I know, I know, but I just don't think I can get past the fact you left me for another man.

AUDIENCE: Ohhhhhhhh!

HOST: Okay, we will have to pause for a commercial break. Be right back and stay right there.

HOST: Thank you for staying with us. Before we went to a commercial break, just in case you just joined us, our guest, Lex, is asking Dimiel for a second chance. Now, Lex, tell us your fondest memory of Dimiel.

Lex: Oh, that's easy. He came over after I came home with the baby. He brought Pampers, milk, and stuffed animals. I knew the love we shared was still there. He really does still care for me.

HOST: Now, isn't that a real man? So, what about it, Dimiel?

AUDIENCE: Awwwwwww!

Dimiel: She needed some help. I was able to help, and I did. That's all.

Lex: He is really being modest. I had a baby by another man after we broke up. I could still depend on him; he was willing to help me out after all we've been through—all I have put him through. I love him.

HOST: Whew, listen to all that love. You two share a special bond. What are you going to do, Dimiel?

Dimiel: I love you too, Lex, but I am still undecided. That is all I can tell you. Maybe it's a man's pride, selfishness, or stubbornness. I don't know, but what I do know is I don't have an answer.

Dreamin'

HOST: That's fair, Dimiel. Lex, do you have anything to add before we go?

Lex: Listen, I am happy I will have him for the rest of my life as a friend, but sad because I believe he is the one for me. I must go on, but it truly is my loss. The whole time I was with my recent ex, I heard the ticking of a clock; I knew time was running out for me to get Dimiel back. Unfortunately, I ran out of time.

Back to 1999

I woke up to my cousin announcing, "We are here! Welcome to Maryland!" She lived in the beautiful development of Marlton in Prince George's County, Maryland—fifteen minutes outside of DC. Her house was a beautiful three-bedroom home. She had a husband and two beautiful girls. They all welcomed me into their home. It was so nice to see them all again because I never thought it would actually happen. Now I understand how easy it was for me to just pick up and go. I had been doing it my whole life, albeit begrudgingly so. Here begins my next chapter, literally…

Dreamin' Playlist
Scan the QR code to listen to the playlist.

Giving You the Best that I've Got—Anita Baker
What I Am—Edie Brickell

NoNDicCuaL

It Ain't Over 'Til It's Over—Lenny Kravitz
Don't Say Goodbye—Walter Beasley
Have You Ever Loved Somebody—Freddie Jackson
Never Keeping Secrets—Babyface
Just Call My Name—Alyson Williams
I Like—Guy
Every Little Step—BB
Looking for a New Love—Jody Watley
What Have You Done for Me, Lately—Janet Jackson
Feels Good—TTT
Always be My Baby—MC
Love Saw It—Karyn White
That's What Love Is—Miki Howard
Pop, Pop, Pop Goes My Mind—LeVert
Is it a Crime—Sade
Something's Going On—Basic Black
I Love me some Him—TB
That's the Way Love Goes—Janet Jackson
Unconditional Love—Hi-Five
I'm So Into You—SWV
Skeletons—Stevie Wonder
Quickness—Michael Cooper
Firestarter—Tease
Heaven in Your Arms—RJ's Latest Arrival
Nite and Day—Al B. Sure
Let's Wait Awhile—Janet Jackson
She's a Bad Mama Jamma—Carl Carlton

Dreamin'

Don't Take It Personal—J Jackson
Start of a Romance—Skyy
Miss You Much—Janet Jackson
Cha Cha Cha—MC Lyte
Ladies First—Q Latifah
Your Sweetness—The Good Girls
Me Myself and I—De La Soul
Heat of the Moment—After 7
All Around the World—Lisa Stansfield
Poison—BBD
My, My, My—J Gill
Gypsy Woman—Crystal Waters
Making Love in the Rain—Lisa Fischer

Albums

Vesta Williams—Debut album
Al B Sure—debut album
Anita Baker—first three albums
New Edition-Heart Break
Christopher Williams—Debut album
Luther Vandross—Any Love
Shanice Wilson—debut album
Prince—LoveSexy
Madame X-debut album
Levert—first three albums
Keith Sweat—first three albums

Angela Winbush—debut solo album

At Will

When I hear "Anytime" by Brian McKnight or anything from that CD (especially track nine), I think of Johnson. He will always be the one who got away—or did he? I don't think I'll ever get over it. I don't know why! Maybe it's because we had three amazing weeks together. We were so compatible; we clicked, connected, and poof! It dissolved like bubbles going down the drain in cold water. In a by-the-way email months later, he apologized—something about not wanting "bad karma" to follow him. Wow! Ouch!

It was July 3, 2002. I ran into him at Dream, a DC hot spot. Funny, I had just been thinking that as much as I went out, I had yet to run into Johnson. It had been three years since the last time I laid eyes on him, but nothing prepared me for anything more than a greeting.

I was in total shock. Johnson stood in front of me and called my name. I stood there for at least ten seconds with my hand over my mouth, as if I had just won the Lotto or been crowned prom queen.

My brain said, *Move, Gump!* I obeyed.

"Oh my God! Hi, Johnson. How are you? Dayum, you look good." That was a pure, unfiltered thought that slipped through my lips—compliments of the apple martini I had just consumed.

Johnson was still beautiful—big, charming, with an infectious smile and sparkling white teeth; soft, juicy lips; Bambi-shaped eyes; and very defined, thick brows, along with his newest addition—dreadlocks. Standing before me, he looked like a cup of Campbell's soup. Mmm, mmm, good! He just looked edible.

We shared the usual small talk as if it were yesterday instead of three years ago. We still had the easy-going conversation, playing catch-up on what we had in common and the people we knew.

Of course, I had to ask him, "Are you single, still racing motorcycles, and hanging out at strip bars?"

"Yes, yes, and sometimes," he replied.

We exchanged a few more words. I made a few dumb comments. I always had that Joan Clayton thing from *Girlfriends* when I was not in control of the situation. I practically forced my number on him and bribed him with offers to take him to lunch, dinner, or breakfast. I was doing it again, kicking a dead horse that wasn't ever going to get back up.

Hey, you can't knock a girl for being a hopeless romantic—the operative word being hopeless.

Thank God my girls came over to rescue me, throwing me a lifeline before I could further embarrass myself. They ushered me away so fast that I don't recall saying goodbye. I didn't run into him anymore that evening, and I didn't think he was going to call me. Hell, I practically coerced him into taking my number, didn't I?

Well, it was very nice to see him again, especially at that point in my life. Besides, I looked damn good that night in the plunging V-neck peek-a-boo sexy top and size five black slimming slacks, compliments of my two-month workout at World Gym in Largo, Maryland. I scored a couple of phone numbers that night. I realized it was harder to meet people in person than it was online, where I had that person's full attention for at least two minutes before they clicked on the next profile. In a club, there were too many distractions to focus on anything.

On Sunday, I was reviewing my weekend as I folded laundry, trying to remember the dumb comments I made to Johnson. Seeing him again brought back all the old hurt feelings, my inadequacy, unanswered questions, thoughts about what could have been, and self-doubting rejection. I had to ask myself why I still held a spot for him to use at will. After all, he had played me like an old Marvin Gaye record. After giving it some thought, it came to me. He was a symbol that represented all the qualities I felt I deserved—the near-perfect description of the type of man I wished I had in my life, with all the right things to bring to the table. However, I wasn't at a stage in my life where I could execute the same. I wasn't emotionally ready. I was still running from my problems, and it was just bad timing for an honest chance with him. Or was it? Did I have a "forever" chance with Johnson? Looking back now…nah, not a chance. It was all in my head. Ain't that a song? It was 1997, when I saw it for the first time: the symbol—the "It Factor." I was a service representative for a cellular company (that was what we called wireless at the beginning of its inception) in St. Louis. I was in love with the Vice President of Marketing, Mr. Daryl Hall. I called it "falling in love" in my mind. My co-workers joked that I was an obsessed borderline stalker. He didn't even know I was alive, only speaking to me because I made myself very apparent and pitiful to him.

Talk about handsome—Armani-tailored suits, wire-rimmed glasses, a sexy, deep, commanding voice, and a confident smile. He drove a brand new 1997 BMW 740. If I was lucky enough to catch him in the parking lot coming or leaving the office, he would always have "Hypnotized" by The Notorious B.I.G. blaring on the car stereo.

He could have taken another route to get to the break room, but he always walked past the part of the call center where I sat. My job was to take incoming service issues, but whenever he passed by, I'd put my customer on hold just to watch him walk by. I mean, a hard stare. He knew I was watching because he always glanced over his shoulder with a cheeky smile to make sure. He would always raise his hand to speak to me as if he already knew he had caught my attention. He definitely had my attention to the fullest, like a recruit to the first drill sergeant in boot camp.

My co-worker, Don, always teased me about him. "Hey, here comes your boy," or "You just missed your boy," or "He was looking for you." I didn't care. I looked forward to each time he made his way to the Coke machine for his daily dose of caffeine.

One time, I was waiting in the break room for him, with a Coke in hand, to give it to him. He looked surprised, smiled, thanked me, and insisted on giving me my dollar back. (Pretty much, he patted me on the head like a good little puppy, with my tail wagging and tongue hanging out.) I still have that dollar today! I keep it tucked in my pillowcase—don't judge me! Sorry, we aren't talking about Daryl. I'll finish that story later.

Anyway, I finally figured it out. The power and confidence attracted me. I wanted to possess it. These qualities were something I was seriously lacking in my life. Now, I have evolved into my confidence, and I'm not the same person I was when I met

Johnson. The girl who waited by the phone for closure is now a woman who doesn't need validation from a symbol or anyone else, nor is she a needy person eager to welcome him back at will. Back to August 1999, Johnson was the first guy I dated after I moved to DC. He worked with my cousin, Mellie, and he was doing his co-worker a favor by taking me out. It was my second week in DC, and I was staying with her until I found a place of my own. Being the cupid-at-heart that she was, she set up our first communication, so I found myself duped into talking to Johnson on the phone. To my surprise, our first awkward, brief conversation flowed easily. I liked that it was easy to talk to him. Still, I had yet to see him in person, so even if he turned out to be a bug, I got the feeling I'd have a good time with him. I could tell he was silly, just like me, so we planned to hang out that Friday night.

Mellie had been telling me about her co-worker Johnson for two years. Ironically, a chain of events had us finally meeting in person. She always spoke highly of him and ran through the whole woman-shopping list of the right potential good man qualities. He had all the right check marks in her mind: a house with a pool, two cars, a beloved motorcycle, no kids, degrees, and he was very handsome. She added that he had just broken up with his girlfriend. My cousin didn't care for that girl, so she was happy about it. A flag went up in my mind. Oh no, rebound! I mean, it was just one date.

Friday night could not have arrived soon enough for me. I was excited. I had never been on a blind date in my life. The closest I came to one was when I was a teenager, and my best friend had talked this guy up. The only thing she got right was that he was

Black. It goes without saying, I never trusted another female with such a task—until now. I was trying to find something to wear. I didn't want to wear anything too sexy or be too diva, just in case. I was ready to venture into the nightlife of the Chocolate City (that's what we called DC).

The doorbell rang. I sent my cousin's oldest daughter—the twelve-year-old—on a mission to see if he was cute. She came back with a smile on her face, happy to report that he was fine! I could hear them engaging in conversation as I wrapped up my beauty session and gave myself one last check in the mirror. Then I joined them in the living room, where Johnson and Mellie were discussing the events of their day.

Damn, he was very striking. My little cousin wasn't lying. He reminded me of Bill Bellamy, lips and all. After the introductions, with the nervous grins and cheese, he asked if I was ready to go. Of course, I was, and we were on our merry way.

We went to a spot called DC Live, a huge club with four levels. Each level had a different theme. There was a fashion show in progress on the bottom level. Johnson wanted to see the show, so we settled in there. The room had a nice-sized crowd, and the music was at a comfortable level, which allowed us the opportunity to talk. He was incredibly open and honest about a lot of things going on with him. I liked the way he welcomed me into his world. I didn't reveal that I knew most of his story already, thanks to Mellie, who can't hold water in a plastic bucket. You tell her about your business, and you might as well broadcast it on CNN. So, I listened intently, as if it were my first time hearing it. He told me about his recent breakup. He really liked her. They got along very well. The sex was incredible, but he couldn't talk to her. I thought that was odd for a man, considering most men would prefer their mate didn't talk. He shared with me what his ideal mate would be, someone who, by coincidence, sounded just like me.

I know it was crazy, but for some strange reason, he had a familiar aura about him. He reminded me of someone I had already met or knew. I tossed that feeling aside. He owned a motorcycle (I knew that, too), had a love for racing, and was remodeling his house. He joked about himself, saying he probably could finish if he just stayed home sometimes.

I was in awe of this beautiful Black man. It was so refreshing to be in the company of someone who had it together. I thought about the last non-goal-oriented jackal of my past that I knew back home. I just wanted to wrap him up, take him back home, put him on display like the Hope Diamond, and show that knucklehead what a real man looked like. Behold, a real man! Sure, we had some good brothers back home, but sisters must have taken them all because I never ran into any of them.

I shared my desperate, narrow escape from St. Louis story with him, and he was very attentive, seeming genuinely interested in what I had to say—as if it really mattered. He complimented me on the courage it must have taken to leave my baby while trying to make a new start for us. No one had ever said that to me. At that time, I didn't consider myself courageous. It was a matter of refusing to eat tuna and crackers for the rest of my life. I had to make it happen.

Our energy was interrupted when a couple of his bike buddies recognized him and came over to say hello. After Johnson introduced us, I excused myself to find the ladies' room. Really, it was to let the boys chat. Besides, I needed to take inventory, check my face, refresh my lipstick, and pinch myself to make sure I wasn't dreaming. I looked at myself in the mirror as I applied a fresh coat of lipstick. I thought about what he'd said to me. This was still surreal. If someone had told me a year ago that I would not marry the man I was engaged to but have a baby with him anyway, and end up in Washington, DC, making double what I was earning, I would have said they were insane.

Now, there I was, sitting in a club, having a bomb conversation with an intelligent, handsome guy. Stop playing! Isn't it funny how life works out?

When I returned to the table, the boys were gone. They had gotten a table close by. The fashion show was at its finale, and Johnson had a confession.

"When you walked into the living room, I knew I was in trouble," he confided.

"Why?" I asked, crossing one leg over the other, and resting my elbow on the table.

"I didn't expect you to be so attractive," he said.

Now, this diva didn't know how to take that one, so I laughed, thanked him for the half-ass compliment, and said, "You aren't the booger I thought you'd be either."

We laughed about that, which led us to share our best stories about our dating mishaps.

I went back to what he had said earlier. I was curious, so I asked him, "Why do you think you are going to be in trouble?"

"I'm attracted to you, and you're related to my co-worker. I just don't want any confusion," he added.

I never gave that idea any thought—not really. Honestly, I was simply happy to be out. I reassured him, "I'm not looking to make a love connection. We're just hanging out." Then I thanked him for taking the time to be out with me, but tonight was just for fun. It had been a long time since I had been out on a date, so I was just enjoying the moment. He nodded in acceptance of my words.

We talked throughout the closing of the fashion show. Afterward, we left the basement level and headed upstairs to dance.

He teasingly asked, "You know how to dance?"

"A little," I answered. I could've been a Luke dancer if I wanted to, I thought to myself.

We danced to my new favorite song, "Vivrant Thing" by Q-Tip. I let him have it (as the children would say). It goes without saying, he would not doubt that issue again.

The night went on, the drinks kept coming, and we kept dancing. The attraction volleyed between us. I was mid-sentence when he kissed me right there on the dance floor. I felt that deep, tongue-touching kiss down to my toes. *Okay*, I thought, *he really doesn't want to go there, with the sexually deprived individual I am.*

Shortly after the tongue dance ended, we quickly grew bored with the scene, so we left that club. It was still early, so we went to another spot called Charlie's in Fort Washington, Maryland. It was an older crowd—my uncle's age, with Stacy Adams shoes and fedora hats on—but don't sleep! It was the only way to really party back home. You never had to worry about a fight breaking out over something as foolish as someone brushing up against someone in an overcrowded, overpriced club. They served wings, and that's a telling sign of a good old-fashioned spot.

We walked onto the crowded dance floor, surrounded by a bunch of electric sliders. It instantly reminded me of home. It was the first pang of realizing I had really moved away, and then my panic set in. I had left everything recognizable behind. I was in unfamiliar territory, and the fear of my unknown future started seeping in. I forced those thoughts out of my mind. I just wanted to enjoy myself for once without sabotaging my happy moment and interrupting my perfected electric slide.

In one of our earlier conversations at DC Live, Johnson said he would take me by his house on the way home, and Charlie's was close to his place. We didn't stay at Charlie's long; we had one more drink that we really didn't need, and we were out.

We got to his house in no time. He gave me a quick tour as promised, which ended in his bedroom, where we got our old-school bump-and-grind show with clothes on. I couldn't take it; it was more human interaction in one night than I'd had in a year. We had to stop before I did something I might regret later, for at that moment, there wasn't one. Blame it on convenient amnesia. Once we both unconsciously came to the same conclusion—it wasn't happening—he drove me back to Mellie's house. He walked me to the front door. I kissed him goodnight and thanked him for a wonderful evening. I tiptoed into the house and quietly closed the door behind me. The light underneath Mellie's closed bedroom door went out. I shook my head as I walked to my room and chuckled to myself. How old was I?

Saturday, Johnson called me. We planned to go to dinner, but afterward, everything was up in the air. I was excited about seeing him again, but reality jumped in to remind me he was nursing a breakup. I shouldn't make too much of it. I didn't want to, but it felt so good to have someone interested in me. Mellie and I went shopping at Potomac Mills that afternoon. I told her all about the evening—he was a perfect gentleman, very sweet, and we were going out again tonight. I didn't tell her everything.

I knew better. She was surprised to find out that he asked me out again. Hell, so was I.

Johnson picked me up, and he took me to the Outback Steakhouse in Oxon Hill for dinner. After dinner, we picked up some videos from Blockbuster and headed back to his place. We got through the first movie: *There's Something About Mary*, one of my favorite comedies. He put in the second movie, *The Waterboy*. I didn't find it as funny as he did.

During the movie, we got comfortable on the couch, with him spooning (or cup-caking). He rested his hand on my thigh. The hairs stood up all over my body; I was pitifully in desperate need of affection. He kissed the back of my neck, and the pulse started. My body was betraying me. It felt good to have sensual contact with a man again, and it was long overdue. He slid his hand between my thighs. I didn't stop him, even though I knew better. I knew Mellie was going to hate me, but the deafening thump of my heartbeat drowned out my reasoning until his lips made their way to the source of the pounding, and he ignited my fire. He didn't continue, and I was impressed with his restraint. I was like, okay, save it for another time, which I was totally on board with. I was going to say "No," anyway. (Insert laughter here.)

He returned to his spot behind me and held me under the blanket that had covered us. We both fell into a light sleep.

After I got home, I went to sleep. My dreams finished what we started. I didn't hear from him for most of the week. I was busy working overtime at my new job, so I didn't notice it right away. I broke down and called him Thursday night, and that's when he told me about the accident. Accident! I was surprised to hear that. Mellie never mentioned it, but we didn't discuss Johnson anymore. I guess she was trying to respect our privacy.

On Friday, we had a date. I was going to pick him up this time because he had fallen off his bike and was scratched up and sore, but otherwise okay. Thank God! Tonight, it was The Cheesecake Factory for dinner and Dave & Buster's in White Flint Mall.

On the way, we had a long talk. He told me I made him forget about her, and his words made me feel good. He asked me, "What will take the hurt away?"

That was the most honest question a man could ask a woman with whom he was interested. I gave him the only answer I knew to be true for heartache. Hell, I was nursing several. "It just takes time."

At that moment, I knew what we were sharing wasn't enough to substantiate a lasting connection. I was merely pacifying his situation. It was up to me not to get caught up because he was being completely honest with me, and he made no promises. Some women, me included, tend to tune out when a man is being overtly obvious because it doesn't align with our own narrative or perspective. I entered headfirst into the zone alone. I should have run far from the obvious, but I stood there wide-eyed and bushy-tailed, like a deer caught in the headlights. We had fun at Dave & Buster's even though he was busted up.

When we made it back to his house, he was still hurting. I made sure he was comfortable, gave him his meds, and let myself out after he fell asleep. He called me Saturday morning, asking me to go to the store for a hot water bottle; his side was aching, and he needed me. Of course, I obliged.

Saturday night, we didn't have any plans to do anything special because of his condition. So, I picked up some movies, and we just chilled. Later that night, Johnson fell asleep, lying on his back. He looked so cute. I intended to repeat the night before and just let myself out. I really didn't want to disturb him. I was crawling over him to get out of bed. I thought I would just kiss him, as my lips touched his. I felt him grow between my thighs, and he returned my kiss.

The soft butterfly kiss I intended, turned into entangled tongue dancing. His hands were on my back, caressing me softly. He grew to a full erection, and it became a little uncomfortable to stay in one spot. I asked myself, "What should I do now?" I knew he was not in any condition to have sex, but I selfishly reasoned it had been a year without it, and my body needed this. (Who said that?) He greeted me with more kisses and caresses.

That's enough. Lights out. Full disclosure: I was thinking about my…um…encounters and whether it was a good idea to go full Zane in this book. When I originally drafted this book, I had fully committed to the explicit details, but now I know that's unnecessary. I don't want to be known for *just* that. It's not the goal or the tone I'm looking for. You just met me (smile). I want you to know me as the well-rounded person I was becoming, and detailed sex scenes would take away from that focus. Besides, I am thinking about all the people who will read my book, and I have a personal responsibility to keep my message clear. Okay, back to the story.

On Sunday, we woke up to the birds chirping. After we showered and got dressed, we went to IHOP in Fort Washington for breakfast. He was concerned—more like afraid—that Mellie should know my whereabouts. By now, it would have been easy to assume the obvious, so I called her, pretending I was unfazed as I told her where we were while we waited for our breakfast to arrive.

After breakfast, we went back to Mellie's house so I could change, and then we were off. We went to the movies first to see *The Sixth Sense*. After we got out, it was a beautiful Sunday afternoon. He proudly announced he wanted to be the first to show me the Baltimore Harbor, which had some of the biggest boats I had ever been close to—bigger and more than those docked on the Mississippi River back home. There was a jazz band playing on the steps leading to the Harbor Mall. We shared a romantic hand-in-hand walk around the harbor. We visited the Bay Lady and played a few games in the ESPN Zone. We agreed it was not as much fun as Dave & Buster's. It was a pretty August day, and the harbor was romantically beautiful—or it was the company I was keeping.

We went back to his place later that evening. He was into watching a motorcycle race. I was just being accommodating by watching it with him because the thought of someone crashing scared me—more like him not being with us for the love of speed. I respected his choice in life and what he did with it, but it scared me, if I'm being honest.

He was sitting behind me on the bed, and he grabbed me, whispering in my ear, "I know you didn't come back here for this." He was right. He read my mind and gave me what I wanted.

On Monday, I felt very self-conscious. I felt like I was losing his connection to me. He didn't call me, which only fanned the flames of my anxiety, but I talked myself out of calling him. My guilt fed all my insecurities. It was just sex, right? I got what I wanted, so why did I feel so pathetic? Why wasn't he feeling the same way I was about him? Damn, why did I sleep with him so early? I beat myself up over it. I had to know—I had scared him away? Maybe I didn't really know what I thought I knew about him. It begged the question: Did I screw it up? I had to know.

To add to my woes, Mellie knew everything. It was obvious when I didn't come home. Even though we didn't discuss it, I could only imagine what she thought of me. I had never been a loose girl, but she wouldn't have known that by my behavior. Hell, we hadn't been in each other's company since we were teenagers. I knew I couldn't expect her to understand. How could she? I knew I had embarrassed her with my stunts. I would have been ashamed of myself, too, if the situation were reversed. How could I be so selfish? Okay, I was feeling him, but I could still hear the song by Zhane, "Love Me Today," in my mind. It was something else we both had in common: we both loved the same type of music. Damn! He had no clue how I had already envisioned us old together in matching rocking chairs, happily watching our grandkids play in the front yard of our home. There wasn't a thing he couldn't ask that I would not have done. I thought I had found the one I had been searching for all my life, but sadly, it was not to be. Poor thing; I was swept away in my own denial.

I broke down and I called him early Tuesday. He said he was going to return his ex's things and that he was done with that situation. It was over as far as he was concerned. I held a small hope that we could or that we would continue.

Mellie invited me to meet her co-workers for lunch, which included Johnson. I thought, okay, I am thinking too much. I couldn't get it out of my head that this thing was over. We talked, laughed, and shared about our weekend; we talked about the movies we saw. He gave me no hint that it would be the last time we would see each other. If I had known that then, I would have appreciated it more.

This is a good time to note again: he never promised me forever and a ring. It wasn't love at first sight. In fact, he did nothing wrong. It was just my self-producing fantasy land dream I was vibing on, based on the times we shared. I was so unaware that a man could be so attentive, so right, so perfectly matched, and so sexually exciting. Oh yes, and so not that into me. I had never experienced it before. I had never met a guy who wasn't feeling me the way I was feeling him. This was new to me. I mean, didn't he notice the tiara on my head? I was a prize, a former beauty contest finalist, a local access TV host, a talent show first-place winner, and a vocalist. I was the shit! Okay, I am feeling myself a bit. (Insert laughter here.) It may have been because his heart belonged to someone else. Truthfully, he never really got to know me because I based my self-worth on what was between my thighs instead of my big heart he never got to meet first.

It was my fault for wishing for something more than what he could give me. I could have fallen in love with Johnson. I would have had his kids, washed his cars with my toothbrush, and lived happily ever after—no question. I would have loved for this to have been the happy conclusion to my story, but it was just the beginning of my long four years of single life in a new city.

He never called me again. The moral of this story: a lesson ignored is a lesson repeated, and you will repeat what you refuse to acknowledge.

"Choke me in the shallow water before I get too deep… Don't let me get too deep," as my girl Edie Brickell said. Fade to black…

Back to 2002, Johnson called me and asked me out to lunch. I had the nerve to be surprised. I mean, I was fly and beautiful. Why wouldn't he call me, right? I had developed self-worth since the last time we met. He caught my new vibe. Either way, I was looking forward to catching up with an old flame.

We chose TGI Fridays in Greenbelt, Maryland. It was close to my job and easy for me to stay if I wanted to. He was already there and seated. I saw him immediately when I walked in. He greeted me with a full bear hug and a kiss on the cheek. He complimented me on my fragrance, and I returned the gesture. He smelled amazing, as usual. He was growing baby dreads. No more berries and juice for him. I teased him about it. He flashed me his 100-watt smile, and I loved it. Then it dawned on me: I wasn't strong enough to resist the temptation. As long as we weren't alone with a nice bottle of Cabernet Sauvignon and old-school R&B slow songs, I would be fine.

We talked about our brief affair. He apologized for how things ended, saying it was awkward between him and Mellie for a bit. I don't think either of us really touched our lunch. We were so engaged in conversation. It was like we never missed a beat. We paused often, gazing into each other's eyes, until one of us broke the trance. We were very hands-on as we talked, whispering in each other's ears to ensure the other was heard. At some point, our server brought us the check. We were too wrapped up in conversation to notice.

So, there I was, getting the personal invite to his pool party. He reminded me about the last time I was over—when the place was a hot mess of construction. Now, he was ready to flaunt the fruits of his labor, to show off like it was the grand reveal on some home makeover show. We wrapped up our little lunch rendezvous, and he walked me out to my car. That's when he pulled me in for one of those bear hugs that says more than words ever could. His lips grazed my ear, sending a shiver down my spine. "Don't forget that swimsuit," he whispered, all smooth like butter. "It was so good running into you again." And just like that, he vanished, leaving me standing there with a mix of anticipation and déjà vu.

You know, I had to hit up my girl Tonya right after. I spilled all the tea about our lunch and the pool party invite. Tonya, that's my ride-or-die, my sister from another mister. We met back at my old gig, Q Communication, and let me tell you, we clicked faster than fingers snapping to a beat. She's the one you call when the plot thickens, and it was getting thick.

Who would've thought picking out a swimsuit could be a full-blown saga? I mean, I wanted to serve looks, but not the whole buffet of my 36 DD blessings. And I sure wasn't about to play it safe with some one-piece Norma number. So, I went for the middle ground: a one-piece from Vicki's Secret that was more hole than fabric, paired with a sheer cover-up that whispered secrets of its own.

Tonya, true to form, pulled up to my house looking like a whole mood. There she was, rocking a two-piece that screamed

"I came to play," topped with a designer cover-up that could've come straight off the runway. That's my girl Tonya—always serving looks that could kill. We rolled out in a two-car convoy, heading to his house. That drive was a trip down memory lane I never thought I'd take. The closer we got, the more those old wounds started whispering, "Girl, keep your head." Because let's be real—he probably had a guest list full of pretty faces. But this wasn't some fairy-tale musical. I wasn't Sandy, he sure wasn't Danny, and life ain't *Grease*.

So, there I was, guard up, ready for the letdown. Because when you've danced with disappointment before, you learn to expect the music to stop. But hey, I was there to have a good time, with or without the drama. Tonya by my side, swimsuit on point, and a heart ready for whatever beat the party was pumping.

His street was littered with cars and bikes. Finally, we found two spots to park, and it was a hike to the house. I was happy I chose simple flip-flops, but my diva friend Tonya was dressed to the tens with heels. Like a trooper, she worked it down the street. The front door was open. As expected, there were people everywhere. His biker friends were there, even some I had met three years ago, some co-workers, and—surprise! —a rack of girls. The ratio of guys to girls was unexpectedly good. He set it up nicely, with a huge tent on one side, with round tables and chairs, and a dance floor with a DJ stand. The other side had a tiki bar and two big cabanas. The pool was large, with a hot tub and a beautifully lit waterfall.

Tonya joked that it felt like we were in Miami. We made our way to the bar to get a cute drink with fruit hanging off the rim and an umbrella in it, just to set it off. Then we hunted for a nice place to sit and enjoy the scene.

Johnson snuck up behind me and wrapped his arms around me. "There you are. What took you so long? I almost thought you weren't coming." Then he hugged Tonya. "Hey, I remember you from the club. You ladies need anything? Come see me. I'm friends with the owner." He winked, and we all laughed. Some new guests showed up. He excused himself, and off he went to handle his hosting duties.

Everyone was friendly. It was very refreshing. Tonya always found the craziest men to talk to. She entertained them, making them feel like they were the man. We laughed with the guys sitting in our area for a while and learned they worked with Johnson. While we were engaged in conversation, my eyes would catch his. Wherever he was, he would smile and wink, and I would smile back. I didn't want to analyze it too much because I wanted to enjoy this second round regardless of how it ended.

After two cute drinks, nature called, so I made my way to the powder room. I took one last look before I opened the door to find Johnson standing there.

"Hi! Were you waiting?" I asked, surprised.

"Yes, for you. C'mon, let's go dance." He took my hand and led me through a crowd of people to the dance floor. The first two songs were fast, and we were seductively dancing. Then the DJ slowed it down and played "Beauty" by Dru Hill. I assumed it was over and attempted to walk away, thinking he was following me, until he grabbed my hand. "Oh no, you don't! I've been waiting for this all night." He pulled me in close for a slow dance.

"Wow! Really? Waiting on what, exactly?" I asked.

"Slow dancing with you, girl. Remember, that's where we first kissed—on the dance floor?" he answered.

I tried to act like I didn't remember. "Really? I don't recall," I said coyly.

He frowned. "You really don't remember?" he asked.

I put him out of his agony as I pressed against his hard, muscled chest. "Of course, I do, 'cause you kissed me first," I reminded him.

"Nah, I'm pretty sure it was you who pounced on a brother," he said, being brash.

"Really? Why? Because you are so irresistible?" I said sarcastically.

"No, no, you're right. I kissed you first. You are cute when you get fired up. Listen, I want you to get in the pool with me unless you're worried about your weave." He chuckled.

"Now you know I do not wear fake hair. All natural here." I pretended to be annoyed.

"I know, I know." He laughed. "I've always liked your curls." He caressed my face, grabbed a curl, and twisted it around his finger.

I gave him the side eye. "Are you trying to seduce me, Johnson?"

"Naw, is it working?"

We both laughed as the slow song ended.

He was still holding my hand. "Hey, I will walk you back to your girl. Looks like she is holding her own. She's got three brothers around her."

"I know, that's my Tonya."

Johnson continued to walk me back to where we were sitting, kissed me on the cheek, thanked me for the dance, and walked away to handle something.

At Will

"See, you were worried for nothing," Tonya whispered. "He has been on you all night, girl. Look, I have to get rid of these flies around me, and by flies, I mean these dudes. Hey, let's get in the pool."

"So, your answer to getting rid of them is to show them your body. Right? Makes perfect sense."

"No, I'm trying to show it to some new prospects." Tonya laughed.

We took off our cover-ups and slow-walked down the steps into the in-ground pool. Tonya was the swimmer; I just played in the water. As I stepped toward the center, I felt his hands around my waist again.

"Gotcha! Why didn't you tell me you were getting in? I told you I wanted to get in the pool with you."

"You are the host, so I figured you'd be hosting."

"You're right. I am in charge. I get to have breaks, don't I?"

"Sure, I am flattered you are sharing them with me."

One of his friends called him. "Hey, Johnson, they need you out front!"

"Out front?" he repeated as he dashed off.

Tonya gave me that you-know-you-are-going-to-give-him-some face as she splashed water at me.

"Stop it! He's just being Johnson, the eternal flirt."

"No, I think it's more than that. I've been watching you guys flow so easily together."

"I'm not getting my hopes up. I am just enjoying the moment." I dipped my head under the water.

Just then, the DJ said, "Officer Friendly has arrived to tell us that the party is over—something about the noise ordinance, and you know Fort Washington don't play. I'm going to play one more song, and you kids have got to go!"

"Well, damn! I guess we'd better get out and dry off so we can go," Tonya said.

The crowd was thinning out.

"Hey, hey," Johnson said, walking up as we were drying off. "Listen, I'm sorry about that. There was a little disagreement between two of the bikers, so they had to go. But the night is still young. I want you to stay and share one glass of wine with me. Okay, a bottle of wine with me. I know you are with your girl."

"Oh, that's my cue. It's okay, darling. I will see you later," Tonya said.

I walked Tonya to her car.

"So, what are you going to do? He is definitely feeling you. He's a great catch," Tonya said.

"I don't know yet. I know the attraction is ridiculous. He said he wanted us to start over, but I'm not sure. I don't want my heart broken again."

"Well, do what makes you happy and something you are willing to live with, but if it were me, I'd go for it." Tonya reached out to hug me.

"I will take it under advisement. I love you, girl. Call me and let me know you made it home."

We broke our hug, and she got in her car. I moved my car and parked in his driveway.

There wasn't anyone left outside. I grabbed a tote from the car that included dry clothes and made my way to the powder room. I removed my wet swimsuit and replaced it with a strapless sundress. I politely stuck my wet swimsuit in his dryer. There were only a handful of folks left inside, cleaning up and getting to-go plates. I made my way back outside. Johnson was at the DJ stand, picking out music. As I walked up, he handed me a glass of Cabernet Sauvignon and turned on an old-school slow jam. Oh, I knew I was in trouble.

We sang off-key through the first glass of wine and several songs. We talked, laughed, and then headed over to the cabana. The candlelight made it so romantic. One of his last guests popped his head out to say goodnight.

"I have been waiting to do this all night." Catching me off guard, he kissed me.

The tingles started from the bottom of my toes. He gently, softly kissed the bottom lip, then the top. I broke from his embrace.

"Wow, ummm. Okay, let's talk some more."

"I'm so sorry. Did I do something wrong?"

"No, you did it right. Woo, that's the problem." I patted my cheeks, attempting to get the red shade back to normal.

We nervously laughed together. Toni Braxton serenaded us with "Maybe" in the background.

He apologized again for how things ended. "Hey, I know it was shitty. Writing you an email was so lame. I owed you a conversation in person, and I blew it. I've thought about it for the past three years, and I promised myself if I ever had a chance, I would fix it. If anything happens between us now, it's because it's meant to be. I want to explore it. I'm asking for a second chance with you. There are no distractions this time. You have my full attention. I was excited when I ran into you at the club that night.

You are just as pretty as the first day I saw you. I couldn't believe my luck that you were still willing to see me." He put his finger softly over my lips before I could respond. "Don't answer now; just let us be in this moment."

Good, because I was speechless. It was everything I wanted to hear. It validated all the hurt feelings from three years ago.

Ironically, "Anytime" by Brian McKnight was playing in the background, reminding me of the journey to this moment. I turned off those feelings and grabbed his shirt as he got closer. My hands caught his face, and we kissed deeply, passionately. I had waited so long to hear those words, and my mind wondered if it was too late.

Zhane's "La La La" played in the background of our moment. I'm not sure why he always caught me in a drought when my better judgment was questionable.

He broke our kiss. "Let's get in the Jacuzzi."

I told him my swimsuit was in the dryer. He excused himself to go retrieve it. He returned and handed me my suit. In a gentleman's gesture, he turned his back so I could put it on. I was so damn wet at this point that it slid right up. He walked me down the steps into the Jacuzzi. Whitney sang "Oh Yes" as we submerged in the water. We walked to the middle of the Jacuzzi, where we slow-danced seductively and then kissed. When the song was over, we walked out of the Jacuzzi. Joe was playing in the background, singing about all the things your man won't do.

We were back in the cabana. I wrapped myself in a towel and excused myself back to the powder room. He said he would meet me in the den. I needed to turn this heat down and think. I stared at myself in the mirror and talked to myself. I had done so much work on myself since the last time I saw him. I wanted this to be real. I really did, but I knew it was only going to be about sex, and we weren't going anywhere else with this thing we had. I wanted something real for myself. I deserved to be courted properly and not just be something to do at the end of the night.

As fine as he was—a nice guy with all the qualities a woman wanted—he was the guy. Just not for me. All the apologies in the world did not make up for losing my dignity and self-respect. All my tears were not for nothing. I didn't want to risk my heart breaking again. Besides, this thing we had was tainted. I had already given him some, so now I was asking him to respect me or see me the way I wanted to be seen. It was too late, and I wasn't going to get what I wanted.

So, there! I had my speech ready. I took one last look in the mirror and opened the door. I made my way to the den, where I found him sleeping—knocked out and snoring lightly. I thought, how ironic? He was sleeping just as he was when I slept with him three years ago. Lessons you do not learn, you are bound to repeat. I got a do-over. I was paying attention in class, and I was going to get it right this time.

All the planning and execution of this incredible party ran its course. I didn't bother to wake him. I covered him with a nearby blanket, gathered my things, quietly locked up for him, and left.

On the ride home, having the conversation in my head, I resolved it was the best decision. I had learned how to be my own best friend. Maxwell's "A Woman's Work" was playing on the radio as I drove home. That was it. The answer was my worth. There was something immensely powerful about that, and it felt good walking away with my head held high. You can't think with your legs open, Nondiccual. No longer used "at will."

This playlist takes me on a nostalgic journey back to my first year in the vibrant Chocolate City. Each song captures those unforgettable days and nights, bringing back my memories of excitement, discovery, and embracing living on my own.

At Will Playlist

Scan the QR code to listen to the playlist.

U Know What's Up—Donell Jones
Faded Pictures—Case
All that I Can Say—MJB
Maybe—Toni B.
Vibrant Thing—Q-Tip
Anytime—Brian M.
So Anxious—Ginuwine
Beauty—Dru Hill
The Love I Never Had—MJB
Happily, Ever After—Case
Sweet Lady—Tyrese
You—Jesse Powell
Get It On Tonight—Montell Jordan
Bills—DC
Back That Ass Up—Juvenile
Moments in Love —Art of Noise
Love Me Today—Zhane

Oh Yes—Whitney Houston
'Til I Get Over you—Brian M
You Got Me—The Roots
Fortunate—Maxwell
Caught Out There—Kelis
If You Love Me—Mint Condition
If You–Silk
Back in One Piece—Aaliyah and DMX
Try Again—Timbo and Aaliyah
He Can't Love You—JE
A Woman's Worth—A Keys
You Know That I Love You—DJ
Heartbreaker—MC
Meeting In My Bedroom—Silk
Quiet Storm—Mob Deep
Who Dat—JT Money
Got Your Money–ODB
Get Gone—Ideal
Get It On Tonight—Montell Jordan
No Scrubs—TLC
All N My Grill—Missy

Albums

Zhane-debut
MJB—Mary
Eric Benét—A Day in the Life
Brian McKnight—Anytime

On My Own

Who would've thought I'd be cashing in my city life for this ticket to suburban serenity. There I was, waking up at the crack of dawn to the sound of a coffee maker on a timer, and going to sleep with the ten o'clock news playing me a lullaby alongside the crickets' chorus. My old life? It was a non-stop party—happy hours bleeding into club nights, stumbling home when the morning birds were just warming up their vocals, and sleeping till noon. But here I am, trading in my heels for slippers, my cocktails for sippy cups.

It's a whole new world—a lane so mundane it's almost surreal; like a Lifetime: Movie of the Week. This is grown-up life in full swing, and I've had Mellie schooling me on the ABCs of parenthood. Who knew this would be my new normal? But you know what? I'm there for it, learning to love the quiet, the routine, and the sweet, simple moments that come with this for-real grown-up me.

Mellie lived in Marlton, a subdivision in Upper Marlboro, Maryland, which was a perfect place to raise a family. I loved the smell of the pine trees in the morning air; it faintly reminded me of Anchorage, Alaska. There was an abundance of wildlife; one could mistake the surroundings for being deep in the woods and not just outside the hustle and bustle of the DC city line. I saw chipmunks, deer, hummingbirds, owls, woodpeckers, and foxes, among others. I even saw bugs I had never encountered before, and as someone who never liked bugs, I still don't. People jogged, rode bikes, or walked, and the neighbors were friendly. Marlton was a golf community comprising of single-family homes, a significant number of townhouses, and a single apartment complex that seemed out of place in the subdivision. It had two elementary schools, a couple of daycares, and churches within the community, which I loved. It also had the convenience of a grocery store, gas station, liquor store, Rite Aid, Bank of America, Domino's, a nail salon, a veterinarian, beauty supply shop, barber shop, McDonald's, and a restaurant with outdoor seating—all within the neighborhood. I felt safe there.

Looking back on it now, 1999 was a good time in my life. Everything felt brand new, exciting, terrifying, and promising, and I had something to prove to myself. I felt like Alice in Wonderland, embarking on some brand-new adventure. The eight-hundred-forty-mile ride was like going down the rabbit hole, with Wonderland being the Chocolate City. My future held so many encouraging possibilities. Memories of that period would resurface whenever I heard songs like "Beauty" by Dru Hill or "So Anxious" by Ginuwine, evoking the feeling of driving home from my new job on Route 1 to the Beltway.

I was thinking I needed something to keep my mind occupied until I went home to get my baby. Being the friendly Barbara that I am, it was easy for me to make new friends. I met a couple at work. I met Patrice, who was married with two kids and lived down the road from my cousin, off Route 301, in a brand-new townhome in Bowie, Maryland, behind the Walmart. She was a member of Ebenezer Baptist Church, and she invited me to go with her.

Let me tell you, I have never been to a church that had a car lot full of nothing but imported expensive cars; it looked like a luxury auto sales lot. This mega-church had an elevator and overflow rooms. The choir sounded like Kirk Franklin & Them, and there was an ATM in the vestibule. It felt more like an arena for a concert than a church in the business of saving souls. What did I know about it, being a heathen and all? I was blown away by all the extras. I called my granny to tell her all about it. I had never been to such an enormous church before in my life.

I come from a down-home church with a mother, a deacon, and an usher board, where everyone knew everybody, your kin, and all your business. The announcements read like something from a Steve Harvey skit. Every Sunday, the choir sang the same song, "God Be with You," before dismissal. After service, in the church basement, they sold $5 chicken dinners. Dollar rolls greased in butter, mashed potatoes and gravy, macaroni and cheese, green beans, greens, yams, cabbage, rice, and a salad. I've gained five pounds just thinking about it.

I grew up in Monumental Baptist Church on the corner of Page and Newstead. It was led by the beloved Pastor White. May he rest in power. I was drawn to this church. As I was turning around in front of the church to run back to our house, I heard the choir singing because the doors of the church were open, literally. The singing drew me in. I was so curious, I stepped inside the church and sat on the pew closest to the door. The sanctuary wasn't very big; it was parted right down the center, anchored by a huge cross in the back of the church. It held about eight extra-long pew benches on each side. There were the pews on the right where the motherboard sat and pews on the left where the deacon board sat; both made up of two smaller rows of pews. There was one pew on each side of the doors against the wall at the entrance of the sanctuary for the ushers and nurses. The organ was on the right and the piano on the left in front of the pulpit. The preacher's pulpit sat in the middle. Climb just two steps from the main floor, and behind the pulpit was the choir. At the very back of the church, hanging on the wall, were pictures of both the current and past pastors. There were three sets of stained-glass windows on parallel sides of the wall on the outside walk of the pews. The carpet and seat cushions were both the same red color.

Pastor White saw me sitting there. He came over and asked me who my mother was; he assumed I was with the choir. I told him she was at home. He looked concerned, so I explained that I heard the singing from outside, so I came in to listen. Just then, I heard Nanny (my great-grandmother) calling me. I ran out of the church so she could see me, and Pastor White followed me. Nanny looked scared, relieved, and confused.

"Is this your baby?" Pastor White asked.

"Yes, she's my great-grandbaby," Nanny answered.

"You know your grandbaby sat down to listen to the choir. It's a sign you should bring her to church this Sunday. We have Bible school for the children."

Just then, my friends saw me and called me to come play, so I ran back to them and left Nanny and Pastor White talking. Pastor White baptized me in this church when I was nine. I became a member of the church. My whole family followed me to the church and joined. That's how my relationship began with God.

Ebenezer was nothing like Monumental Baptist Church. I felt like a grain of sand dropped on a beach. It was large, and I felt disconnected. It wasn't the church's fault. I found myself distracted by all the insignificant things, and I needed to learn to be open to change. Did you ever feel that when you finally went to church, it seemed as if the preacher was preaching his sermon directly to you? You understood the message, took away some food for thought, and tried to apply it to your life or circumstances.

Oh, the other thing I noticed was the young women looked like they had just left the club to come to church. Maybe it's me, but cleavage showing, a tummy exposed, and wearing jeans with the thong hanging out for all eyes to see aren't appropriate church attire. But hey, you've got to save souls, and there's nothing wrong with coming as you are, as long as saving your soul is why you are there.

My next focus was locating a place to live on my own, losing the rest of my baby fat, saving my money, and then going back to St. Louis to get my baby. The job that brought me to the DC area was in Laurel, Maryland. I was so excited about my new position, the money, but the facilities seriously left a lot to be desired. The office space was an oversized copy room. It held six small cubes, and they packed us in there like sardines. It reminded me of my past jobs with tight quarters. Some people were nice enough. It took a minute for me to grow on the women, but the men didn't have a problem introducing themselves. I was the new cute girl. It was nice to be new and anonymous. I sat sandwiched between Mandeep, a beautiful Indian woman, on my left, and Dwayne, a brother, on my right. I thought that was ironic.

In the short time I was there, Dwayne and I were friendly enough. I even bought him lunch twice. He would skip lunch a lot. He was my age and married with five kids. Dwayne showed me around the office, schooled me on office politics, and let me in on a secret. He was leaving the company as soon as his references cleared. He would start working at another telecom company, Q Communications.

Back in 1999, good old wild Bill Clinton was still president and was getting impeached behind the Monica Lewinsky scandal. My two cents on the subject, not that anybody asked: this was between him and his wife. Thank goodness I didn't have a friend like Linda Tripp, who took it upon herself to record their conversations, hoping it would gain her some positive notoriety. It was bad that she kept the dress with semen on it and told them about the cigar in her privates. I have done some things I would never want to repeat. Hey, with friends like that, who needs enemies? I felt sorry for her. Monica, that is.

Moving on. The telecom industry was booming on the East Coast. The consulting agencies were fighting to hire folks who could name their price. Pop-up Internet/telecom companies were all over the DC metro area. One company even offered a BMW with a two-year signed contract. It was crazy money to be made back then. Of course, I asked Dwayne to hook me up once he got in. I was all for making more money. I don't remember a lot in that two-month period that I worked there, except a very brief encounter with a co-worker who worked in our Columbia office. A week before Dwayne left, we visited the Columbia location for training. That's when I saw him. His name was Joseph. Dewayne introduced us. I reached out to shake his hand. There was an electric sexual charge that ran between us, and that was it. He had milk chocolate, baby-soft skin, cold black curly hair, and pretty brown eyes with Bambi-long eyelashes. He was slender, about five-foot-nine, well-dressed, smelled good, and he was so damn sexy. Coincidentally, he was a writer. He was writing his first novel, so we had something in common besides the mutual sexual attraction. He only had one tiny flaw: he had a girlfriend, or should I say, his fiancée.

It started with emailing him. I was feeling frisky that day. I was fishing to see if he would bite, and he did. Our brief encounter was mostly phone calls and emails. The one time we got together, nothing happened. Let's say he was too excited to see me and leave it at that. We made better friends anyway. He finished his book, and he would let me read samples, asking for feedback. He got his book published and now he is a very accomplished writer doing very well these days, with several books under his belt.

I kept my fingers crossed that Dwayne would hook me up after he got settled at the new gig. Let me tell you, in this corporate game, it's all about the grace you carry and the kindness you sprinkle like confetti. You never know when those paths will cross again, especially in the tight-knit world of telecom. Back in my MCI-WorldCom days, I was soaking up knowledge like a sponge, learning the ins and outs of designing transport circuits. That skill? It was my ticket to doubling my salary and strutting my way into the DC scene.

My daily after-work routine was to walk four miles with or without Mellie, sit in my car listening to quiet storm music while I drank three beers, and went to bed. Rewind and repeat. One day during my daily walk, I saw a for-rent sign on a townhouse in the neighborhood. Perfect!

It was too good to be true. I thought about moving into the apartments in the neighborhood, but I knew I would need a co-signer, and I couldn't even imagine asking Mellie. It wasn't because I thought she would say no; she might have, but I wanted to get it on my own. This opportunity just fell in my lap. What was the worst that could happen? All they could say was no. I was so happy I took the risk.

I made an appointment to see it. I fell instantaneously in love with it. It had a bay window in the kitchen, a fireplace, a deck, a fenced-in backyard, three bedrooms, and two and a half bathrooms. It was more space than where I had been living for the past couple of years. I could see myself in that space. I don't know what would have happened if I had not been so blessed. God showed me grace, and I am thankful. The owners were pleasant people. I begged them on my knees, in the kitchen, with tears in my eyes, not to rent it to anyone else. Well, they actually went with a different couple, but the couple had taken another place. The wife must have felt compassion for me. I got the townhouse! Look at God!

Being humble was becoming normal for me. I wasn't too proud to beg. It wasn't until that moment that I truly grasped the meaning of those words; before that, they were simply lyrics from a TLC song. God was blessing me all the way through. I couldn't wait to tell Millie the good news. I had been in her space long enough. I had gotten there at the end of July, and I was gone by the end of September. What's that? Two months! My family would never accuse me of freeloading. My God was working miracles in my life, and I knew Nanny and Granny were praying hard for me.

I was getting used to making it on my own and would not stop now. I was excited to be moving to a place of my own. I was nowhere near on my feet yet, but I would get there. She seemed genuinely concerned that I was moving out too soon, telling me I should wait a while longer before diving in. If I have to pay to live somewhere, then it might as well be in a place with my name on the lease. I wasn't ungrateful. I appreciated everything she had done for me, and that was a lot! If it weren't for her kindness and willingness to help me, I would still be in St. Louis, trying to figure it out. I'm not leaving any unclaimed blessings.

I had given the owners, the Roberts, the deposit at the end of September. I moved in on October 1, 1999, with two duffel bags, a stereo, a sleeping bag, and a thirteen-inch TV. That was all I owned. Kinda sad but sweet. There wasn't anything in my new place but an echo, but it held mammoth peace. A huge blessing. The freedom I felt on the first night was indescribable. It felt like the dance scene from the movie Risky Business (if you don't know what I'm talking about, Google it). An oasis away from all the madness I had encountered back home in St. Louis. The fireworks of emotions still exploding inside me, I finally had a place to call my own. I could, for once in my life, let my hair down without the whispers of judgment and ridicule. I was on my way to getting some things checked off my list. Next up was to save some money, buy some baby furniture, and then get my baby from my grandmother, who was taking care of her while I got on my feet.

The other friend I met from work lived in Baltimore. We were about the same age. She was someone I could hang out with. She introduced me to Baltimore and the DC nightlife. We went out to a few places: 2K9, Silver Shadows, and Republic Gardens, and we hit two spots: Melba's Choices and Mariah's in Baltimore. She was mysterious about the details of her life, but I was okay with it. I was never the type to pry anyway, but I talked about my business with anyone who would listen, and I was happy just to be getting out. She was a mother of three: two girls and one boy, who was about nine months older than my baby girl. She was very empathetic to my situation. Later, she would give me a baby crib and a dinette set. It was the first piece of furniture I had in my new place, and I will always be grateful to her. We eventually fell out of touch as time went on, but I will always remember her and her kindness.

    I missed my baby so much that it hurt inside. Now I was idle. In St. Louis, I was so used to running around for her all the time, for doctor appointments, the grocery store, and Wally World (that's what us Midwesterners call Walmart) visits. It felt weird not having to do anything for someone else. I knew I should have enjoyed my break, but I felt so guilty for having a good time without her. She was my responsibility. Having to take care of my daughter was a burden for my grandmother. I had a lot to learn about trying to be a good mother. I hated myself for a small, selfish feeling of relief that she wasn't with me. Split between my feelings, I felt remorse for her because she had me as a mother. I wasn't worthy of such a beautiful gift from God. To be honest, deep down, I never wanted to be a mother. I just didn't want the responsibility of possibly ruining someone's life by screwing it up. I didn't believe I had the skills to do it. I felt very selfish because I wanted my carefree life back so badly. I felt like I was being punished, like Cinderella, because I wasn't going to the ball ever! No fairy godmother! There was no prince to save me! I was completely alone in this charge, and I hated my new responsibility. It seemed so unfair. All he had to do was pay child support. Hell, he wouldn't even do that, and here I was stuck with the lone burden of raising a human being.

I hated myself for the implication that she was a setback instead of a step up or growing up. Those thoughts depressed me because they were so selfish! I prayed to God that He would take the fear, selfishness, and negativity out of my heart. Fear came over me constantly. What if I hurt or neglected her? What if I were some terrible monster in a fit of rage who couldn't control myself and tried to harm my baby, like you see on the local news? I didn't want to go to jail! I don't like small spaces! I really wanted to just die, so I didn't have to deal, but I knew my life no longer belonged to me. I didn't have the right to end myself anymore. I had all these crazy thoughts that came out of nowhere. I was indebted to her well-being, and my goal had to be for me to get it right. So, I learned how to suck it up and do my best because she deserved it.

But these thoughts constantly haunted me. I couldn't sleep at night. I hated being alone in a city where I had no family outside of Millie. No one to talk to about this. Maybe, I was suffering from postpartum depression. My anxiety was in overdrive, so I started drinking more—I could fall asleep without thinking about the entire world on my shoulders. I was always a social drinker. But I had turned into a functioning alcoholic. There are rules to this and as long as I followed the rules I stayed away from the deep end. So, what are the rules for alcohol? One, never drink before 5pm on a weekday and never before noon on the weekends.

Two, never drink past the quota. Three, never drink back-to-back days. Four, always buy alcohol before you go home. Five, no alcohol before you put the baby to bed. As long as I followed the rules, I felt like I was in control. This was a part of my life I am not proud of. If I'm being honest, I didn't resolve it by the end of this book. I come from a family of alcohol abusers, but I was different. I was only kidding myself. I maintained as a on and off functioning drinker. I was in a really bad place emotionally; I just couldn't let myself grieve over the pain I left behind in St. Louis. No matter how hard I tried, I couldn't shake it off. I tried to mask it with fake affection, but that only led me down a long, dark road of anxiety, insomnia, loneliness, and depression. Ooh, that was new. Just a little attempt at humor here.

I had the peace to have a mental breakdown without the judging eyes of others or the jeers of negativity relishing in my struggle. As exciting as it was to start over, I am ashamed of the first two years of my time in DC. I'm not proud of some of my actions, but they served a purpose. I had to go through it to understand where I never wanted to be again. It was my learning curve, and I had taken my lumps in morality and maturity. My will to subsist brought me back from my psychosis, but it would be a long, well-traveled journey before I accepted the truth about myself. Like a trooper, I just kept moving forward and hoped this stuff would work itself out. I gave it to God, and I stayed prayed up.

Changing gears, Dwayne kept his promise. He helped me get a gig at Q Communications, where he worked. The new telecom job in Ballston, Virginia, was a hump from Upper Marlboro. It took an hour and a half on a good day, but I was chasing dollars, and the DMV area was jumping with telecom jobs.

So, this new job in Ballston was a whole different vibe. It was packed with beautiful young Black folks, and the place felt more like a college campus or a buzzing club than a corporate office. It was a corporate meat market playground, and everyone acted like it was the most normal thing in the world—it was wild! The amount of hookups happening in that building could rival any cable network's reality show. I wish I had thought of it. Of course, my little country bumpkin butt, I got swept up in the chaos, exactly what I didn't need. There's a lot of truth to the saying: Never sleep where you eat, and I learned that lesson the hard way.

David was the biggest player in the entire building. As the new girl, I hadn't made any friends yet, so I wouldn't find this out until later—much too late to take my tutu back. I was learning the frame of mind of some DMV area men. He was a book-worthy example, with a dedicated separate tab, who hit on every girl in the building. He was attractive, very funny, down-to-earth, from Virginia, and he got a lot of play. I took none of his bullshit as truth. By the time I got to him, I was just about getting the hang of the sex-without-strings mentality, believing men when they show you who they are. He had big dreams of becoming an actor and proudly shared his black-and-white, eight-by-ten headshots and samples of his work with me via videos. I felt privileged to get a glimpse into his aspirations. I offered him some advice, suggesting he focus on comedy or stand-up—not because he was a bad actor, but because he was genuinely hilarious. I truly believed that humor would be his ticket into the business. I had a bit of insight into the entertainment industry he was eager to break into, and I wanted to see him succeed.

I didn't have any unrealistic expectations of him. We acted more like boys, drank beers, and watched basketball games together. Hell, I even helped him, and his brother move into their first apartment in Woodbridge, Virginia. It didn't bother me. What was I doing other than looking at the walls of my new spot alone? It felt good to be useful and needed, and it kept my mind off my own issues. On our first date, he took me to Old Town of Alexandria, VA for dinner. He ended up back at my place. I have to give it to him. He was like the Energizer bunny. I think it was the weed. As I stated before, he was a man whore. So, the Monday after our weekend romp, of course, I was feeling like shit. Now I had to work with him.

I met a few good people on the 8th floor. In particular, my friend Jamal, who was from Pittsburgh. He took me under his wing and treated me like his little sister. I really appreciated his kindness and his big heart. He shared his observations about the job, management, and the happenings on the eighth floor where we were. It was a serious soap opera going on up in there. My little tryst was only a drop in the bucket compared to the rest of the mess going on. He was looking out for me and shared how to handle the situation with David, who was sleeping with several girls in our department. Now I knew why some girls didn't care for me. Hell, they could have had him. I didn't need nor want the drama. The thing with David was short-lived. It didn't take long to figure him out, and we made better friends, anyway.

It was refreshing to get a male's perspective. Jamal was a lifesaver, helping me fix my reputation and steering me clear of David's drama. Lawd knows I needed it! Jamal and I spent a lot of time together during my first couple of years in DC, and we're still friends to this day. I also made some other important connections; friends I'm still in touch with. This was where I met Tonya and Janice—whom I affectionately nicknamed Super Mom. It's hard to believe I was only there for six months; it felt more like six years because time flew by!

Millie did her best to entertain me after I moved out. Between her graduate classes and tending to her own family, she introduced me to The Ascott, a Friday happy hour spot in DC on 17th and L Street. It was my kind of spot—two-for-one beer and good, grown folk music. I loved it! It reminded me of home, one of the few clubs that operated under an old school platform. We made our way there a few times.

Right after Turkey day, I had a weird conversation with my grandmother, who had been caring for my baby since I left STL back in July. She asked for cash to watch the baby. This came out of left field, but I realized it was just time to go get my baby, bring her to her new home, and end my crazy single life. It was heartbreaking to take my daughter away from my grandmother because she had grown so attached to her. My granny was retired, so taking care of her kept her busy. I was happy to be getting my angel back. She brought so much meaning to my life, but I was on the fence about giving up a carefree lifestyle and taking on responsibility.

I found out that my mother connivingly convinced my grandmother that I should pay her for watching her great-grandbaby and talked her into calling me and asking for money. What a shame. I never left my grandmom without food, Pampers, milk, or clothes. I gave her money and went back to St. Louis every month to shop for her. Southwest Airlines offered a $99 round trip in 1999, so I returned every month. I wasn't supposed to pick her up until January, but I had to rip the Band-Aid off and just do it. It wasn't going away, and I was going to have to accept it. The scale would eventually tip toward the acceptance of motherhood and less about being in the streets. It would take me some time, but I would figure it out. I would have to.

Millie went with me to St. Louis to pick up the baby, but before we left, she found Trevvy, who was a babysitter who lived in Forestville, which was on the way to work. I was happy with her; the baby responded well to her, and Trevvy, whom I affectionately called Tricky, fell in love with my little heartbeat. Her family adopted us.

Paying for a private sitter was brand new for me. I was just stupid. We laugh about it now, but it sure wasn't funny back then. Some women think mothering comes naturally. Well, it does for some, but not for all. I was clueless; I read all the baby books. All right, I didn't read all the baby books. I asked a lot of stupid questions, and I was open to all suggestions. I had to be humble—this was my first experience with a baby. Hell, I had never even babysat as a teenager. I knew nothing about babies, and I didn't have my mother to ask. Thank God Lexy didn't get sick before I got benefits because I was still consulting, and COBRA health care was something I couldn't afford.

When I brought my little Lexy to Maryland, we were making do without a crib. She cozied up in a playpen while I waited for a hand-me-down baby bed from a friend in Baltimore. Meanwhile, I graduated from the hardwood floor to an air mattress—courtesy of my day one, Reggie. Don't knock it; that air mattress was a slice of heaven compared to 'da flo'. Reggie, he's been my rock since the days at The Max nightclub back in St. Louis. He was slinging drinks, and I was a weekly visitor to the spot. Fast forward, and he's still got my back, flying out to see me nearly every month after I struck out on my own. Mellie, bless her, hooked me up with some furniture—a dresser, a chest, and a living room set that had seen better days but still had plenty of life in 'em. And that ex-coworker from Baltimore? She came through with a dinette set and a crib that might as well have been made of gold to me. It's wild, you know? The way kindness can turn up from every corner, from family to strangers who become friends. Like my neighbor, who passed on his nineteen-inch TV. So, I set up Lexy with the thirteen-inch tv in her room, and let me tell you, she was all about that Scooby Doo life at nine months old. It's the little things—the helping hands—that make a house a home.

A blessing in disguise happened right on time when I got into a fender bender with a telecom utility van, of all things. Instead of getting my car fixed, I bought a mattress to put on my brand-new IKEA bed frame I had bought months prior. I know it was ghetto to spend the money, instead of getting my car fixed, but I was tired of sleeping on an air mattress on the floor. Reggie and I put that bad boy together. I had a bit of money left over to get us new bedding, curtains, and decorations for the baby's room. I felt so grown-up, buying bedding and curtains. It was something the elders in my life would do, not me. Yup, things were changing! Six months at Q Communications was all it took for them to try and play me, rolling me over to permanent with a $7,000 salary slash. But I wasn't about to let that slide. My faith held strong, and would you believe it? My God showed up and showed out, handing me a golden ticket to a major telecom gig right in Greenbelt, Maryland. And talk about a small world—the manager from my very first job here in Maryland put in a good word for me. That's the kind of blessings you can't plan for. My new spot was a stone's throw from home, a short 30 minute ride with none of that bumper-to-bumper headache, and just a beat to my babysitter's doorstep. I started in April, my birthday month; it felt like the universe was throwing me a personal party. They welcomed me with a management title, a shiny laptop, company trips, a corporate card, bonuses, and a prime cubicle with a window view. Not bad for a Midwest girl making her mark.

Sure, the new job had its characters, but it was a yawn fest compared to the last place. Picture this: a sea of seasoned ladies and married men with wandering eyes. A few familiar faces from Q Communications popped up, and I even got one of my old co-workers, Janice, in the door. Being the fresh-faced, single, and yes, dare I say it—attractive, I drew some looks I wasn't asking for. But a girl's got to navigate the corporate waters, right? Unwanted attention or not, I was there to climb that ladder.

My job at TVI Cable in St. Louis was a whole different world. It was my first real gig, and I stuck around for seven whole years. We were all customer service reps, but more importantly, we were like one big family. We had each other's backs and celebrated our kids' birthdays together like they were national holidays. Sometimes my co-worker Mandy didn't have a ride home, so I played chauffeur. Working late meant the bus and that wasn't an option. I would have felt terrible if anything had happened to her. We all hung out after work, swapping stories and making memories. Honestly, the stuff that went down there could fill a juicy novel. I might just write it one day—watch out, bestseller's list!

During my stay/sentence at TVI—why sentence? My mother wouldn't let me quit that job, no matter how much I hated it.

She actually got me the job there through someone she knew. I hated the job, but I loved the people. She enjoyed the free cable I received from working there, so she was going to pimp me out as long as she could. I started working there when I was twenty. It was 1990. Hey, I'm telling my age. You could smoke in the building and at your desk—that's how old I am. It was a dank place on the 4900 block of Delmar between Euclid and Kings Highway, across the street from the Nationals grocery store, sitting in the nook of a mini strip plaza between Payless Shoes and Woolworth, with plenty of parking in front and on the side of the building. The office consisted of two floors. The ground level was the customer lobby. You had to be buzzed in to go upstairs. Employees were never supposed to come in that way. There was a separate entrance with a security guard who let employees in. I always raced up the stairs to sign in on time. I was a customer service rep and talking on the phone was my game.

Welcome to the jungle—there was always chaos on the floor. Let me set this up for you. The first floor was the hub for the techs, the equipment room, and where the girls took payments in the lobby. Upon entering the second floor, ringing phones, the constant chatter of phone conversations between the reps and customers, and the introduction "TVI Cable, how may I help you?" would greet you. The reps would explain bills, why their service was disconnected, the latest movies debuting on Showtime or HBO, in an attempt to upgrade their service, and explain why the tech wasn't there with an eight-to-noon appointment, and it was going on one o'clock. There weren't any cubicles. They were desks with a phone on the back wall, a huge computer monitor/keyboard, and two thin walls on each side. No privacy. The chairs were broken, ragged, and not uniform. When we finally got new chairs, we had to put our names on them so part-timers wouldn't take them. There were quite a few grievances. No one else was brave enough to bring it up to management, but I did. Such as not paying for holidays and off days, lack of security, spraying pesticides during work hours, and broken equipment. We won by going over the office manager's head directly to HR and things turned around for the better, but the office manager hated me for it. He got me back by only giving me a two-cent raise, twice. I started there in 1990, making $5.25. When I left there in 1997, it was $9.32, and I only got that much because the new people were starting at $9.25. Seven years! While I was there, I tried my hand at everything: taking and keying in payments in the lobby, reports, rides with the techs, doing inventory in the warehouse, and finally hosting a company-sponsored cable show called The Cable Connection. I would do anything to stay off the phones. I grew to hate talking on the phone because I had gotten tired of repeating myself.

In 1994, I decided I wanted to go back to school. I did not want to be a customer service rep for the rest of my life. I was going to be a paralegal (said in my hard Southern dialect). After I successfully won justice for the office grievances, I wanted to go into law. I felt so behind. All my friends were graduating from college and here I was just figuring it out. I was supposed to be a star by now! Or at least, well on my way. I guess it worked the way it was supposed to. I graduated from the two-year college program with a paralegal degree in December 1996. I found a job in Clayton, Missouri, at the beginning of 1997. I always wanted to work in Clayton. I loved my job, but I was bored to death. It was too quiet, believe it or not. I had gotten used to the chaos. Then, outta nowhere, a blast from my pageant past rings me up with an offer I couldn't refuse—Ameritech, with a paycheck that had me seeing dollar signs. Heck yeah! It was back to the phones I went. Ameritech was 100 percent better than TVI. We had cubicles, new equipment, and a restroom that didn't resemble a bus station rest stop. Then, in October 1998, I heard MCI WorldCom was hiring. They were looking for people with a telecom background. I was pregnant at the time, but I concealed it in an A-line dress during the interview and, of course, I got the job. The building was right across the highway from Ameritech. It was a beautiful building with skywalks, indoor waterfalls, a huge indoor/outdoor break area, and a full gym. It was there that the idea of DC started to take root. My cousin dropped the hint, and with my telecom know-how, I was ready to take on the capital. So, I packed up my dreams and set my sights on a new stage, ready to shine.

Okay, back to the current situation. I was trying to get myself together and prove myself worthy of my new position. I had a whole new level of maturity to achieve. I also discovered I am competitive. I wasn't there long when the company's union members went on strike. We were management employees and had to fill in for the 411 operators. The company sent us to five states where we had service centers. I could not travel because I had the baby, so I requested and received a justification. So, I didn't have to go out of town, but I had to work twelve-hour shifts. Well, my team thought that was unfair, so it was hate on me and it just went on from there. It seemed like we changed managers once a year. In the three and a half years I was there, four managers came and went.

As a circuit design engineer, I was all about growth—sticking close to the folks who had the know-how, soaking up every bit of wisdom they offered. My skills? Sharpened. My confidence? Sky-high. And when the boss tapped me for team lead over Mr. Popular? Well, that put me square in the spotlight—a place I usually love, but not this time, it came with a side of envy I wasn't craving. I wasn't trying to be the arrogant new queen bee; I wanted that family vibe, that TVI kinship. But despite my best efforts, some folks just couldn't see the team spirit through the rumors. They whispered that I brown-nosed my way up, but let's set the record straight—I was at my desk grinding, had the answers locked and loaded, and my stakeholder relationships? Solid gold. I even bagged a couple of awards to prove it.

Management saw the real deal, and they made their call. It wasn't about favoritism; it was about the right fit. And sure, the cold shoulder from a few colleagues stung—they thought I didn't earn my stripes just because they had a soft spot for the other guy. But this wasn't a high school election; it was business, nothing personal. They pegged me for a snitch; that's not my style. I'm about lifting folks up, not tearing them down. I made it clear snitching was management's game, not mine. I was there to lead, not to tattle. And that's how I played it, straight up and with integrity. All of that happened in the latter part of my time there. In the midst of the daily grind, there was this co-worker, Janice, a gem from my last gig. We weren't the kind to hang after hours, but at work, Janice was my go-to—my Super Mom. Married with a squad of four, she was the MVP of motherhood, schooling me in the art of juggling life and kids. I doubt she even realizes the depth of her impact on me. I'm talking gratitude on a whole other level. She blessed me with hand-me-downs that were more treasure than secondhand—designer duds for Lexy that kept her clothed and chic for a solid three years. No shopping sprees needed; Super Mom had us covered. Being in her orbit, soaking up her wisdom, it was like the most nurturing boot camp. She and Trevvy showed me the ropes, laid down the blueprint for parenting with grace. I soaked it all up, aiming to mirror that blend of love, patience, and strength they embodied. What a blessing they were, shaping my journey into motherhood.

So, let's back up a bit, I got this great job in April 2000, my birthday was coming and there I was staring down the big three-oh. I felt ancient. All thanks to the chorus of elders in my life singing the blues about getting older—how it's all downhill from youth. They never did pinpoint the age when the curtain falls, so my mind set it at thirty. Now, I can't speak for all the ladies out there, but turning thirty? It hit me like a ton of bricks. Memories of birthdays past—those carefree, champagne-bubble days, my friends singing happy birthday to me—played on repeat. Maybe I was homesick, missing my family, or just the weight of all the changes.

Celebrating thirty should be a great milestone in life, appreciating the journey that led you there, and then there was me. Leaving my twenties was like death. Actually, it was the death of my twenties because I could never go back. Woe was me! Drama queen, much. Guilty as charged. Listen, my entire world is a dramatic musical of my own making. I have always been one for the dramatics. Every single event in my life is permanently etched into the melody of a song, even songs I didn't like. I know you can relate to that.

For example, as I waved goodbye to St. Louis in 1999, Brandy's "Broken Hearted" and Lauryn Hill's "EX Factor" were the anthems of my heartache. Fast forward to the year 2000, and Monica's "Ring Da Bell" and Kelis's "Caught Out There" became the soundtrack—see the irony? But when April rolled around, and thirty came knocking, it was Carl Thomas' first CD that had me my attention. Now, those tunes are like time capsules—whenever I hear them, I'm right back there, drenched in Bath and Body Juniper body spray and tangled up in thoughts of Eddie, the IT guy who had me all kinds of twisted.

Thank goodness for Reggie, who swooped in like a knight in shining armor that weekend. We hit DC's club scene, dancing away my birthday blues. He pulled me out of that ridiculous pity party I was throwing for myself. I mean, who was I to wallow? I was blessed, yet there I was, sinking into a funk. It was a cycle I was all too ready to break, even if just for a weekend. I felt renewed. I decided I would try to focus on work, get better at doing my job, and learn all I could from the guys on my team. It was lonely but peaceful. My routine when I got home from work around 6:00 p.m. was to fix the baby's dinner, bathe her, make her a bottle, and put on her favorite cartoon, Scooby Doo. She'd be asleep by 8:00 p.m., and I got myself prepared for bed. Sleep and repeat!

Introducing 2n2me…

In the dawn of the internet era, the notion that you could find all of your heart's desires online was the snake oil folks were buying. As if the internet were the genie granting wishes—if you wanted a husband, just go to a husband search website, scroll through the catalog, choose, and voila! You were planning a wedding. It sounds like something out of a sci-fi movie, but there were real dating sites created to do just that. Before, you met someone the old-fashioned way—in person. For example, on the internet, you could find a social media site where you could meet someone from Spain, London, or even Brooklyn, while you sat comfy in your bedroom in Maryland. Then someone came up with the bright idea of having to pay to meet someone online. For twenty bucks a month, a woman could find her Prince Charming. This was now a million-dollar industry, but back in 2000, it was revolutionary. The details seemed so trivial now. There was a lot of caution and skepticism applied to the internet. Some people believed it was dangerous. People imagined an axe murderer at their door because of the internet, and by people, I mean Mom. She has a flair for dramatics. I guess that's where I get it from. It must have been all those Stephen King novels she read.

Anyway, Porn was popular on the web. Yup, porn was the internet's first successful million-dollar commodity. There was clickbait on websites that tricked people into clicking on them, taking them to a porn site. Computers needed regular scrubbing of cookies and cache files. Mom thought people could find out where she lived and kill her if she were online. Yeah, she wasn't having the internet in her house. There was a time when there was peace to surf the waves of the web in private. In the land before teenagers got laptops for Christmas, GPS, and invasive algorithms, there were only working grown people out there online. The internet chat sites with pictures. They were so primitive that they had to be less than 25kb to be uploaded. The webcam was nowhere near the scale of what it is today. It was bulky and stationary, and it wasn't ready for mass consumption back in 2000 like it is now. I fell into internet dating by accident. Mel, my co-worker, introduced me to this new website, BlackPlanet. It was a safe distance interaction with the opposite sex. It's laughable now because it became anything but that. I was home alone with my baby most days, so it was, by appearance, innocent enough, just something to pass the time. This was how I rationalized it in the beginning.

Mel and I worked in the same office, and she and I were unknowingly dating the same IT guy.. She told me he was married with four kids, sleeping with the chick in accounting on the seventh floor and another girl in a different building. I didn't have sex with him. Thank my lucky stars for small favors. I don't remember how the conversation came about, but we started talking in the break room. That's how I found out that Mel and I were messing with the same dude. We became friends. She invited me to go to happy hour with her at Jasper's in Greenbelt on a Friday. We laughed about the whole thing over drinks. I was enjoying myself for the first time in a while. Hey, I found a new hangout spot, almost equivalent to Hadley's in U-City, Missouri, minus the catfish nuggets and familiar Friday night faces. I met a bunch of lively fellas. Ironically, all named Brian, but with different nicknames. I looked forward to hanging out with my newfound friends every other Friday. It was the human connection I missed the most. At least I would get something normal in my life again.

Back to the internet. It allowed me to be socially adventurous without ever leaving my kitchen table. Yep, that's where I set up my laptop. Back in the day, before the magic of wireless, we had slow-ass dial-up, so I hooked my computer into the nearest phone jack outlet. Remember that? Ahhh, the wonderful sound of the dial-up connection. I still feel some hint of excitement when I hear the now nostalgic sound of the internet connecting.

BlackPlanet.com was the newest Black internet site in 1999. Before BlackPlanet, in 1997, it was Black Voices, but its platform was hard to use. BlackPlanet was very user-friendly. Registering meant creating a username. I chose 2n2me because I wanted to be cool and unique. I got it from M'tume, an R&B group popular for their song, "Juicy Fruit." N2ME was taken, so I ended up with 2n2me. Next, I had to add a picture, but in 2000, right before digital cameras exploded on the scene, and before the price point was cheap enough for the regular consumer to buy, I had to scan my photos into a computer or a flash drive before I could upload the pictures to the site. Back then, scanners were not cheap, so I had to go to Kinko's—now called FedEx Office—or most folks would sneak and use the one at work. I never did that. Guilty as charged!

I had to add something cute to say in my bio like, "I hope the hit was worth the click." Mmm-huh, cool, right? Okay, it was corny, but I thought it was cool. So, once I completed my profile, I was all set with the new account. The site highlighted the new members. That's how the hits started when people clicked on my username. They would either sign my online guest book or leave me a note. If I were really fancy, I could add code to have a cool background and add music, animation, and different fonts.

Before BlackPlanet added the instant messenger feature, there were other alternative ways to communicate because the note feature was really slow to return messages. So, I also signed up for AOL, Yahoo!, and MSN instant messengers. My typing speed increased because I had to keep up with the person I was chatting with.

The first week, I found a lot of guys in my area. It was a feature of the site. I could search for guys in my area, age range, body type, and height. The first page I encountered was justforladies. This was her username. She had the cream of the crop of men in her guest book, where men would post pictures and leave the links to their individual pages. I couldn't believe these dudes really existed. They all looked too damn good to be true. This was before catfishing got started because the limitations to get pictures added were challenging, or copy-and-paste fake photos were easy to recognize. Again, this was just before digital, so 90 percent of the time, it was truly the person. I could double-click on their usernames and go to their pages. Man, talk about entertaining—it was just fun clicking on the pages of hot men without ever having to communicate with them at all. Based on the details of their pages, I could tell the character and mindset of who they were.

Now, if I were to become bold, I could leave a note (message) in their inbox and wait for them to respond. Of course, after seeing my photos on my page, if they liked what they saw, then they would leave a cute reply. This was how it all got started.

My then-obsession was getting more photos of myself to add to my page. This was all before face filters. I had to be creative to take pictures of myself—now known as selfies. I was the self-proclaimed queen of taking selfies in the bathroom because the light in there was perfect for pictures instead of taking my photo in the mirror. I thought it was tacky showing the background of the bathroom, toilet, tub, or holding the camera in the picture. So, I turned the camera around so I could pose at just the right angle. I just wished I had longer arm. Then I got the idea to put the camera on a timer so I could run and pose. Either way, I got very creative with taking pictures.

There was a bit of self-marketing involved. I wanted the traffic to come to my page so my hit number would increase, and I could have more choices to choose from. So, there was a lot of effort and attention paid to getting the right new picture to add to my page. I never posted too provocative or half-naked pictures. I didn't need or want that kind of attention. One time, I added a picture of myself in a swimsuit, and my page exploded with hits—a lot of negative sexual comments and private messages, so I removed it. Besides, there were a few co-workers on there that recognized me, and I did not need that shit at work.

There were a few guys who caught my attention. I don't recall their usernames, but none of the first three were of American descent. Troy and Kenneth were Trinidadian, and Ali was Brazilian. Fascinated by the diversity, their backgrounds, the accents, and the decent chat conversations, it was not uncommon for me to have at least three or four IMs (instant messages) going simultaneously. I would give my number to a few guys who piqued my interest so we could chat offline. I interacted more with the opposite sex than I had met anyone in person since I came to the area. For a moment, I had their complete attention and got the shallow shit out of the way. They could actually see me and recognize I was a bomb diva and hopefully get to know me, versus being in a dark club, where some random drunk guy with nothing to lose would grab my arm. Online, I held their attention, and it wasn't by chance.

I had three dates in the first week. That was amazing to me. I hadn't had a real date in months. The first one was Ali, who worked in downtown DC for the Department of Somebody. I met him at a barbecue joint next to Zanzibar. His pictures were incredible. He had dark features, thick ebony eyebrows, shoulder-length curly hair, nice lips, and a pretty smile. Notice that I said nothing about his physique. All of his pictures were of him sitting down or in a jacket. I didn't pay it any mind at all. As I met him in the restaurant's lobby, it became quite clear. Oh, he was tall, six-feet-two, but if he had turned sideways, he would have disappeared. I mean skinny. Now, I was a size 6. Both of his legs would fit in one of my pant legs. Child, skinny. At least that explained why he never took a picture standing up. He was waiting for me with a dozen roses and a Mother's Day card. It brought me back around to the reality that he was a nice and charming person. We had a great lunch date. Afterward, we continued to chat online and, on the phone, but never much more than that. We became great phone friends until we fell out of touch. Now, he is a famous environmental activist with a doctor's title. Who knew?

I met Troy for lunch on that Mother's Day Sunday. That was interesting. I loved his accent and amazing hazel eyes. His head was clean-shaven, putting me in the mind of Mr. Clean. He had a fantastic deposition, and he wanted to be a model. His pictures on his page were particularly good, but he had nothing else going on in his life—no real-life goals. He was working as a deejay in a salsa club in Dupont Circle. He had major sex appeal, but that was about the gist of it. We lost touch after that.

I met Kenneth at the Pentagon City Mall for dinner. We decided on Ruby Tuesday. It was the only place that didn't have a wait. Now, in his pictures, he didn't smile at all. I thought it was odd, but I didn't sweat it too much until we met face-to-face. He looked exactly like his pictures, minus one teeny, tiny flaw—

he was missing half of a front tooth. I tried to ignore it. I don't know if I was any good at it. It explains why he didn't share any beautiful fronts.

One of the two dudes I met for lunch was straight out of a comic script. I can't remember the name, but he had great pictures on his page. He was tall, well put together, and slightly older than me, which was a change because most of the guys I met were younger. I thought nothing about the fact that he wore sunglasses in all of his pictures because he took poolside shots. We met in Beltway Plaza Mall, close to both of our jobs. How about that? We worked in the same area. I met him in front of Three Brothers Italian Restaurant inside the mall. I recognized him, and he recognized me. He walked toward me. I think I had a smile on my face and then I saw it. He was cockeyed. Lawd, it took all I had to keep from bursting out into laughter. Do you know how hard it is not to stare at a person when one of his eyes is on the wall and the other on you? I just tried to focus on my food because every time I looked at him, my eyes would water. I'm not playing. I'm not a shallow person at all. I dated a guy with half a front tooth missing, didn't I? Honestly, I can't tell you what our conversation was about, but I know I didn't have any interest in finding out anything more. Call it what you will. Moving on.

Then there was Michael, and he was extremely attractive. I was excited about meeting him in the same mall. I guess I should have researched him a wee bit more. He seemed normal. He was just as fine in person as he was on his page. He worked out at Gold's Gym in the mall. I had a short lunch that day because I had to get back to a meeting. He was really cool. I thought his conversation was so easy. We exchanged numbers and talked both on and offline. I was thanking my lucky stars I had met a normal nice guy. Child, come to find out, he was into S&M and vibrators. I mean, he liked them on him. Okay! He was looking for a mistress to spank him, stuff her underwear in his mouth, put a vibe up his ass, and become her love slave. I thought about it for a quick, hot second. Then I shook my head. Any man that wanted a vibrator up the ass wasn't healthy dating material for me.

Oh well, it was back to the drawing board. I became a quick expert at examining a guy's page, determining if he was telling the truth about his height. Some guys liked to show off their upper body. I could tell if they were short by looking at the nipple-to-navel ratio. If the area was tight, then they were short, and my calculation was never wrong.

I loved the fact that I could be anything I wanted to be without ever exposing myself. I showed only the side I wanted others to see. I was adored for my slightly above-average pretty face. Throughout all the time I spent modeling or participating in contests, I had never experienced such feelings. I had never seen myself before. Growing up, we didn't have a digital camera to take selfies, let alone use the term selfie. We took regular old pictures, but nothing with great detail or frequency. I did some modeling for a major beer label, so I knew I was cute, but I had never really seen myself—the angles of my face, or which side was my good side. Growing up, I spent hours playing with makeup. Now I could see what everybody else saw. It was crazy, but it was like I was being introduced to myself for the first time. I loved the admiration I got from the site.

BlackPlanet was the most shallow-minded, superficial, ego-stroking, false-validating site ever created, and it was great as long as you didn't have to deal with the real world. The more hits (folks who visited my page) I got, the more mentally empowered I felt. I, too, was a bleeding heart, insecure, and bored with my circumstances. Sad, but true. However, in retrospect, it had become my only source of communication with the opposite sex, my only source of entertainment. I became so obsessed with this site; it was like it became my companion. I believe I lost about a year or two of my life. It became a part of my daily routine. Of course, I functioned like a normal human being, with the day-to-day stuff, but I couldn't wait to get home to log on again. I had grown to like being entertained by the click of the keys, and the jingling sound of AOL's instant messenger notifications. Someone was always waiting to talk to me. In those moments, I was beautiful, sexy, important, and, most of all, wanted. It was easy to slip into the fantasy, which fed the need to validate and be validated. Here was my rationalization, and I feel this to be true even now—I didn't have to waste $30 for admission into a club and parking, hoping a decent guy would start a bomb conversation, buy me a drink—and, if I was lucky, maybe exchange numbers—then wait for him to call me back, possibly set a date, just to find out that he was not my type. The internet cut out all the legwork. I could chat with a face I liked, within the first couple of Ims; I could tell if he was cool or out to get some ass. Let's be honest. All of them were out to get some, some finessed better than others. It was easy to tell if a guy was lying about his background, a bum, sleazy, a player, married or, God forbid, not the guy in the picture. The latter never happened to me, as I became pretty good at my craft. I could probably write a how-to book about it. Hey, imagine that!

It was June 2000, and I had just returned from dropping off my daughter in St. Louis for the summer. My grandmother asked to keep my angel for the summer, and I obliged her. I was excited about the freedom, but the freedom to do what, exactly? I didn't have anyone to paint the town with me until my best friend, Cindy, arrived in town later that month. So, I found my entertainment online. I started chatting with Jackie, a guy in Brooklyn. We started very innocently. Meaning, the chats were about general subjects, the usual things. He sent me more pictures of himself. He was a model; he was a beautiful man, and he had plenty of good conversation.

One day, the conversation changed. There was a storm, my lights went out, and the only thing working was the laptop. I was in the shower, washing my hair, when the lights went out. It was still light outside, so I could find clothes and towel-dry my hair. It started getting dark outside. He IMed me while I was in the kitchen, looking for candles. The only light I had was the blue hue from my laptop. It was a terrible thunderstorm with lightning. I hate storms. I come from a land where my grandmother would make us get off the phone, turn off all the lights, and head to the basement when there was a storm. I relayed this to Jackie. He calmed me down. He asked me to visit him in Brooklyn, and I said I would. I was excited to go back to New York and more excited that I would be sharing it with my BFF, Cindy.

A year before meeting Jackie, I didn't even know how I was going to live, and now I was planning a trip to New York with my best friend, a great job, and my own home—look at God!

I picked Cindy up from the airport as planned. She was giving me shit about my new car. Long story short, I went to the car dealer in Saint Louis before I left. There was a nice little

Hyundai I had my eye on. I was turning in my 1995 Honda Civic Coupe. I needed a family car. I was tired of pulling the car seat out of the two-door. The salesman said I would need to put down additional money for it. Of course, I didn't have any additional money to give. There was a 1999 red Buick Century Custom I could get with no more money down. Yes, a Buick! I was kind of desperate because I didn't want to come to DC with a busted car. By that, I mean I wanted a new car. Well, the Buick was new. The perfect granny car, equipped with the stalk. Don't sleep; it was the smoothest ride I had ever had. It floated, and it had lots of room. My granny loved it. But of course, she did.

Anyway, I was ready for another caper with my best friend. Since I left Houston back in 1986, we vowed to always keep in touch and visit each other. It was her turn to visit me. The DC area had so much more to offer than Saint Louis. I had been talking about my new pastime with BlackPlanet and all the guys I met virtually and some in person. It was not her cup of tea, so she was very concerned. She let me know she thought I had lost my mind. She would not let me go to New York by myself to visit a man I didn't know. How sweet! We were going to die together. Sarcastically, of course.

We prepared to drive up to Brooklyn to hang out with Jackie for the weekend and come back on Sunday. I hadn't seen my bestie since 1998, right before I got preggers, so we had a lot to catch up on. As we always did, we revisited everything we did together. All the boys we liked in school. She would catch me up on all the old friends we both knew. We'd share the latest in our mama dramas. We laughed about the fact that we were so close, we even shared over-controlling mothers and how we were lucky we missed the crazy gene. We talked so much on the way we were exiting the New Jersey Turnpike before we knew it. We made great timing for a Friday rush hour. Well, it was summer, so there was less traffic until we got to the Brooklyn Bridge.

Jackie lived in Brooklyn Heights, in a two-level condo. It was very Art déco, very nice, complete with a spiral staircase. He offered us a glass of wine and then led us to the roof to see the breathtaking view. I'm usually terrified of heights, but I didn't even notice because the view was so mesmerizing. I couldn't take it all in with just one glance. The beautiful lights flickered like stars, and the mammoth-sized buildings stood like majestic giants. Besides seeing my daughter's face for the first time, I had never witnessed anything so incredible. The gentle warm breeze and the hum of traffic created music in my ears. It was simply magical. So peaceful, I didn't want to leave. Cindy, on the other hand, was also afraid of heights and complained a bit. I promised myself I would come back to soak it all in before we left. I tried to capture the moment with my simple Kodak camera, but it just couldn't do justice to the astonishing view. When Cindy and I had a moment alone together, she whispered, "He doesn't look like a serial killer. I hope he doesn't poison our food." She always has jokes.

Jackie was just as fine in person as he was in his pictures. He was an editor of a magazine. He was older than me, but he didn't look like it. He was an intellectual, so Cindy and he could banter all day. He was a little intimidating for me, so he kept my neutrons firing. We would always joke that Cindy was the smart one and I was going to be a superstar. See? I had reasonable goals.

He was the perfect host. He woke up early that morning to make us breakfast while we got dressed. Man! The best damn eggs

I've ever had. He sprinkled some paprika on top, and it tasted like steak. I whispered to Cindy, "If he did poison the food, at least it was delicious." She nodded happily in agreement. I think she was letting her guard down at that point. We went sightseeing to the Statue of Liberty, the garment district, the Brooklyn Bridge Park, and ate at Grimaldi's Pizzeria, the best New York pizza ever. Child, we did a lot of walking. Cindy and I took a nap when we got back to Jackie's condo. He was mocking us with that sexy Brooklyn accent.

"You guys are amateurs. We didn't even walk all that much. You guys could never be New Yorkers."

We shooed him away, and I responded, "That's why God made cars." We passed out on his living room twin couches for a light nap.

We hit the clubs later that evening. One of the biggest clubs I'd ever seen in my life. It was as big as a basketball stadium, I don't remember the name of the club. Oh, we had a good time. I wish we had taken pictures at the club. We danced the night away, all of us. It looked like Cindy was cock-blocking that whole evening, but I wanted her to. I needed to keep some distance from the pouty lips, washboard abs, and the Superman arms.

We made it back to his place in the wee hours of the morning, buzzing and tipsy. Cindy fell asleep in her clothes on the couch, and we put a blanket over her. We headed to the roof with a bottle of wine. I had to see that view one more time—so amazing and overwhelming. We talked for a while. It reminded me of the Mariah Carey song, "The Roof." He was a diehard Prince fan like me. We went back inside to play some of our favorite Prince songs. It was making out time—nothing really heavy. I excused myself to the bathroom to change clothes and check on Cindy, and he had dozed off, waiting for me to return. So, we cupcaked all night as we slept.

The next morning, we were up early to hit the road for home. Cindy had a flight to catch. Hugs and kisses, thanked him for a wonderful time, said our goodbyes, and we were on our way. I love my best friend. She sure could talk. Her superpower was making the time pass, and she did. She complimented me on Jackie. She understood why I liked him—not as crazy as she thought. We didn't die and we couldn't stop talking about those damn eggs.

Our conversation led to talking about old boyfriends again, and the one we always came back to was—Fran. I always held a soft spot for my first puppy love. We reminisced about how we met Fran and Phillip. I really love talking about that memory. Of course, we talked about the first time I came back to Houston one year after I left.

It was 1987. My epic return. What happened was, a close friend from my old school, Troy, invited me to attend the prom with him. He was my Prince ride-or-die co-fan. He played bass in the high school band. He knew everything about Prince. We would talk for hours about the whole Purple family and listen to all Prince's music. We were going to start a band before I left. He knew all about my bleeding heart for Fran. I thought, Man, I could shock him and show up to the 1987 Jack Yates prom, which was his prom. I remember contemplating what I would wear. This was after I had come home, got my gap closed, and started modeling and performing, so I learned a few things about how to fix my face. I was an ugly duckling who had turned into a swan. I couldn't wait to walk through those doors and show off. Wouldn't you know it? Fran didn't come to his own prom, but I caught up with him that night. It was magical for my seventeen-year-old mind. Then Cindy reminded me it was him and I bumping and grinding on a car while she and Phillip were doing the same in the back seat of the car. We laughed really hard about that. Especially the part where my older cousin, Darny, came outside to break us up. Both of us still had our virginity intact. We made a pact that if one of us lost our virginity, the other one would have to do it, too. It was to keep with our friendship of sharing everything and holding each other responsible for the other. Ironically, we ended up losing our virginity the same week. We called each other, afraid to say it, knowing the other would have to do it. We laughed about it.

I got her to the airport right in the nick of time to catch her flight. We hugged for an extra-long time like we always did. We said our "I love yous," and she was gone. I got home and called Jackie to let him know we made it, and Cindy made her flight. I was exhausted. I took a shower, lay down for a nap, and reminisced about the weekend we had.

As we approached the Fourth of July holiday, Jackie was giving a cookout at his condo. I wasn't sure I was going until he called and said he needed me there. I was on the next flight out, just in time to catch the fireworks. It was truly quixotic, watching the display of fireworks from his fire escape outside his living room window. What transpired after that defied comprehension. Let's just say I would look for him in the daytime with a flashlight. It wasn't just sex. It transformed into something multi-layered. I never wanted to leave.

But it wasn't to be. My quest wasn't over yet. We weren't going to be a long-distance couple. We've remained friends and love each other to this day, but it's strange because we can't give what we have a title. We are more than friends with the options open. The best way to describe it is that Prince has a song called "Old Friends for Sale." This is our song.

The rest of the summer was boring except for one incident—Mr. Saturday Afternoon. I was driving home from his apartment, and the feeling of a garden tool came to mind. I realized I wasn't any good at the one-night-stand stuff—straight sex without feelings. My morals battled me with the thought of the lack of respect I had shown myself. How was he to know this was my first time doing something like that? I'm sure, as fine as he was, he got this situation all the time. I don't know how my girlfriends do it or deal with it, but it doesn't work for me. It only leaves me empty. It's too late for guilty girly stuff now. I cursed myself for needing to push the envelope, wanting to be adventurous, but it was necessary then. At least I found out what my boundaries were. I chalked it up as a lesson learned. "I need someone to help me forget the guy that just walked out of my door," is a line from an old Prince song. Once again, I was nursing a self-induced heartache, this time over Jackie. He told me he wanted to remain friends. I needed to keep my mind occupied and definitely off of him.

Here's the story:

One day at work, I was chatting with Mel, who was telling me about Run and Shoot in Forestville, Maryland—a gym where she worked part-time. She gave me a two-week visitor's pass but warned me it was a meat market, although extremely attractive men came to get their ball on. It was just the thing I needed. I promised her I would stop by and check it out.

One evening, I was getting ready to go check out Run and Shoot when my phone rang. It was friends asking me to meet them at Zanzibar for happy hour. I told them I would catch up with them later. I had my gym clothes on and caught my reflection in the mirror, thinking, *She is going to kill me*, but I couldn't go to the club in sweats, could I? I switched from gray cotton sweats to a rayon and silk all-black outfit, along with a nice, comfortable pair of high-heeled sandals—as if those two words go together: *comfortable* and *heels*. I knew she was going to shoot me, but at least I was keeping my word. I showed up, satisfied with my decision, as I jumped into my grandma ride on the way to the gym.

Entering the gym, I could hear the screeching of tennis shoes on the court floor, the thunderous sound of basketballs pounding the surface, and the echoing voices calling fouls and boasting rhetoric. I was in my club gear, and it got a lot of attention from the court. I located Mel, who fussed about my trying to work out in heels. I was just about to explain when I saw him. He was sexy as hell, and I couldn't take my eyes off him. Mel snapped her fingers in my face to bring me back. I had to make myself remember what I came to tell her. He noticed that I was trying to come back from a *Joan-from-Girlfriends* moment because he smiled as he ran down the court. I just shook my head at God's amazing creatures—MEN.

"Girl, I'm so sorry. I am on my way to Zanzibar to meet some friends. I know I promised this time, but the pass is just about to expire. You weren't lying; there are some cuties up in here, so I must come back. Who is that angel over there in the red tank top?"

"Oh, you mean Lloyd? I see he's been checking you out as well."

"Oh really? So, I have noticed. Do me a favor, girl: if he asks about me, give him my number."

"Okay, Ms. Thang, but I must warn you, he is a ladies' man."

"Good, just the way I like them." I looked at my watch. "Okay, I still have enough time to make happy hour. I'll see you at work tomorrow."

First thing the next morning, Mel came to my office, full of tea. "Listen, the moment you walked out of the gym, Lloyd made a beeline for me, asking about you. I must admit, I am a little jealous. He wanted to know who you were, what your name was, etc., but I caught him off guard when I told him you would be expecting a call from him and handed him your work number. He looked completely dumbfounded, like an unsuspecting fly trapped in a web. He said he liked your style and that he was going to call you. He was going to give me his phone number to pass on to you, but I told him to call you and give it to you himself. I may not be so honest, "cause he is fine."

Okay, I would wait and see if he called. I expected it wouldn't be today. If he were a player, like my girl said, he would be way more laid back. I gave him two days.

Hello, he called on the second day. I am very impatient—a typical Arian quality. I offered to take him to lunch that day. My boss was away at a conference, so I could disappear longer than normal. We met at a restaurant on M Street, just down the street from Zanzibar—it was some rib shack. He was a contract lawyer working in DC and originally from Boston. I loved his accent. It was just sexy. Oh, he was smooth in his black Brooks Brothers suit, Versace tie, and Kenneth Cole shoes. He was tall, about 6 foot 2, a light-skinned Black man with lips and eyes to die for. I wondered if I would make it through this lunch without slobbering.

What I wanted wasn't on the menu. He was standing right in front of me. He was very charming. He paid close attention to details and listened attentively. I liked that. There was this underlying strong sexual attraction. It was so thick you could cut it with a knife. Each sentence could easily serve as a double entendre. For example, I was asking about playing basketball at the gym. "Do you come very often?" He answered, "Every chance I get." He took full advantage of every opportunity to turn it into a sexual overture, and I allowed it because it was a turn-on for me. Needless to say, the lunch went well and was over too soon. He promised to call so we could get together again very soon.

The next Saturday morning, Lloyd called. He wanted to know what I had going on and asked me to stop by for a visit. I knew what he had in mind, but I went anyway. He didn't live that far away; he lived in some apartments off Silver Hill Road. I parked and located the apartment, and as I was walking up the stairs, I asked myself, "How did I get here?" Under no circumstances did I have any intentions of sleeping with this complete stranger, no matter how fine he was. Do you think I was sending the wrong signal by dropping by wearing hip-hugging jean shorts (no underwear) and a short, cropped top that exposed my belly button and cleavage? You think! So, what? I wasn't having it. Even if he did resemble a Black god, he could get it—but not today.

Okay? I was bringing the goods to his front door—uh-huh, not!

I knocked on the door. I could hear him rumbling and scrambling inside. Finally, his footsteps made it to the door. He opened the door and moved aside to allow me to pass. I walked through the door, and it was apparent he had just stepped out of the shower. His beautiful black curly hair was still wet, and he was rubbing it dry with a towel. He greeted me with that million-dollar smile and said, "Hey, you, c'mon in."

He offered me a beverage and a seat. I sat on the leather loveseat next to his fifty-two-inch TV. He was DeBarge-family fine—light-skinned and natural curly hair. His personality was easy enough to make you comfortable with general conversation. I thought about my goal and debated whether he could 'get it' at a later date, and I knew the answer. Even though he was a lawyer, he had a real laid-back attitude. His demeanor spoke more of a mailroom clerk in a law office than an actual lawyer. As he made small talk, he reminded me of the A-list of boys back in high school who had it going on when light skin was in. Back in the day, most of the guys like him would just pass me up. Now we were on an even playing field. We were both beautiful people. Something hit me. At that moment, I decided I was going to do a hit-and-run. Did I say that?

Okay, you can say it. I'm a little off on the deep end. Step away from the edge, diva, and straighten your crown. Alright, I know, I need some time on the couch to talk about it. I don't even know why this was triggering or why I thought I needed to prove something, but my silly simple self was on some different shit then. I knew my worth, so this was not needed in my development. Anyway, I can't say he deserved or cared what I was about to do, but so what? Men did it all the time, right? I didn't care if he never called me again or what he thought of me. This was all about me and what I wanted. Hell, I just wanted to know if I had the balls to pull this off. It was all about power and control. Get laid and go—no desire to wait by the phone, no girly stuff, and definitely do not hang around long enough for the wet spot to dry.

Okay, back at the scene. I think we were discussing a basketball game as he sat down beside me. I blinked, and he kissed me. It was the weirdest thing because it came out of nowhere. Damn, my eyes were still open. He was a little surprised. I wasn't responding, so he stopped to look at the blank expression in my eyes, but he continued to kiss me. Lawd knows it wasn't him. I really wasn't interested in having sex. I know what I said earlier, but I did it anyway. It was in the middle of the afternoon—not that sex in the afternoon ain't the bomb, but the setup was all wrong. It lacked ambiance, mental foreplay, a failure to capture the essence of a moment, and no mental stimulus. Women need that stuff, you know? Oops, now he was moving down to my top.

Oh no, he just pulled my top over my breasts, exposing my really cute bra that gave me cleavage from hell (I'm a 36DD). He moved the bra aside, exposing my nipples. I was actually enjoying watching his lips wrap around my nipple. You know, he really had amazing smooth skin—I wondered what moisturizer he was using—long curved lashes, and beautiful shiny black curly hair. He was absolutely wonderful eye candy, but I still was not in the mood. He was going to have to work for it, and my ginseng hadn't kicked in yet. I wondered what he was going to do when his probing hands discovered I was not wearing any underwear. Here we go. He just picked me up (I love that). We were moving to the black leather chaise. I assumed he didn't have enough room to explore the things he was trying to reach. He laid me down and slid on top of me. He started kissing me again. Hmmm, this time with a little passion. Now he was piquing my interest. His hands were on the move again—lower, lower, lower—bingo! He struck gold. He finally discovered the no underwear thing. My body wasn't aware that my ginseng hadn't affected my mind yet, because the lips between my thighs were famously incredibly wet. When he slipped his finger between my lips, his demeanor changed. The look on his face told me he had just found something he liked, and a smile crept across his lips.

"Should I get a condom?" he asked.

"Yes. Do you want to continue in the living room or the bedroom?"

I know what you are thinking, but I am such a sucker for a big… Ummm, pretty face. He was a tad bit skinny for 6 foot 2, with Cape Verde beautiful almond-shaped eyes and heart-shaped lips… oh, how I really love lips, and he was exactly right for right now.

So, he was standing there nude in his bedroom. The sunshine was sneaking in between the half-closed blinds. He had a black wrought iron four-poster bed, and the dresser was cluttered with jewelry and cologne, but no pictures. His room looked as if he had just done a quick clean-up job decent enough for company. The bed was partially made, and his closet door was slightly open, exposing his club clothes and the Kenneth Cole collection of shoes. He had big feet. I wondered when was the last time he changed his sheets or how many women had been there before me. "Stop that!" I said to myself. "Just do it!"

I reached up to grab his face, my palms on his cheeks. I began kissing him. He walked me backward toward the bed as I met the foot rail. I lowered myself to the bed. We continued to kiss. I thought it was smooth the way he opened the wrapper and put the condom on without interrupting our deep tongue-locking kiss. Yup! My ginseng kicked in. I took the lead. I am agile and flexible—double-jointed, but who's bragging? He started sweating all over me. Yuck! I didn't know him like that. "Stop it!" I told myself. We were on the final stretch. He nestled in my neck to muffle his cry of release. Honestly, I was relieved it was over. He rolled off of me, still breathing heavily and complimenting me on the sex. Wet with his sweat, I got up and headed to the shower, and he was right behind me. His phone rang. He stopped to retrieve it. I didn't wait for him and showered alone. Thank goodness, I was relieved because I didn't want to shower with him! I dried myself off and moisturized with his lotion, disappointed that it wasn't anything different from what I had used before. I put my clothes on and retrieved my things. He was still on the phone. When I pulled out my keys, he quickly ended the conversation. I planted a kiss on his cheek and thanked him for a beautiful Saturday afternoon.

He acted surprised when I was leaving. He asked me to stay, saying he didn't have any plans until later and wanted me to keep him company. I declined, telling him, "A girl never overstays her welcome. Besides, I have some things to do."

"Maybe we can do this again sometime," he said, and with that, I was gone.

I knew I wouldn't be doing it again, ever! I could check this off my bucket list if I had one. Well, I had done it! I must say it felt good to be in control of the situation. I left with my power firmly intact. The mission was a success! I heard the Rocky theme music in my mind and almost threw my arms up in victory as I descended the stairs. Truthfully, the sex was good. He was a decent enough person, and he sounded sincere about wanting me to stay. I could have stayed and done another round, but what would have been the point? This was not going to be a love connection. Ironically, I saw him every single time I went out that summer, reminding me of the moment I was trying to forget. That's what I get! Can you believe years later, I turned on a cable reality show about finding love and his ass was on it? Man, I'm telling you, the luck I have—always the hints of fame haunting me, so close, but a pretty face away.

My summer of freedom was almost over. I had been on a mission—a home-making quest for my little one: a new toddler bed in the shape of a Volkswagen Beetle for her to dream big dreams, bedding, curtains, and toys to fill her room. And then, there it was—my very own thirty-six-inch TV, a DVD player, and a TV stand to crown it all. Mellie had to help me dragged the big ass TV box into the house. Standing there, remote in hand, I couldn't help but feel like I'd just stepped into the shoes of adulthood. My space, once a blank canvas, was coming alive into a picture-perfect home. It's almost there, this little world of mine. It's more than a collection of things; it's love, care, and the touches that say, "This is me. This is us." My house, my sanctuary, is becoming a home, all on my own.

Music has always been a character in my life, but when I moved to DC, I couldn't bring myself to play any of my beloved old tunes because each song is tied to a memory. It hurt to listen because I missed my old life so badly. So, this playlist was created with all the new jams I was listening to.

On My Own Playlist
Scan the QR code to listen to the playlist.

You Don't Know My Name—A Keys
A Long Walk—J Scott
U Know What's Up—Donell Jones
He Loves Me—J Scott
You Got Me—The Roots
Meeting in my Bedroom—Silk
Didn't Cha Know—Erykah Badu
Country Grammar—Nelly
My First Love—Avant
Best of Me—Jay Z w/Mya
Bag Lady- E Badu
I Just Wanna Love U—Jay Z
Too Close—Next
Shake Ya Ass—Mystikal
Just Be a Man About It—T Braxton
You Should've Told Me—K. Price
Fill Me In—Craig David
Happily, Ever After—Case
Just in Case—Jahiem
I'm Missing You—Case

On My Own

Try Again—Aaliyah
Ms. Jackson—Outkast
What Chu Like—DaBrat
No More Rain- A Stone
Faded Pictures—Case
Heard it all before—S Anderson
How You Gonna Act Like That—Tyrese
Emotional—Carl Thomas

Albums

Tyrese—Debut and 2nd album
Joe—2nd and 3rd album
Carl Thomas—debut album
Jill Scott—debut album
Musiq—debut album
India Arie—debut album
Tweet—debut album
Mariah Carey—Butterfly and Charmbracelet
Aaliyah—Aaliyah and I Care 4 U
Angie Stone—Debut album
D'Angelo—Voodoo
Toni Braxton—The Heat
Mary J Blige — Mary
Silk—Tonight and Love Sessions
Erykah Badu—Mama's Gun
Donnell Jones—Where I Wanna Be

Rooted

My summer of freedom was done. I went to St. Louis to get the baby. My grandmother loved having her around and gave her lots of attention. Mom was more supportive, too. She looked after her while she was there, but she didn't show up to greet me when I came back for her or to bid her farewell.

I didn't mention it before, but Mom and I hadn't spoken since I left for DC a year ago. She was sad about my spur-of-the-moment move to the DC area, but she was too full of pride to reach out to me. My grandmother tried to persuade me to go upstairs to see her. I guess I was on the path of least resistance to her. With as much gentleness as I could muster, I explained that the next move had to be Mom's. I had done all I was going to do. I had nothing to say to her. Everything I wanted to say was in the letter I left for her a year ago.

She could not get to me because I was no longer under her control. I was out of her reach. So, during the first year I was gone, she resorted to spreading lies about me. Get this! She contacted the father of my child and told him that her ex-boyfriend, Bill, was really the biological father of my child. Here's the trip! The sperm donor had the nerve to entertain it. Now, Bill called me to tell me about it because he had just cursed her out and hung up on her. He was livid!

"Out of all the things that woman could say, why that?" He reasoned; the question was more rhetorical. "I have always thought of you as one of my daughters, but she gets that drink in her, and I swear she starts talking all kinds of crazy shit! Excuse my French. She is missing you and doesn't know how to deal with the fact that you left her."

There was more. "Your mother had the nerve to say that you must be on drugs because you have gotten so skinny."

I could picture him shaking his head as he talked. I burst out laughing. The walks in the neighborhood were doing me justice, I guess. I assured Bill that I was unfazed by Mom's gimmicks. No, I wasn't on drugs, and I appreciated him thinking enough of me to call. I was genuinely humbled by that and embarrassed that Mom, once again, made herself look like a villain. I wasn't mad or hurt. I had just become numb to all the bullshit, and I wasn't entertaining her negativity. I was putting myself first so my mind would stay healthy.

So, yeah… Granny, there wasn't a reason to contact her at this point, but I loved the fact that she was spending time with her grandbaby.

My cousin/brother Ronnie was picking me up to take us to the airport. My grandmother was complaining because I was leaving much earlier than I needed to before the flight. I tried to explain as nicely as I could that I had other family members to visit before I left. This would be the argument every single time I came home. Once I moved away into a place of my own, coming back to stay at my folks' house was never the same. It had bad energy. I would become anxious, and I could never shake it. I couldn't stand being there. I loved the people in it, but I just didn't want to stay there when I came home. It triggered my anxiety. End of the story.

I was so happy Ronnie arrived to rescue me from the guilt trip my granny was taking me on. During our drive to the airport, we shared a moment. I caught him up on all my adventures in DC so far. We have grown up side by side; his mother was my grandmother's sister, and although he's technically my first cousin, only four years older than me—he is more than family; he is magic. Imagine Six Flags and Disneyland merging into one enchanted realm—the thrill of roller coasters, the wonder of fairy tales—the hero of the story all wrapped in his presence. I was never disappointed when I was with him. Just saying his name conjures a Polaroid snapshot memory: sun-kissed summers, secret hideouts, and whispered dreams. In the quiet chambers of my heart, he's not just family; he's my brother—a blessing I hold close.

Back in the day, around 1986, Mom and I would beef every third of the month, about the social security money I received after Dad died. The words on the check read to Mom (her name) for me (my name). It was the crux of our monthly argument. Mom thought she could use it how she wanted and give me an allowance. She said she used some of it to help Grandmommy with groceries and utilities. How could I argue with that? It was about six hundred dollars a month. That was a lot of money back in 1986. It would be worth one thousand dollars today. I would hide in the basement to be by myself in the dark. I would just sit on the stairs and cry. Mom had turned into a person I no longer recognized. At an early age, I learned money changes people. Sometimes, it makes them do things they wouldn't normally do.

I could hear Ronnie talking to Mom, asking where I was. I don't know what Mom replied. I could hear his footsteps coming my way toward the basement door. I was embarrassed. I just knew he was going to give me shit about sitting on the steps, crying in the dark. The door opened. He turned on the basement light. I looked up as he looked down. It blinded me while my eyes adjusted to the light. He just smiled and sat down beside me. He gently nudged me with his shoulder.

"You know your momma ain't right. Why are you sitting in the dark? Ain't you scared a spider gon' get you?" he said jokingly as he looked around, searching for the insects.

I instantly felt my heavy burden lift a little. Ronnie always knew how to make me feel better. He had been my hero for as long as I can remember. One time, a bully at school terrorized the kids walking home. I told him to leave us alone, and he poked me in the eye. I cried all the way home. The next day, my mom stormed into the school to have a word with Principal White about what went down. During lunch, Principal White asked me to point out Ralph. I was terrified, but I did it. Principal White yanked him out of the lunch line. He grilled him about why he put his hands on me. He had the nerve to say something smart. My mom lunged at the boy like the lioness she is, but Principal White held her back, surprised that she would try to lay hands on the boy.

Man, my mommy was my hero. She didn't take that crap, but she chilled out and kept quiet. Principal White slapped Ralph with a one-day vacation. Later on, Ronnie found him and beat him up in the alley behind our house. He never bothered anybody again. In fact, I never saw him again. Ronnie was always my big brother. He took me everywhere with him once I got back from Houston in 1986. I was sixteen, and he was twenty. Once he joined the National Guard and started working as an assistant manager at McDonald's, I didn't see him as much.

Ah, the holidays with my mom's side of the family—where the turkey was as dry as our sense of humor and the stuffing could double as desert sand. Ronnie and I, the culinary critics we were, developed a whole semaphore system for navigating the dinner table. A subtle cough for 'pass on the mashed potatoes,' a raised eyebrow for 'stuffing's a no-go,' and a discreet nose scratch for 'Auntie's Watergate salad has landed.'

Chitterlings? I refused to eat them. The mere whiff sent me into an existential crisis—why would anyone eat something that smelled like poop? In a desperate bid for freedom, I once flung them out to the dogs, but even they had standards. Mom caught me in the act, and let's just say my behind remembered that lesson well. She took pride in those chitterlings, and Ronnie, bless his heart, actually enjoyed them. He'd wait for my 'all clear' signal before braving a serving. Sitting at that table was like being in a food-themed comedy show, where I was both the star and the punchline. The family would prod and poke about my choices, turning dinner into an interrogation session. And oh, the lectures about the "poor kids in Africa"—as if guilt could season the food to my liking. Can I eat?

Anyway, Ronnie was a man's man. He could fix anything in the world. He was the smartest person I knew. He was always helping somebody fix something. Our family kept him busy with free labor. He would never say no, but it might take him a minute to get to them, and they had the nerve to complain. I would always say, "You can pay somebody else to do it," and then they would digress and, under their breath, grumble. I always had his back, just like he had mine.

We tried to fill in the four years that were lost while I was in Houston. Sliding down Art Hill in Forest Park in the winter, the arcade Funway Freeway in River Roads Mall, meeting his numerous girlfriends—he was quite the ladies' man. He was my family, but he was fine, so the ladies were always in his face. Going to the haunted house on Laclede's Landing and bowling. Just like a sibling, he would talk to Mom for me and try to advocate on my behalf on several topics. Usually, they were about going to some party and how he would make sure I got home safely.

I was there for all his firsts, as he was there for mine; like meeting the woman he would spend the rest of his life with. His first house. His first son—what a joy that baby was. He helped me find my baby's furniture. He was there at the hospital when I had the baby, and he was the only one there when I could finally take her home. He also helped me navigate getting the baby in the car for the first time. Pulling out of the hospital parking lot, I heard "No Scrubs" by TLC for the first time. I thought, How ironic. Of course, when I finally left the sperm donor, Ronnie was the first person I called. All he said was, "I'm on my way." I could always count on my Ronnie.

Speaking of counting on someone, there was another cousin, Darny. When I wasn't with Ronnie, I was with him. He helped me get through my high school years. We were thick as thieves. When you saw him, you saw me. He was a year older than Ronnie. We had so many things in common—we loved to sing, we loved the same music, and we loved to dance. We were going to be stars, honey! I was never at home, thanks to him. He introduced me to the cool modeling group run by a guy named Robert Tolliver, who practiced at Harris-Stowe College. It's where I learned how to model-walk down a runway. Oh, the memories of practicing sashaying down the runway and hitting the mannequin turn to jazz grooves like Kenny G or Alex Bugnon.

Only for reference, he was Mom's brother's wife's baby brother. Got that?

Okay, back to the story. He was always around because we were family, but we got close the summer Dad died. He called and asked me to go to a modeling meeting with him. I joined the group, and that was it. We were inseparable. I entered my first beauty contest at sixteen at his encouragement. A few other girls in the modeling group were entering; I think I placed in the first sixteen out of fifty, something crazy like that. We went to all the movies together. We attended concerts together. We would pull out a blanket and watch the stars in my front yard on Page Boulevard or down at Gateway Arch Park downtown. We would just drive around in ole Bessie (his car was a 1979 Granada) and play music, like Anita Baker, René and Angela, Luther Vandross, Freddie Jackson, Surface, Prince, Michael Jackson, Ready for the World, Keith Sweat, Tony Terry, and Janet Jackson (he would scream whenever anyone said her name). We wrote songs together. When we weren't together, we were on the phone. I could share my deepest thoughts with him about Mom or the memories of Dad. I would share my adventures in Houston or Anchorage. He would tell me about his issues. He would sneak me into adult clubs with a fake ID. I would be so nervous because I didn't look anything like the face in the picture, but it worked most of the time. I just love the memories of our relationship because it was the most beautiful friendship I have ever had. He is just a beautiful person; I will forever love him with childlike wonder. It remains unconditional to this day. Whenever I hear "Happy" by Surface, his spirit pops into my mind, and the feeling of his love overwhelms me, just like it was the first time. He was there to support all my performances. The one that stands out in my mind right now is when I performed "Pleasure Principle" at the Euclid Sarah Fair in the Central West End. He was right there, taking pictures to memorialize the event. We did a lot of modeling shows together with the group we were in.

We would walk up and down Euclid Avenue in the Central West End on the weekends; it was the thing to do. You had to be from St. Louis in the eighties or the early nineties to understand that one. Hershel's was a full restaurant with a bakery and a bar. They had the best desserts in the world. We would always stop in there for their triple chocolate cake or their famous brownies. We loved each other unconditionally. We remained close until Dimiel and I got serious. Life took over, and we started fading. The song that comes to mind that kind of explains our fade is "Don't Say Goodbye" by Walter Beasley. Even now, I can't listen to it without tearing up. Sometimes, growing up sucks.

Since I'm bringing up the male figures in my life, this is a good time as any to bring up my dad. He died when I was sixteen, six months after we returned from Houston in 1986. As I stated earlier, he was a heavy beer drinker. I'll come back to the end, but let's start at the beginning.

In 1948, my father was born in Mobile, Alabama. He had twelve siblings, and he was the middle child. His family was part of the mass movement of Southern Blacks who went north to seek a better life, and that was their aim, too. They faced segregation, discrimination, and violence in the South, and hoped for more freedom and opportunity in the North. Many of his eldest brothers and sisters settled in St. Louis, where they found jobs. Some went further north to Chicago, Illinois, Flint, Michigan, or west to Compton, California, where they joined vibrant Black communities that celebrated their culture, music, and faith. As the story goes, Dad's dad worked as a carpenter. He was very violent and angry, maybe because of the hardships and injustices he endured. My grandmother eventually left him with the younger children still with her. She was a brave and strong woman, who wanted a better future for her kids.

Later, I would trace Dad's ancestry back to the 1700s to his great-grandfather Daniel, with the help of a website dedicated to finding your roots. He was a free man of color! That's right! Not only was he free, but he was of West Indies/Caribbean descent. He owned acres of land and a cattle-raising business with his wife, who was half Choctaw Indian and white. His children were all free and passing. They got in trouble for marrying whites. The lawyer got them off by claiming that the "color" wasn't African but Indian or Spanish, and their cases were overturned. This was all documented. Ain't that something? As long as it wasn't Black, it was all right! His oldest son was the executor of his estate and heir to the land and business after his passing. Dad's family had money and property! It is unheard of for Black people to be able to trace their ancestry before the 1800s because most arrived here as slaves. However, Dad's family ancestors were not slaves, and I could trace it back to the early 1700s, six generations before his father. How different would things have been if Dad had learned his heritage? This knowledge fills me with a sense of honor.

Okay, what was I talking about? Oh yeah, his oldest sister, Auntie J, who was twenty at the time, came to Mobile, Alabama, to visit her mother and siblings sometime back in the 1950s, when she witnessed her father hit her two-year-old brother. The plan was developed to leave their abusive father. Auntie J convinced her father to let her take her mother, my grandmother, and her siblings on a vacation to Saint Louis. Auntie J, my grandmother, and three more siblings quietly started packing while he was asleep. They hid the bags under the front porch. He went to work the next day, and they made a run for it to St. Louis. About a month later, my grandfather came to St. Louis to get his wife and family back. He found them by discovering a letter Auntie J had written to my grandmother. He showed up at Auntie J's house demanding to see his wife and children and causing a scene. He was trying to go around Auntie J to get to my grandmother, but she stood in his way. He was no match for Auntie J. At five-foot-two, maybe a buck-oh-five dripping wet with combat boots on, she had many years of abuse at his hand. She was not afraid of her father anymore.

"My momma and brothers and sisters ain't going nowhere with you, but you 'bout to go!" Auntie J told her father. "Now, are you leaving by the door or the window?" she asked him, giving him a choice. "I ain't going no damn where without my wife and kids, and you ain't gon' stop me. Them are my wife and kids!" my grandfather said as he tried to push past Auntie J.

So, Auntie J pushed her father out of the window, just barely catching his legs. Everyone in the house held on to Auntie J until they could pull him back inside. He was so shocked that his oldest child was so defiant and strong. He retreated, jumped in his car, left St. Louis empty-handed, and it was the last time anyone saw Grandpop. Well, that was until my grandmother returned to Mobile for court to settle on the family property that she actually owned. Her husband tried to sell it without her permission. Back in the day, they didn't recognize women owning property, only husbands. They awarded her half of the proceeds from the sale. So, that's how Dad ended up in St. Louis. Auntie J was no joke! When all the siblings had settled in St. Louis, before they moved on, they all lived within a five-mile radius of each other.

There was an incident where Dad's second oldest sister, Auntie A, was married to Uncle Jamie, who was abusing her after a night of drinking at the neighborhood bar. He was angry because his food was cold and began to beat Auntie A. Her children ran to Auntie J's house to get her help. Auntie J ran all the way to Auntie A's house and commenced giving him an ass-whipping for putting his hands on her sister. She warned Uncle Jamie if he continued to put his hands on her sister, she was going to put her hands on him.

Auntie J was no joke. In fact, she put a beating on her own brother, Uncle C, for slapping his wife in her presence. The fight was so bad that Uncle C called the police on her, but not before she bit him and took a chunk of flesh out of his side that left a scar. When the police arrived to take her away, she was still threatening to beat his ass when she got out if he put his hands on his wife again. I guess she decided she was never going to watch any man hit a woman ever again as long as she was around.

She was the first sibling to go to college; she attended Dillard University. She had to leave school because she got into a fight with her roommates. She refused to join the sorority, so one of the girls poured soup on all her clothes. My Auntie J beat up all the girls because she didn't know who did it. They kicked her out of school. She kept right on moving forward. She got a job working for the local workers' union. She also became the PTA president of Laclede Elementary School while she was in St. Louis. Later, she moved to Cape Girardeau, MO, with her young family. She became the union vice president and Shop Steward for a popular seamstress business. She brought the AFL-CIO union to Cape Girardeau. Auntie J was a force of nature, a whirlwind of righteousness, and yes, an absolute badass. Her legacy? A family that knew the value of standing up for what's right, come hell or high water.

Auntie A and her family moved to Compton, California. Her son, my first cousin Don, would invent the Campbellock, better known as locking, a style of dance that would become world-renowned. Freddy Rerun Berry would move to Cali from Saint Louis, join his group, and you know the rest.

Uncle S was the oldest brother and the first one in the family to work at Chrysler. He was a lead teamster. He got his brothers hired on. One night, he was driving home late from work and pulled over to take a nap. The police tapped on his window and asked him for his driver's license. As he was reaching for his wallet, the white cop shot him in the legs. He survived, thank God, sued the county, and won. My uncle was one of the first Black men to buy a house in the previously all-white University City, a county in St. Louis, in the sixties. Auntie C and Dad would follow suit in the seventies and buy homes.

There was a big difference between my parents. Mom was born in St. Louis at St. Mary's Hospital in 1950. I'm mentioning the hospital because most Blacks were born in the segregated hospital, all-Black Homer G Phillips. As I think about it now, I wonder how well they treated my grandmother at the all-white hospital. I can only assume there was a separate Black section. St. Louis wasn't the most diverse place to live in the fifties, but it was better than Mississippi and Alabama. Mom's mother moved from Amery, Mississippi, to St. Louis to attend nursing school with her sister and a cousin. They were migrating from the oppression of the South. They all lived together until my grandmother met my grandfather and got married.

Mom's father was Seminole Indian and Irish. His father owned land in Arkansas. There were six children, including him, and all of them were "passing," which meant they could pass for white. My grandfather served in World War II. When he got out, he became a firefighter until a car hit him, and he lost his leg. He used the settlement money for a down payment on the family home. They bought a two-family flat on Page Boulevard between Pendleton and Newstead. It was a huge three-thousand-five-hundred-square-foot lot, with eight bedrooms, two bathrooms, two kitchens, two back porches, a basement the full length of the house, a two-car garage at the back of the home, and a huge backyard with fruit and vegetable gardens, peach trees, and a playground. Then it was a well-to-do neighborhood, with teachers and doctors, so my grandmother used to tell me. They paid off the mortgage in 1970. I'm bringing this up because there was a huge contrast between my parents, as mentioned. Mom and her brother attended Catholic schools. It wasn't called a private school back then, but that's what it was. Mom went to Sumner because she didn't want to go to the all-girls Catholic high school.

My father lived with his mother's sister's family, in the Lewis Place neighborhood on Newberry Terrace. His older siblings were doing well for themselves. As fate would have it, they would meet at Sumner High School after Dad got kicked out of Vashon High School for fighting.

Fast-forward to 1974, when Mom and Dad attempted to reconcile two years after Mom and I had been living at the family home on Page Boulevard. My parents were house hunting and fell in love with a house in U City, short for University City, where his two older siblings were already living. I remember house hunting with them. It's amazing what you remember as a child. Mom and Dad in a car together; pretty memorable, considering I only have one memory of it, and there is a picture of me in front of a house.

Welp, the story goes, Dad bought a house on Trenton in U City. Mom was all set to move in. She came to the house to drop some things off, and Dad was moving in with another woman. Ouch! Now, I don't know how any of that really happened, but I know there wasn't a woman living with him until much later. Dad loved the ladies, so there may have been a woman there, but she wasn't moving in. Regardless, Mom was a "woman scorned, a soon-to-be ex-wife, and a bitter baby mother." Those were Dad's words. I believe Dad sabotaged the reunion because he was not ready to be tied down. He was a mixture of the suave Marvin Gaye and the silliness of Richard Pryor. My father certainly had a type—beautiful, long hair, short, and fair skin. They all looked just like Mom!

Worth noting: He owned his own home at twenty-six. He used to say that he lived among the Jews. He was right. A large Jewish community still populated the side of U City where he lived, behind the Jewish cemetery. As much as he was a ladies' man, he was also a family man. He made sure he took care of his mother. He loved his brothers and sisters, and, like any other sibling, he had his favorites—Auntie Cee and Uncles Bee and Jay. They were all close in age and were always together at each other's houses. The nucleus was Big Mama's house on the 5800 block of Terry between Hamilton and Goodfellow in Wellston. They always gathered there every weekend to hang out with family, drink, eat, listen to music, and laugh.

Dad had a good job at Chrysler. He started on the assembly line when he was still a teenager in school and worked his way up to foreman. Not bad for someone with only a high school education. The money was good. His favorite line of all time was: "Money talks and bullshit walks!"

Known for throwing parties, he was the fun uncle. The teenagers in the neighborhood, and my older cousins, knew he would allow them to drink and smoke at his house. Everyone loved Dad. Too bad I never knew him like that. I don't mean it condescendingly. I guess I was too young to appreciate his fun side. I would hear family members talk about him fondly, and for me, it was like they were talking about a stranger. The man I remember wasn't fun or cuddly. I want to say this carefully: He did the best he could with the time he had with me. He knew nothing about being a father or a husband. How could he, based on the examples he had? His beginnings were less than meager. They were horrifying. He was removed from the situation early, but was the damage already done? I knew he loved me in his own way. Often, he would say, "Guess what?" and I would say, "What?" and he would say, "I love you!"

He would spend limitless amounts of time ranting about Mom, how she left him and took me away from him, and how he still loved her. He messed up their relationship, and he regretted it to the point of it tormenting him. He'd play The O'Jays, "Use ta Be My Girl" on repeat and sing it off-key. Then he would switch the album to Teddy Pendergrass' "The Whole Town's Laughing at Me." The more he drank, the angrier he got, and the more intense. He fussed about how he had to pay child support, how she didn't let him see me as much as he wanted, and that she didn't need the money. That's familiar. He would protest, "Look at all the boyfriends she's got!" He would spend hours talking to me about it, sometimes in graphic detail, from the ages of five to ten. Charming content for my age group, wouldn't you say?

I recall I didn't know my home phone number from memory. So, he made up melodies with the phone numbers so I could remember them, and it worked! He would buy any toy I asked for, but he didn't allow me to take them home with me. That part was okay, but when I returned, they were always gone with some weird explanation. I could go on about the examples, but it would only make me sound petty and spoiled now. But as a child, it hurt my feelings, and it has stayed with me.

The money was good at Chrysler while it lasted. The first layoff happened in 1980. It would be the shorter of the two times. He was optimistic about going back. However, I would miss this event in his life because I was moving around the United States with Mom. We came back for a brief stay in St. Louis in 1981 after we left Alaska. I was home for one year before Mom came and got me, and we moved to Houston. I only have a couple of memories of Dad from that year. He was still laid off from

Chrysler. It turned out to be one of my favorite summers. Not to be insensitive to his circumstances, but I was a kid and didn't understand the gravity of it all. I stayed with my cousin, Mellie, who lived a few houses down the street from Trenton. I played every day with the kids in the neighborhood. My cousin's house was the place where all the kids gathered. It was a joy to have family and kids to play with; I didn't want to go back home on Page. We walked all over U City, sometimes to the Target over on Olive, or getting candy from the corner store on North and South, or the 7-Eleven on 82nd Street. I would go over to Dad's and get money from his gigantic piggy bank. He was sad, disappointed, ashamed, and angry, and he stayed intoxicated.

By the next summer of 1982, I left for Houston.

We came home twice while we lived there: Christmas 1982, we flew home, and in the summer of 1984, we drove back to St. Louis for a visit. Mom had this ridiculous notion that if Dad wanted to see me, he needed to come get me. He had lost his car by this time. Mellie was old enough to drive, so she came and got me. I saw Dad. Still laid off and unhappy, I said my hellos and left because it was hard to see him like that. The lights were cut off, and there was no food and no air. Ronnie came back to Houston with us. He was eighteen, so he helped Mom drive.

When I say I didn't know Dad, thinking back, I didn't even know his favorite color. I don't remember his favorite food. However, there are some details I know: he liked to play chess, he loved music, he had the wit of a comic, and he loved football. His favorite football player was Tony Dorsett. He always reminded me of Richard Pryor, who was his favorite comedian. He had a way with stories, even history. He told me that Columbus didn't discover America. He said, "How are you gonna put your flag on someone else's car and say I discovered this? The native Indians were already here." He had a point. I share his wit.

Dad loved music. He had the nerve to try to sing. He had a baritone voice in the group. Yes, there was a group. He started it back in high school, but it didn't get very far. The fellas came over to Dad's house to hang out one time when I was there. They broke into "Special Lady" by Ray, Goodman & Brown. They had great harmony, and I was surprised. It was special to see him interact with his friends because I had only seen him with his family. It's a great memory because they were really into it, and the joy I saw on his face…I will never forget it.

I know he took pride in his home because it was always clean. He had an addition built onto the back of the house. I believe Uncle Cee built it; a room equipped with patio sliding doors, a closet, and a built-in A/C unit. He held parties in the basement. He had a deejay stand built in under the stairs with huge speakers and a long bar built in. I think Uncle C built that, too.

Minus the obvious reasons, we spent time together. He picked me up often, but it wasn't consistent and never during the week unless it was a holiday week.

Halloween? Six Flags? Forget about it. I would be so jealous to hear the stories about Dad taking my cousins trick-or-treating or to Six Flags. I believe Mom said, "No." I knew he wouldn't leave me out on purpose, but I still felt slighted as a child.

Dad finally got to take part in my birthday party festivities. It was my eighth birthday party. My friends in the neighborhood had other plans because it was an Easter weekend. I'm an April baby. Mom dropped her pride, called Dad, and told him to bring over my cousins for my party. Well, in Daddy fashion, not only did he bring my cousins, as well as some of my cousins from out of town, but he brought some of the neighborhood kids, too. It was like nine deep! It is still my favorite birthday of all time.

Mom tried to set up the movie on the projector, but once the sugar hit, the party was off the chain. Somebody threw ice cream, and it was on. Of course, Mom blew it out of proportion. No one was watching the movie anyway. To this day, she never let me forget it!

Did I say it was the best birthday? It was! I wish Mom had included him more in my life instead of always keeping it separate. She never invited any of my cousins on Dad's side to any of my parties. I didn't have a lot of parties, but I think it would have added more balance to my life. There was so much hurt between the two of them, so it was not to be.

In 1986, we returned to St. Louis, the same year Martin Luther King, Jr.'s birthday became a holiday. I don't know the full story, but what I do know is Chrysler called him back to work. He tried to work, but it was too late. The alcohol had taken over. His job had done right by him. They sent him to rehab twice. He had DUIs, so they took his car. He lost the house. He was living in Big Momma's basement. He had hit rock bottom. He was in a terrible way. It would hurt me to see him that way. I can only imagine the disappointment he felt with himself as a man. He had always been a provider; he was respected at his job and in his community. It must have been embarrassing and humiliating to lose everything, so he drank his life away. He was only thirty-seven.

I remember the last conversation I had with Dad over the phone. He was tipsy, not fully drunk. He briefly talked to Mom first, then he wanted to talk to me. I was sixteen and had grown tired of the drunk man who was Dad. It was sad and embarrassing for me. He started with, "Hey, I gotta tell you something. I got cancer."

"You don't have no dang cancer. Stop it!"

He laughed, and I did, too.

"Would you miss me if I did?" Then he changed the subject. "Father's Day is coming and all I want is a pack of Kools and some matches. That's all I want." Then he would always add, "You know what?"

"What?"

"I love you."

Irritated, I asked, "Why don't you stop drinking?"

"No."

"Can you stop drinking for me?"

"No. I can't do it for you."

I got mad and hung up on him. It was the last time I spoke to him. He died two weeks later.

I was sixteen, thinking with a sixteen-year-old mind. If I had a time machine, I would go back and handle it differently. I was ashamed of what he had become. It hurt so much to see that he was living in my grandmother's basement for the last days of his life.

A couple of months before his death, we all gathered at Big Momma's house. It would be our last time together, but it was significant. I think it was spring break, Easter weekend. A lot of my cousins were there, including Mom. Dad showed up later. It was special because it was all caught on video. My cousin, Vernon, was an amateur videographer and recorded it all. We were acting silly; they were drinking and loud. The interaction between my parents was unusually sweet. They were taking shots at each other, but it was all in good spirits.

For a long time, it was hard to watch the video because I knew what was next. I hated what happened to him while I was in Texas. He had lost an eye and wore a patch. Funny, I never got a clear answer on how it happened until years after his passing. I remember the day I heard the news. It was a Sunday, and I had just left church with my grandmother. Mom was sitting in the living room when I came in and told me he had passed. I thought she was mistaken. It was the last thing in the world I thought would be true, and it hit me like a ton of bricks on my chest. He was supposed to be around to embarrass me for the rest of my life with his antics, but most of all, he was supposed to be my dad, here with me.

In another small way, I was relieved that I didn't have to worry about him anymore. No one would hurt him because I was afraid for him. I hung up the phone that day because it hurt to care about him, and I didn't know what to do with those feelings. That's why I started his story with his beginnings, because, as an adult, I could appreciate his journey. Even though he never talked about his upbringing, I knew it was bad. Later, I would learn just how bad it was. I wanted to celebrate his successes. He made a great living, bought a home, had a nice car, and took care of his family. He lived the American dream. RIH! I love you, Daddy!

Back to 2000
Returning home with the baby put me right back into Mommy mode. Tricky was happy to have her baby back. It was

also back to Black Planet for some daily ego stroking. I met someone briefly. I think it lasted for like three months. We didn't end on bad terms, but he just wasn't what I wanted, and I wasn't willing to compromise anymore. I enjoyed the company; it was nice not to be alone, but his coming over to do his laundry every other week had run its course. He got a benefit from me, but I got nothing out of it in return. I recognized it and removed it.

It was nearing the Christmas holidays. I was broke broke and Lexy was a year old, so I didn't have to buy her much. My cousin was still around the corner, so I could always spend Christmas there. Out of the blue, the phone rang, and it was Mom. She wanted to reconcile. She offered me an olive branch and sent tickets for us to come home for Christmas and New Year's.

I took her up on her offer. I was open to trying to repair our relationship. I was actually excited about going home for the Christmas holidays, but I vow I will never go home without access to a car again. Man, I couldn't escape from there for shit. I was at her mercy, and she loved that; she liked being in control. I wasn't able to make my rounds to all of my family because she wouldn't allow me to use her car.

Dimiel was having a 2000 New Year's Eve party. Heck yeah, I was going. I got my really good friend, Reggie, to drop me off at Dimiel's house for the party. He stayed for a bit, and then he was off to his own party downtown. Dimiel agreed to take me home. Man, it felt so good to hang out with familiar faces and folks from the old crew. Everyone was home for the holidays. Everyone wanted to hear my story about how I escaped St. Louis.

"What are you doing now?"

"Oh my God, you had a baby? I didn't even know you were pregnant."

"You look great!"

I think I repeated my story maybe three or four times that night. I was used to it by this time. Dimiel and I sat up into the wee hours of the morning, talking about the good old days. Then he drove me back to Mom's house.

Okay, okay! We fooled around a little, but I was distracted because I needed to get back home to pack. After all, we were leaving on New Year's Day.

Ronnie came and scooped up me and the baby to catch the flight back. I don't think I slept at all. Ronnie walked me to the gate. I sure appreciated it because I had the baby and all the baby stuff. She was really good on the plane. She slept straight through the flight.

It felt good to be back home where I had peace, and no one was demanding anything of me or expecting me to be a certain way. Mom and I were back on speaking terms, which was a good thing, but I knew it was just until I disagreed with her or something petty like calling my grandmother without calling her first. We would ride the emotional rollercoaster for years to come. I would just enjoy the good feelings as long as they lasted and appreciated having Mom back in my life, no matter how short it might be.

2001 started slowly and quietly. My baby turned two in February, and I took her to Walmart to take a birthday picture. I decided then I would get her picture taken every year on her birthday. I stopped at Food Lion to get her a cake. The only thing they had that looked like a birthday cake was red velvet, so I got it and vanilla ice cream. I lit the candle, sang "Happy Birthday" to her, and taught her how to blow out the number 2 candle. I didn't have friends outside of work, and I didn't know anyone with kids her age. I promised myself the next year would be different. I would try to have a real birthday party for her.

Speaking of birthday parties, I got an invitation to hang out at Jasper's for a birthday party for Big B, a guy I hung out with at Jasper's periodically. Tricky would agree to watch the baby. It was nice to be out like a normal person. I spent a lot of alone time in the house with the baby and Black Planet. I met someone new that night. Two songs come to mind when I think of him: "Superwoman" by Lil Mo with Fab and "Take You Out" by Luther Vandross.

My birthday was coming up. I was planning my birthday party at where? Yes, you guessed it, Jasper's! This year, I would not be at home, depressed about my birthday and alone. I planned a party. I invited the boys from the Jasper's crew, the new guy I met, some co-workers, my girl from Baltimore, and my boy, Jamel, from my old job. You know what? Everybody I invited came and celebrated my birthday with me. Jamel took me to DC to continue my birthday celebration. Oh, Jamel, we were just friends, but he had my back like a brother. He always treated me with respect, and we never crossed the friend zone. My girl from St. Louis was in town and met us at the club in DC and the new guy came, too. I had a wonderful time, as my Auntie Cee would say.

This relationship? Oh, it was brief! I mean, I wasn't even checking for him—I had my eyes on his brother, okay? But this dude? He was all up in my face, selling himself like he was the last iPhone at a Black Friday sale. And let me tell you, he checked all the boxes: light-skinned, curly hair, eyes that could make a girl forget her own name, and tall enough to reach the top shelf without a step stool. Plus, he had this fancy assistant director gig, rocked the suit-and-tie nerd look, and sprinkled just the right amount of bougie on top. But don't get it twisted—he was still down-to-earth. I would meet up with him at Jasper's when I could get away. We hit it off and started a sexual relationship.

Now, let's talk about communication—or lack thereof. You know that friends-with-benefits mess I claimed to hate? Yeah, well, I walked right into it. No defined relationship, no expectations laid out. I was like a GPS navigating without a signal—lost and clueless. And this guy? Self-absorbed doesn't even begin to cover it. Our convos went like this:

"So, how was your day?" he'd ask, all casual.

I'd start spilling my tea, and what does he do? Interrupts me like he's the star of his own reality show: "Enough about you. Let's talk about me."

Not kidding. It was like my words evaporated into thin air. But guess what? I woke up. I realized I was giving him chances like they were free samples at Costco. There were chances he didn't deserve. He was a Cancer, which wasn't a bad thing. It was just that the sperm donor was one, too. It was not my first choice. I had PTSD with that sign (insert laughter here).

He had old-man tendencies. The sex was just okay. He wasn't into buck-wild freaky sex or oral. Just normal, run-of-the-mill, and there wasn't anything wrong with that! I told myself I could live with it. We were planning a trip to the Essence Festival. There was a large group of us going from the Jasper's Friday night crew.

One night, a couple of weeks before the trip, he and I were hanging out on his patio, sharing a bottle of wine, and he was enjoying smoking a cigar. He let me know that this thing we were doing wasn't serious, but he loved spending time with me. He didn't really date women with children, but he was making an exception for me because "your sex is the bomb!" His words. As if his mediocre sex was a prize. I'm a package deal. No love for Shortie, no love for me! Besides, he was planning to ask another woman for her hand in marriage, which I found out later from the B crew. I guess I dodged an emotional bullet.

Whelp! We didn't hang out anymore. I lost some of my money for the trip because I definitely wasn't going. I can't be mad at him. It was my fault. We should have had that conversation long before we slept together. I should have defined the relationship upfront. I could have saved a coochie coupon and hurt feelings. You can't think straight with your legs open. I should have gone to the Essence Festival anyway because Cindy was there. Heck, a lot of my family and friends were there. I would have had a good time without that situation, but I didn't know that then. I didn't find out about all my folks attending until afterward.

Back to my sanctuary, I went—Black Planet, Jasper's hangouts with the boys, and my deliciously guilty pleasure: Lady's Night at The Classics. That spot? Pure bliss.

Now, let's talk about that raise. Picture me doing a happy dance for you! An $8,000 bonus? Cha-ching! With my base salary of $84,000, that's a grand total of $92,000 a year. More money than I'd ever seen! But here's the kicker: no one to high-five or clink glasses with. So, what did I do? Bought a couple of champagne bottles and shared the bubbly love with the lucky strangers beside me. Yeah, it might sound a tad pathetic, but hey, life's about making your own party, right? And as for those frogs? Oh, honey, I puckered up and kissed a few. Some were more tadpole than prince, but that's the game. Still waiting for Mr. Right, though. Maybe he's stuck in traffic or lost his GPS. Speaking of that, we will call him 25 for the sake of anonymity. He was the next new shiny thing I met on Black Planet. He favored Shyne, and I had a small crush on him. I see why they call us cougars or MILFs. I knew there wasn't an intellectual component to this friendship.

But the sex! Oh, it was incredible! It wasn't because he taught me new tricks. It wasn't because he had swag, because he didn't. It was the shape. It had a mushroom head, and it rubbed me the right way. He was hard to leave alone, but there was no substance, and I couldn't convince myself I could live without it. The substance, that is! I was figuring out who I was, but I would dabble with 25 for tune-ups.

I met a girl at Jasper's while hanging out with my crew. They all knew her. They told me she was bisexual, but that meant nothing to me because I'm not. I genuinely thought I was meeting a new friend to hang out with. I guess I was being naïve. In the beginning, she didn't express to me that she was pursuing me. She lived in Laurel, Maryland. She invited me to a cookout at her apartment. There was a beautiful lake and a playground where my Lexy could play. It was nice to have activities that included my Booboo. We went to a Howard homecoming game together. We talked on the phone a lot. She had a son, so that was our connection, and we shared our stories about our children's fathers. I talked about my fascination with 25 and how there wasn't a deep connection with him.

We met up at Jasper's with the fellas one Friday. I invited 25 to meet me there. She didn't like that I invited him. I didn't understand why. I charged it to the fact that I had told her that the relationship wasn't going anywhere, and she thought I was leading him on and nothing more, so I paid no attention to it. I thought of her as a friend, and I thought we were just sharing. I left with him that night. Some time had passed, and I hadn't heard from her in a while after Jasper's, so I called her. That's when she told me she liked me.

I said, "I like you, too."

"I mean, romantically," she said.

Taken aback, I didn't understand how we got there. I never gave her any signs of being into her. I mean, I was used to my friends complimenting me, as I would do the same to them. When she realized I wasn't on the same page, she told me she didn't want to be just friends and ended our connection.

This was new to me. I wasn't used to having females trying to have a relationship with me. I accepted her words. We never spoke again, and I never saw her at Jasper's again. When I saw the fellas at our next meet-up, they were teasing me about it. They were commenting, "We told you she wanted you." Sure, they made jokes during our brief friendship, but I didn't pay them any mind because I was secure. I thought I was clear—I wasn't into girls. I didn't judge her. I was only interested in making friends. Listen, live your truth. I appreciated the fact that she could tell me her intentions. I am just in love with men! Real talk: I believe women know how to satisfy women, depending on the man, probably better, but it's just not my thing—that's all.

At the end of the summer of 2001, a friend I had made at my last job had returned to my little boring world to give it some life. Tonya was about three years older than me. You know the meat market I talked about earlier at my last job. Well, she had gotten pregnant. Anyway, now her youngest was turning one, and she invited me to the birthday party. She lived close by in Upper Marlboro and was divorced with three girls. The other two were sixteen and twelve. She was trying to get the baby's father out of her life because she had met someone new, and she was excited about this new relationship.

Girl, Tonya was that chick—petite but mighty, a five-foot-one powerhouse with long nails. Her skin? A flawless shade of caramel. Her hair? A flow of auburn waves that danced down her shoulders. And her style? She was the high priestess of haute couture, strutting her stuff in Gucci, Chanel, Prada, Versace, and Louis Vuitton. Her signature fragrance was Angel by Mugler. She turned sidewalks into runways. Tonya was the type of woman who drew you in. She was funny, thoughtful, and had a knack for getting her way with everyone. Most of the time, it worked on me. She had a way of getting people to tell her all about their business, and she was always full of good advice. She was a busybody in the kindest way—she genuinely cared about you, and she always followed up. Her only downfall was choosing the wrong guy.

She was always there, calling all the time to tell you the simplest of things. She had a knack for storytelling, sometimes TMI, but always entertaining. She would make a trip to the grocery store sound like an episode of *Girlfriends*. We would talk for hours. We would watch TV together while talking on the phone. We liked the same shows. She still worked at Q Communications after I left. I loved having someone to talk to, and she was a talker. So, when she reentered my life, she was trying to get rid of George, her baby's father, but he wasn't ready to leave, even though he had a baby at the same time Tonya did, with another girl. We had that in common. He was very possessive. I think she actually liked it. Somehow, it made her feel loved, but he drank a lot and was violent toward her, and she really needed to leave him alone. Since they had this baby girl to raise together, it was going to be tricky. She was stuck on the sex they had. Does that sound familiar?

She told me she invited him and his family to the birthday party, so this was going to be interesting. I was actually excited about having somewhere to go for a change. Not having any family here made places to go and things to do rare and far between, so this was a step up for me. My cousin, Mellie, had moved to Texas with her family, so I was alone. In true Tonya fashion, she was not ready when I got there, so I helped put up decorations, helped finish cooking, moved furniture, and helped her set everything up. I didn't mind when I thought about the alternative of being at home alone. The party started without a glitch. The clown showed up and entertained the little ones, including my two-year-old daughter.

George showed up after the clown had left, tipsy as hell, and was giving Tonya the blues. The party continued. We sang "Happy Birthday," cut the cake, and passed out the ice cream and cake. The birthday girl opened her presents, and then I helped her clean up the mess.

As the party ended, George took off with her cell phone because the new guy's number showed up on it. This was about the time I left to go home to put my baby to bed. The next day when Tonya called, she told me she finally got her phone back, but not before George acted like a damn fool, called her new guy from her phone, and broke some vases in her home. I told her in vain, again, she needed to leave his ass alone, but some folks have to find their own way to things. Lawd knows I had to, so who was I to talk?

Two weeks later, the world fell. I believe everyone can remember where they were on September 11, 2001, but none more than the people in the areas where the tragedies happened. I worked close to the Pentagon. It was one of the scariest days of my life. I could see the smoke from the Pentagon blazing from my office building on the eighth floor. The threat of being next was very real because I worked for one of the largest telephone companies on the East Coast. My coworkers and I watched the TV from the office conference room—the horrendous events taking place in New York. I thought about my friend Jackie in Brooklyn. The phones were out, so I IM'd him. I was so relieved when he finally responded. He told me the smoke and ash were everywhere; he even sent me pictures of the horrific scenes from his window. My company dismissed us to go home to be with our families.

While I was driving home on I-95, the fourth plane was making its way to the U.S. Capitol when it went down in Pennsylvania. The highway was a parking lot full of traffic. I couldn't get to my baby fast enough. When I finally got to her, all I could do was hug her so tight and run home. I think I watched TV for twelve hours. The phone lines were still out. I could make local calls, but no long-distance calls at all. So, my family couldn't reach me, and I couldn't tell them I was okay. I talked to Tonya for most of the day. I was relieved to have someone to talk to.

I confided in her about the new guy I met. I told her I was unsure about dating him because of the age difference. Of course, she told me six years didn't make that much of a difference if he treated me right. She admitted the new guy in her life, Rafael, was younger too. As I said, she liked talking on the phone a lot; she even liked adding Rafael on a three-way sometimes. That was just the way she was.

So, Rafael was supposed to hook me up with his friend, Juan. He warned me that his friend was very forward in his approach. Never truer words were spoken. Child, we met them at the 1223 bar. When I tell you, Rafael's friend was half octopus. I thought I was going to have to two-piece him if he didn't keep his hands to himself. He was all in my personal space. Hate that! It was a no for me. I continued to meet my B gang on Fridays at Jasper's and sprinkled in 25 here and there. Still checking in at Black Planet—it wasn't as bad as the first year, but I wasn't ready to put it down. The audience was getting younger, and that was the beginning of the end for me.

Tonya moved over the Thanksgiving holiday to an apartment in Largo, Maryland. On a crazy whim, I drove home for Thanksgiving. I wanted to spend the holiday with my family. The weather was great; it was chilly, but there wasn't any snow or rain. I called Ronnie and told him my plans. He gave me his travel suggestions, but I had already pulled up MapQuest. This was 2001, the land before turn-by-turn voice GPS. I left at 5:00 a.m. and made it to St. Louis by 6:00 p.m. It took me thirteen and a half hours to get there. I only had a bag full of tapes to keep me busy along the way because the Buick I bought only had a tape player. Satellite radio didn't exist yet. I called folks to keep me company when the service worked properly. Luckily for me, I only took restroom breaks when I needed to fill up, and my baby pretty much slept most of the way. I couldn't believe I did it. I felt so accomplished. Mom drove from Houston to St. Louis a few times, which was eighteen hours. Every year, the Hall family reunion was all over the Midwest, so I grew up liking road trips. I could endure it. Going to St. Louis was fun, but going home sucked because everyone was coming home at the same time. We were stuck in traffic for too long for my little trooper. It was painful, but we made it safely. Thank God.

After our first adventure to St. Louis, it was the beginning of December. I was excited to buy my first Christmas tree. My hunt led me to Walmart. I bought an artificial, thick, seven-foot tree for $129.99. I dragged that big-ass box into the house all by myself. I was excited. I bought red, green, and gold decorations. I lit my fireplace for the first time, put on my W.H.U.R. Christmas CD I bought at a kiosk in Forestville Mall, and drank my favorite Christmas liquor, Bailey's. I thought, *This will be my tradition every year.* I felt so grown-up. I was hiding the Christmas toys in the trunk of my car and couldn't wait until Christmas Eve to pull them out and place them under the tree. It reminded me of my childhood Christmas experiences—the wonder and anticipation, believing Santa would come down the chimney with the red bag to bring all my heart's desires. I watched all the old traditional Christmas cartoons with my baby, and I introduced her to *The Wiz.* The Christmas songs had me missing family, but I wasn't isolated anymore. I had Tonya. We ate Christmas dinner over at her place. Her family came up from North Carolina, and our babies played together all day. On New Year's Eve, my friend Reggie came to town. He stayed with me so he could go hang out at his favorite gay bar. I didn't have a babysitter, so I couldn't go anywhere. Tonya had plans with Rafael, so I was at home toasting the New Year…alone.

Welcome, 2002! Lexy's birthday was on Groundhog Day. I took Lexy to Jeepers in the Greenbelt Mall for her third birthday. Her day fell on a Saturday. We started the day by getting her birthday picture taken at Walmart. I got the red velvet cake and ice cream and went to Tricky's house to celebrate. I took Lexy and Tricky's kids to Jeepers. Lexy was too little to get on most of the rides, but the ones she could, she was on them repeatedly. Jeepers was like Chuck E. Cheese on steroids, with a roller coaster and a few other rides you would normally see at an amusement park. Man, I would rather go to the dentist for a deep scaling instead of dealing with a bunch of screaming kids running everywhere, but parents sacrifice for our babies, right? I'm learning. Mom would say, "It's payback for that birthday when the kids were throwing ice cream." She was always bringing up old stuff (smiling to myself).

Tonya talked me into joining World Gym with her. It was just around the corner from her apartment in Largo. We were there every other day getting our workout on. We had plans to go to Miami that summer, so we were getting in shape. It didn't hurt that there were some fine men in there. I was nursing a heartache from 25.

Long story short, the sex was incredible. He was just a boy playing at love, and I had no time for games. My heart was learning to let go sooner, even if each loss stung with the might of what could have been. But there was joy in the distraction, in having a partner in crime, and Ms. Tonya made sure our days were packed with everything but idle moments.

My job gave us our well-earned bonuses. I bought a laptop, a printer, and a digital camera. You know what that means? New pictures every week on Black Planet! Yup! I was still on there every day, but not as long as I used to be because I was having a life in the real world, and it felt good. We hit a lot of DC clubs together that spring like we were twenty-one again. We hit 1223 a lot. We ran into Michael Jordan and the African ball player, Dikembe Mutombo. Then, one of the many times we were in Dream, I saw Johnson for the first time after he dumped me, and you already know that story.

We were always coming up with new places to hang out and meet new people, and by people, I mean men. It was basketball season, so we would head out to the sports bar in DC off 14th Street and New York Avenue. We had something going on every single weekend, and it always included church on Sundays. We have to give God the glory. Amen!?

It was coming up on the Memorial Day holiday. I decided I was going home for Auntie Cee's birthday. She was my favorite auntie. When I was young, I used to think she was Tina Turner because she wore a ponytail like her, and they favored a smidge. She was Dad's favorite sister. They were always together. So, I wouldn't miss this for anything because all the relatives were coming. It was going to be a small family reunion. Yes, I was going to brave the road again. Wow, what a difference a year makes. I was alone with no friends, no social life outside of Black Planet, and now I was enriched by a lot. I had made some friends and had a social life outside the computer. What an idea! I finally had some roots.

Rooted Playlist

Scan the QR code to listen to the playlist.

Special Lady—Ray, Goodman, and Brown
Good Times—The Jacksons
Got to Give it Up—Marvin Gaye
Come Get to This—Marvin Gaye
Brandy—O'Jays
Back Stabbers—O'Jays
Fire and Desire—Rick James
Happy—Rick James
Love TKO—Teddy P
Forever Mine—O'Jays
Weekend Girl—SOS Band
Square Biz—Teena Marie
Humpin'—Gap Band
Smiling Faces—O'Jays
After Party—Koffee Brown
Separated—Avant
Love—Musiq Soulchild
Dance Tonight—Lucy Pearl
How Does It Feel—D'Angelo
Take You Out—Luther Vandross
Just in Case—Jaheim
Rock the Boat—Aaliyah

NoNDicCuaL

Superwoman—Lil Mo
The Pleasure Principle—Janet Jackson
Lovey Dovey—Toney Terry
I Want Her—Keith S
Heaven in Your Arms—RJ's Latest Arrival
Teddy's Jam—Guy
Piece of My Love—Guy
I'm Coming Home—New Edition
Happy—Surface
Angel—Anita Baker
Feel the Need—Anita Baker
Let's Wait a While—Janet Jackson
Slide Over—Ready for the World
Cutie Pie—One Way
Tell Me If You Still Care—SOS Band

Homecoming

Eight hundred forty-three miles might as well be a million when it comes to the distance between me and my family in St. Louis. Let me tell you, this move to DC got me feeling like I got swindled out of the family time you can't get back. Missing out on everything from the milestones to the 'pass the salt' moments—it's a steady ache that no amount of painkillers can fix.

Birthdays, holidays, and those 'I need you' emergencies—I've racked up quite a list of absentee moments. And let's not even talk about the simple stuff, like going out to eat, retail therapy, or just watching TV together. Trying to squeeze a lifetime of catch-ups into a weekend visit? It's like trying to read the entire Bible during a bathroom break.

Maybe, if I'd stayed in St. Louis, the wounds of the past would be all healed up by now. But every time I hit the road back to my present zip code, it's like life hits the pause button, only to hit play again when I return home to St. Louis. It's like my heart's stuck on replay, reliving all my trauma. But hey, I chose this road trip life, so I'm rolling out one mile at a time.

Let me tell you, I was feeling all kinds of accomplished—and completely exhausted—when I finally saw the Arch welcoming me back to St. Louis. And yes, I had my toddler co-pilot with me, making that long haul once again. We only stopped for gas, food, and those gotta-go moments. Road trips are my jam, my annual tradition, and Highway 70? That's my old friend—I could cruise that road blindfolded.

Seven states, y'all: Maryland, West Virginia, Pennsylvania, Ohio, Indiana, Illinois, and then, sweet home Missouri. I've got my favorite pit stops, like checkpoints on my personal racetrack. Now, don't side-eye me for this, but I've got a little highway hack—I find a speed demon and tail them from a safe distance. Let them clear the way and snag those speeding tickets. It's like an unspoken bond, me and this stranger, teaming up against the slowpoke brigade.

Thirteen hours in a car—pre-DVD players, satellite radio, or FaceTime? You gotta make your own fun. So, it was me, MJ's *Invincible* album, and a playlist of hits keeping me company. And "Unbreakable"? That track's my anthem, my pump-me-up jam.

Rolling down the highway, I was homeward bound for Aunt Cee's birthday over Memorial Day weekend. Now, this wasn't just any birthday—this was a victory lap for my beloved Auntie Cee. After staring down two brain tumors and breast cancer, she came out swinging cancer-free. She's my shero, the embodiment of strength and grace. Having her here with me, still calling my name, still giving me orders, still filling the room with her laughter—that's a blessing I don't take lightly. The miles couldn't keep me away, not when it meant basking in her light just a little while longer. She's the heart of our family, stepping into the role my dear grandmother left behind. It's been years since we lost my grandmother and my father, but Aunt Cee? She's the glue, keeping us all together. Because when you've got a shero like her, every moment, every memory is precious. And let me tell you, her birthday? It was more than a celebration—it was a reminder of the resilience that runs deep in our blood. And let's just say I would fight a cousin over her amazing greens and mac and cheese. I called ahead to have her hide some for me.

Thoughts of Auntie Cee lead me to think about my Big Momma. It's funny how I remember the smallest details of my grandmother's home at 5877 Terry; she lived in a four-family flat, occupying the first floor on the left side. Walking in the front door, there was the living room furniture and lots of light from the picture window next to the front door. There was an old 1970s big, beige-and-green flower-patterned couch, accompanied by a matching love seat and a rectangular coffee table. It was where, as a child, I once bumped my head right above my right eye, resulting in thirteen stitches and leaving a scar on my brow that I still bear. The hardwood floors had oval space rugs on them, and a La-Z-Boy chair, which Big Momma adored, sat next to a floor-model TV that looked more like a piece of furniture than a television.

An oval cutout led to the dining room, spacious enough to accommodate a six-seat dining room set, a China cabinet, and a record player/AM-FM radio credenza. The galley kitchen on the left was small, with just the basics—nothing fancy like my other grandmother's house. It had a small eat-in kitchen set on the right, pushed up against the wall. The only bathroom was the next room, beside the kitchen. The main bedroom was past the bathroom. There was an enclosed porch she used as a second bedroom, just past the main bedroom; separated by a door. It was always cold in the winter, so she used a space heater to keep it warm. It's where the kids slept sometimes if we came over during the summer. But most of the time we made pallets on the floor in the living room or slept on the couch if it wasn't a lot of us.

Some say Big Momma died of a broken heart after losing her beloved son, my father. He was one of her favorites, even though he was troubled. He was the first of her children to die beyond childbirth. He had a heart attack in her bathroom, and he wasn't discovered until it was too late. I believe that did something to her. There was a lot of guilt surrounding the details. Big Momma repeatedly played "On My Own" by Patti LaBelle and Michael McDonald. Whenever I hear that song, I can hear her saying, "Play it again, Debbie, play it again." Debbie was my elder cousin, who operated more like an aunt because she was a few years younger than my mother. I can't imagine the pain of burying a child.

My maternal grandmother could relate because she knew that grief. She handled her pain internally. I never saw her cry, but I knew she was devastated. Uncle Donnie was that uncle. You know the type—every family's got one. He was a walking, talking lover of life, well-liked by everyone, very popular, charming, handsome like his father. He was full of affection, kisses, noise, and a whole lot of happy. I remember when I was just a little thing, how he'd light up the whole house, it was always entertainment with Uncle Donnie. But then he went and got married and moved out. Child, you could hear a pin drop in that big ol' house. He was the light in my grandmother's eyes. She was never quite the same after he passed. He was the baby, the only son, and easily her favorite. Mom and her brother were two years apart. Although Mom had an older half-sister, it was just the two of them—Mom and Uncle Donnie.

I was surprised when I found out later that he was in a band. He sang and played drums. Wow, the arts ran in my family on both sides. Born a blue baby (congenital heart defect), he is in the medical books for being the first baby ever to have open-heart surgery and survive. He wasn't supposed to make it past five years old. By the grace of God, he lived to be twenty-seven, and he died of a heart attack. He was married with one child and another on the way, who never got to see her father. But let me tell you, in those years, he lived more life than most dream of—singing, drumming, and a loving family of his own.

I remember it like it were yesterday. It was in 1979. I was nine; I was sitting in the living room looking at the New Yorker magazine, trying to work the crossword puzzle in the back of the magazine. I knew it was too mature for me, but I would always try, anyway. I was waiting for my mother to pick me up because at that time we were living in Laclede Town Apts. *Entertainment Tonight* was coming on television. The intro music is ringing in my head as I tell this story. I had answered our loud ringing white Southwestern Bell rotary dial telephone and heard the screaming in the background, and a voice I didn't recognize saying, "Let me speak to your grandmother." I handed the phone to my grandmother. Little did I know I was handing her the worst news of her life. I don't even remember her reaction anymore. It was an awful time. My grandmother and Mom were never the same after that. I believe that's how the crazy-ass idea of moving to Alaska was born. I think she just wanted to get away. I mean, away, away. Shortly after we left for Anchorage, her father was diagnosed with cancer. Their strained relationship improved while we were in Alaska. He wrote to her all the time and called long distance. Back in the day, it was a big deal to call long distance, especially to frickin' Alaska. Without an AT&T calling card, it would have cost an arm and a leg for a fifteen-minute conversation. Oh yeah, AT&T was a long-distance carrier in the 1980s before it became the communication wireless mogul it is today. She had an urgent reason to return to St. Louis. She would have never forgiven herself if we hadn't made it back to the States in time so they could spend that time together.

Now, where was I? Oh yeah. Big Momma was our family's nucleus, and after my dad passed, my aunts and uncles did their part to keep her going. She was a traveler, visiting her children from the sunny coasts of Cali to the windy streets of Chi-Town. But then sickness reeled her in, and the visits became less about visiting and more about necessity. I was a high school senior caught up in the whirlwind of caps and gowns, too wrapped up in my own world to know any of the details of her condition. Call it teenage tunnel vision. The one memory that cuts through it all? I was being summoned to her hospital bedside. Mellie, bless her, drove me there, knowing how much it meant to Big Momma to see me. But those hospital walls, the beeps, and the hissing of machines—it was like stepping into a nightmare. Big Momma, once so full of life, was now bedridden. I've always despised hospitals and seeing her like that—it twisted the knife. It's one of those moments you wish you could erase or replace with something, anything brighter. The last time I saw her, she was staying at Aunt Cee's house. She looked so pretty; she was alert and sitting up in bed, but I can't remember anything about our conversation. It was the last time I saw her alive. It broke my heart when she passed. I had been looking forward to having her at my graduation, but it was not to be. Her funeral was on Senior Day, so I went to the funeral and made it back to school just in time for the Senior Luncheon Awards. I was there, physically. My fellow seniors awarded me "Most Outgoing" and "Best Body." Go figure. It must have been the black shiny mermaid prom dress I wore, designed like the dress in the movie *School Daze*. I didn't get a chance to be in *that* moment. I was mourning my grandmother.

Auntie Cee and Cousin Debbie were my graduation angels. They brought with them the spirit of Big Momma. Their presence was a gift in itself, a reminder that family is more than just blood—it's heart, it's soul. Cousin Debbie handed me a piece of history wrapped in love—a photo of Big Momma, her, and little ol' me. There I was, a three-year-old in her arms, on the day of her own high school graduation. That picture—it was like a time machine. That photo, a snapshot of legacy and love, got lost in the shuffle of my many moves. It's one of those things that gnaws at you, the loss of something irreplaceable. I hate that it's gone, but the memory. That's mine forever.

Back to 2002, I was coming home with a new attitude. I was renewed, and I was in a completely different headspace than I was when I first left St. Louis in 1999. I held my head high instead of watching my feet as I walked. I didn't think I had accomplished anything noteworthy, but I had survived. I was making a good living, and it was enough. I should have celebrated my big accomplishments. I was simply happy I didn't screw it up. I owed it all to Him on High. My great-grandmother, Nanny, my mother's grandmother, was ninety-eight and still kicking, so it was important to me to return home.

I made it home to St. Louis just in time to make it to my favorite Friday night spot in U City. Hadley's had the best two-for-one drinks and catfish nuggets in the world, according to me. I met my old girlfriends there after I caught up with Dimiel at the Auto Zone down the street on Olive. It was a very quick meet up. He wanted to see me. He didn't want to join me at Hadley's, so it was a quick hug, and "Damn, girl, you still look good," and I was on my way.

Hadley's wasn't popping, so we hit a new spot. Well, it was an old spot with a new name. Who did I see as I got in the door? The sperm donor and all of his friends. They greeted me with excitement, which was surprising and strange because I figured he had bad-mouthed me enough that they wouldn't say anything to me. Instead, they greeted me with respect and welcomed me in. They gave me my kudos, and that made me feel validated. Walking around the club floor was like walking through a tunnel into the past—the same old folks who were in the club when I left were still there. So was the décor. It sucked! Stuck in the 1990s, much? You know, after I had been to DC and NYC nightclubs, the familiar spots back home failed in comparison.

I couldn't help remembering one of the last times I was in that spot. It was for the Ms. Colt 45 contest where I won second place. My friend Kathy won. Always a bridesmaid, never a bride; it was where my last hope of the things I dreamed of doing was laid to rest because it was to be my last contest.

There were a lot of small reunions for me. It felt good to see some old familiar faces again, something I missed in my new home—running into anybody who knew me was extremely rare to never. I used to be a club bunny. I would hop from club to club with a crew full of pretty girls. I was always out dancing or holding the table; I was the coat holder/seat saver. I loved people-watching at a club. I remember thinking, Damn, am I going to be one of these people in a club past my prime?

Anyway, I was running into folks I hadn't seen in years. I must have answered the same questions a thousand times.

"Where have you been?"

"What are you doing now?"

"I heard you had a baby?"

"You still look the same."

It felt good to answer all the questions with positive responses. It was the first time I felt good about how far I had come, even as I was sad that St. Louis hadn't changed one bit. Wherever I stood, I could still feel those eyes watching me, judging me, sizing me up. Those beady little eyes belong to the father of my child, whom I affectionately call the sperm donor.

After a while, he walked up to me and said, "Can I have a moment of your time?"

"Sure, what's up?" I said, kind of curious, kind of not.

He started in on his reasons, his excuses, his symphony of blame for why he hadn't been the father he should've been. I could almost hear the sad violins playing in the background of his sob story. Always the one to cast blame everywhere but on himself, and to this day, he's still dodging the mirror. I sat there, nodding along, giving him the Oscar-worthy performance of a lifetime because, truth be told, I couldn't care less. His absence in her life spoke volumes, and whether he chose to step up now or fade away didn't matter to me. But for my baby girl, I'd play nice. I'd let him weave into the tapestry of her life because of her smile when she saw him. That was pure and true. And then he had the nerve to spill about his troubles with the other woman—the one I left him for. Oh, the irony was as thick as molasses. I knew all along I was the best thing that ever happened to him, and it took me three long years to stand firm in that truth. He noticed how I was glowing, and child, that was the sweetest validation, even if it was served with a side of too little, too late.

"I see you lost all your baby weight; you look good," he said reluctantly.

"You didn't think I'd stay two hundred pounds; you know me better," I said.

"Of course, you are all too vain," he said, rolling his eyes.

"It's not vanity, it's self-love. If you don't love yourself first, no one else will. You should know that, darling," I said, self-assured and confident.

I started feeling like I was Alexis Carrington talking to Blake. Characters from the 1980s show *Dynasty*. Google it. They both loathed each other, nurturing their hate by jabbing each other every chance they got. It became a game. Only he was the one trying to deliver the blows, but they were fruitless. I was so over him, numb to anything he could say. He was sensing this about the new me, so he tried a new approach by bringing up the past, the good parts.

"So, have you found anyone new to cook you barbecue?" he asked.

"You mean like you did when you had the whole apartment full of smoke because yo dumb ass forgot to close the balcony door?" I added, "I started choking as soon as I stepped off the elevator."

We both laughed about that one.

He asked me to bring the baby to his job the next day. I agreed.

It was nice not to despise him anymore; we could still laugh and enjoy a moment of peace. He noticed the male suitors hanging around, waiting on their chance to step up and put their bid in, so he politely excused himself. No one would ever accuse him of being a cock blocker. It was very enjoyable to get the old ego stroked. I've got to give it to St. Louis men on one thing: they don't mind giving ladies their due. I chatted all night with old friends and admirers, but I had to go. I was so tired. I had dropped Lexy off at my grandmother's, so that's where I laid my head that night.

My dear mother took a break from all her pointed drama. I never thought I'd see the day when she would beg me to stay in her home again, the same place she kicked me out of several times before. I remember a man once said, "You can only kick me out of the house so many times before you don't have to worry about me returning." That man was her ex, Bill. I understood those words because that was how I felt now. I didn't want to hurt her feelings, but I didn't want to make myself uncomfortable more.

My nickname for my mom is Sybil. You never know what personality you are going to get. Who's going to show up today, Sybil? Oh, why Sybil? Google it! It's from a movie in the seventies, a woman with multiple personalities. I'm not intentionally being disrespectful, but I still didn't trust her intentions. Maybe they *were* pure, but how could I know? With all the meaningless drama I have endured, I am too far gone to blindly trust her with my feelings. I pray for my feelings to change, but with time, I have built up a wall to protect my heart. She is still my mother, as if that is any consolation. I don't mean to be harsh, it's just my bruised heart talking. I felt sorry for her because I thought she really was trying, but I was not ready yet. It was too many years of unpacked baggage between us, but it wasn't too late to be the grandmother to her granddaughter and embrace it with her heart open wide. My little angel gravitated toward her Grandmommy on sight. She wanted to spend the night with her, and I asked her if she was sure, as if she would understand the meaning behind it. It was hard to leave her there, but I did. My baby girl has a knack for picking out poor souls who lack love. She was ready to spread her ray of light and love on them, comforting them from all that was wrong with the world. I know it well because she always does it for me.

It was wonderful to remember what it felt like to be a part of a family and share with my little shorty that she, too, was included, just like it was when I was small. All the family gathered at Aunt Cee's huge house in U City in celebration of her life. Three generations of relatives, to be exact. Now my baby would have her own set of cousins in her age bracket, just like it was for me. She is the youngest girl, too. I had taken all of this for granted; we need family, and we can't do it by ourselves. It is a blessing to have lasting relationships with both sides of my family, despite my mother's manipulation. "My family good, your daddy's family bad," were her words to me. It's funny how it took being eight hundred and forty-three miles away to make me realize how close I am to my family. I appreciate the wealth of resources I have with people who think like me, look like me, and enjoy the same activities as I do. I learned one thing: I will never take them for granted again. I stayed with my cousin Ronnie the rest of the time, much to the aggravation of my maternal grandmother. Listen, I was well past pleasing other people at the sacrifice of my peace of mind—not even for a night. I love you, but no. I was going to stay where I felt comfortable. They had the baby, so that should have been enough. After all, she was the prize, right?

Every trip back to St. Louis had its non-negotiables—my most precious eateries: Pasta House for that famous salad, Chong Wah on Lindell for the best damn fried rice, and Imo's Pizza because, well, it's not a homecoming without it. Nail those three and baby, we're talking about a hall-of-fame visit. Being wrapped up in the warmth of my family and friends? That's the good stuff, the soul food you can't order. But like all good things, we had to return, and it was time to hit the road once more. This trip? It was one for the books. But the ride back? Lawd, it was like every soul with a set of wheels decided to join us on the road. We were cruising until we reached the mountains, and the Pennsylvania Turnpike decided to show us its teeth. But nothing, and I mean nothing, tests your patience like that final stretch on Interstate 95. Those last one hundred fifty miles? Pure, unadulterated traffic madness. But we made it, safe and sound, back to our own beds, with the next adventure just on the horizon—sending my Lexy off to summer with her godparents, Ronnie and Pam. The cycle continues, and so does the journey.

Child, let me tell you about the summer drama that had my mom and granny up in arms. The minute Lexy's preschool closed its doors for the season, I was on that plane faster than you can say "summer break." But Lawd, the family back home? They threw a fit like I was trying to ship Lexy off to the moon! Here's the deal: Ronnie, bless his heart, had a house full of kiddos, Lexy's age, so it was a no-brainer she'd summer there. He'd even offered to chauffeur her to see the matriarchs. But nope, they wanted her parked in front of the TV, watching game shows and the stories (soap operas). That wasn't gonna fly with me. I remember those dull days from my childhood—no playmates, just me and the tube. I couldn't let my little one wilt in boredom, not on my watch. So, I made my stand, and let me tell you, catching that flight back to DC felt like lifting a weight off my shoulders. It's like every trip home comes with a side of drama, a test of how many hoops I can jump through. They love us, sure, but sometimes that love comes with a heavy dose of "my way or the highway." They acted like I was abandoning Lexy in some back alley, not with family who'd spoil her rotten. I adore my folks, truly, but when it comes to family, they've got tunnel vision. It's all about finding that balance, and this summer, I was tipping the scales in favor of fun and games over daytime TV.

Stepping off that airport shuttle, I could feel it—the sweet taste of freedom. I was this close to pulling off a full-on "Oh what a feeling" Toyota leap right there in the parking lot. Two whole months without baby duties? Child, it was on and popping. Tonya and I were about to turn the heat up this summer. We had our sights set on Dream Nightclub, the spot! We mingled, we laughed, and wouldn't you know it, we got scooped up into the social whirlwind—fight parties, poolside shindigs, and cookouts. It was a season of living it up, of saying 'yes' to every invite that came our way. Because when you've got a break from mom life, you don't just dip your toes in—you dive headfirst into the fun. I was at Jasper's every Friday and, oh yes, The Classics!

It was Eye Candy Tuesday at The Classics. Standing in front of my closet, I pondered what I would wear. It had to be something black and sexy. "Maybe I'll let my hair down," I thought aloud. As I considered my outfit, another thought crossed my mind, "I wonder what his favorite color is or what his real name is." I was seriously tripping. I was certain that not all the women at the club were as lost as I was, and deep down, I knew he probably didn't care about my choice of sandals.

I had been going to The Classics on Ladies' Night Tuesday for about two years for the male dancers. I would watch my favorite dancer, Dream, perform and then leave. Every time I went, I had the same routine: get there early to get a good spot. My favorite spot was in the back, to the left of the stage. It was in the section with a mirrored wall, a counter, and bar stools. It was right at the stairs next to the kitchen window, where they sold the chicken baskets. I'd buy a couple of beers and wait for him to come through the left-side entrance door where I sat. I watched every single move he made, and all of this was before he performed. I would always say I was going to buy a dance, but I would chicken out by the time I got to the club. I had dreamed up one million ways to approach him—one million and one wrong ways. So, it was easy to scratch out that idea because I was not that bold.

"Tonight, will be different," I told myself because I was going to give him a note as soon as I got up the nerve. My dumbass came up with this brilliant idea to write him a note, inviting him to dinner to discuss the topic of male exotic dancers, which was part of my research for the book I was writing. Writing the note was easy. Getting up the nerve to hand it to him was scary, but the possibility of him saying yes would be unbelievable.

It was crazy, I know, because as beautiful as he was, he probably had some lucky-ass girl in his life. It didn't stop the fantasies running through my mind. For example, I would book him for a show in a hotel room, and I would be the only one there, and—sorry, maybe I'll share that another time.

The atmosphere in the club was dimly lit with a laid-back vibe. It smelled of liquor, cigarette smoke, and fried chicken grease. The ladies came in all flavors, shapes, sizes, and levels of status to pack the twice-a-week ladies' night. The early goers got the best seats in the house. I had only one observation: spandex ain't for everybody. However, if there was ever such a place a woman could feel sexy, I would have to say, "Do what you do, boo, because this is the place."

The structure of the club was like a huge square, with a two-tier dance floor in the center. The chicken line at the back of the club was next to the large bar. The line for the chicken was always longer than the line to get to the drinks. The music in the club was loud enough to break the sound system. The show usually started around 8:30 p.m. when the chicken started running out. The MC enticed the ladies to bring their dollars to the stage to tip their favorite dancer.

The show usually started with the newbies just getting their feet wet at the strip tease game. I watched the first set of dancers perform a needless buildup in anticipation of my reason for coming. Finally, my wait was over. The DJ played a male dancer's classic, "All the Things," by Joe. All the women would sing, sway, and dance in their chairs along with the music. Then the MC announced the next dancer. "Ladies, coming to the stage next is a man who can make all your fantasies a reality. Ladies, he wants to make you cream. He will make you want to scream. He goes by the name DRRRRRRREEEEAAAMM!"

All the ladies screamed as he came out to R. Kelly's "Sex Me." He wore a lime green spandex top cut right below his pecs, showing off his well-assembled chest and abs, with white shiny pleather pants and his belt in his hands. He seductively strolled past the tables, flexing his pecs and slapping his belt in his hand as he made his way to the dance floor, now used as a stage. The song changed to "Adore" by Prince. He flexed his abs by rolling his stomach up and down, and then he rotated his upper body in a full circle. He ran, grabbed the rail to the upper dance floor, leaped over the railing, and turned to face the crowd of screaming ladies. He removed his pants, exposing his G-string-covered, twelve-inch penis. He leaped over the rail again, grabbed a chair, and stood in it with his ass facing the crowd. He bent over, placing his penis between his thighs, where you could see it clearly standing out from between his ass cheeks. It always made the ladies lose their minds, me included. The music changed again to something fast. The MC asked the ladies to bring their dollars to the stage. The ladies rushed to line up with dollars in hand or on their bodies, waiting for their chance to put the dollar in the strap of his G-string and free touches. He always thanked the ladies for the dollars with kisses on their foreheads or their cheeks. When his time was over, he took a bow and headed backstage to change into his street clothes so he could come back out to mingle with the crowd and pass out his cards for private parties. He had a certain charisma that made you aware that it was friendly, exacting business. I could tell he had been doing this for a long time and he had worked it down to a science. He was approachable, friendly, and cordial to familiar faces.

"Okay, here is my chance," I said to myself. I had already consumed a couple of Heineken bottles of liquid courage. I made my way over to where he was interacting with the patrons and passing out his cards. My heart was beating like a racehorse. I asked for a card. As he handed me the card, I gave him the note and mumbled, "I understand if it isn't okay." I didn't wait for a response. I pivoted on my heels and walked away, trying hard to keep from sprinting. I didn't dare look back and headed for the exit of the club. I cursed myself all the way back to the car. Oh sure, I do dumb shit, but by far, I had reached greatness. I actually had the nerve to wait for my phone to ring. I didn't return to the club for a while. Hopefully, if I go back, he will have forgotten what I looked like.

Maybe you have figured it out by now. I'm not wrapped too tight. I know I might be in good company. For the sake of argument, I really come by crazy honestly. I had to do some digging to understand where my attraction to male dancers originated. It's not a thing that generally entertains women. It's an acquired taste. If you think about it, male dancing hasn't been in existence that long. I am not a historian by any means, but I can take an educated guess that it probably started in the late 1970s or early 1980s. I suspect the first version of it was innocent enough; the concept started with the birth of rock and roll and the performances of the crooners of the late 1950s and 1960s. It hit me. It all came back to me. It was the first time I saw *Purple Rain*. I can still remember when I was a teenager, sitting in that cold movie theater (you know the spot is always cold). I watched in awe as Prince performed, "Darling Nikki," and he was shirtless with sexy black button pants, licking his fingers, pouting lips, thrusting, and rotating his hips, simulating making love on top of a speaker. I have been corrupted ever since that day. It would become the blueprint of how I would assess what is 'sexy' to me. I am still a true diehard Prince fan—the whole family, the images, the clothes, the music, and, of course, the people: Jesse Johnson, The Time, Sheila E., André Cymone, The Family, Vanity 6, etc. Hot pink, purple, and black became the flag symbolizing a new order of sexuality, the progression of things to come within me.

Man, back in the day, I wanted to be Vanity—the black lace teddy, the thigh-high black boots, the ebony shiny straight hair, and the sexiest eyes in the world. I have the eyes, if I do say so myself, but I looked more like Susan with my curly hair than Vanity. But that was okay, too. I would always have a brass ring to reach for. Gazing at a man while he seductively takes his clothes off to slow, sexy music is the greatest mind-sex there is, in my opinion. It is completely suggestive. There isn't any physical touching, and it allows your mind to take you places your body can't begin to grasp. There are no condoms required, no HIV testing needed, and no wondering if he is going to call you the morning after. All you need to do is show up, and he's there, ready to re-fuck your mind as many times as you can tolerate watching him perform.

I never had the inclination to take it to the next echelon or put the last touches on the fantasy by making it a reality, but the prospect of it sends me on an ultimate natural high. A few dancers, in my years of voyeurism, had piqued my curiosity enough to at least learn their real names or be acknowledged by them—it must be an ego thing, I suppose. In my mind, they are all strands of the original host, but a little more accessible if I ever chose to reach out and touch, as opposed to salivate from afar.

This brings me to the current fascination, Dream. He was the type of scrumptious person who made you think if only you had the opportunity; you would do this and that. You know what I mean, unspeakable things. You know, 'ho stuff.' As if 'yo stuff' would be any better than any person he had ever been with or like it would be his first time, right? The thoughts danced around in my mind until reality hit me like a ton of bricks or like my mother's reality spin on anything I ever wanted to do. "He doesn't want you!" You (meaning me) are just a customer with a tip, nothing more, nothing less. The idea is to make that money, maybe a new friend, but most definitely a repeat customer, so don't you dare get it twisted. I treated myself to that eye candy every once in a while. Why? Because I was almost afraid I would humiliate myself someday and say something stupid if I went regularly. My thoughts went so far. I saw us married with kids. Honey, it stayed with me for a while. Sad to say, he had become my twisted dream man. All I wanted to know was, did every woman in that club share my sickness? I kept three real thoughts in my head as I watched him perform a simulated head job on a lucky girl whose girlfriends had the decency to purchase for her: One, I had to meet him somehow; two, I had to give up the idea of him ever taking me seriously—bittersweet but true—and three, I had to stop it!

The whole butterflies flying in the stomach experience was very real for me. I felt like a fan who just met her favorite star, who kissed her on the cheek, and she vowed never to wash her face again. It was that bad. I actually had a picture of it—him kissing my cheek. There was something seriously wrong with reality when you lose it for a guy you have never met. I mean, what if he turned out to be the biggest asshole? Now that would dash out the flame. I had played out this scenario in my mind repeatedly, but I would never know that if I didn't approach him, right?

Three weeks later, I had given up all hope of ever hearing from him. I was doing my usual Saturday cleaning when the phone rang.

"Halloo," I said, being cute.

"May I speak to the unknown author who wrote me a note?"

It's him; it's him! I shouted in my head.

"This is she." I laughed and thought his voice was as deep and sexy as I had imagined it would be.

He laughed, too. "You left so fast; I didn't get a chance to respond."

"Well, I am surprised you called. I didn't think you would. I'm sure you get all kinds of things thrown at you all the time."

"Nah, I do, but not as creative as research and dinner." He laughed.

"Okay, okay, fair enough. I know you are a busy man, so when are you available to give me my once-in-a-lifetime opportunity?"

"Okay, I see you are very straight to the point," he said. I think he was slightly thrown off.

"Well, I appreciate you taking the time out of your busy schedule to meet with me, so I don't want to be rude and waste your time," I said sincerely.

"Well, I haven't agreed yet. I'm curious about a couple of things. Let's get that out of the way as I decide. First, why did you pick me? Second, what kind of research are you doing? Third, will you be in something black and sexy?" he said jokingly.

I joined in, playing along. "Okay, that's three things. To answer your questions, I picked you because you are the best at what you do, as well as being a veteran of eleven years in the business. The research is based on a more human side of what you do, what it takes to be successful, how you manage to continue to maintain your fan base, and last, if that is what it will take to get you to accept, then it is a small price to pay."

"Wow, I see you have done your homework, sweetheart. I accept. I'm going to be working all week, but Sunday, as far as I know right now, looks good."

"Okay, Sunday it is. Now, where would you like to go for dinner?"

"Umm, I don't really have a preference. How about you?"

"Well, as a matter of fact, I do. How about Zanzibar on Water Street?"

"Okay, let's do it. Seven o'clock. I'll meet you out front. If anything changes, I'll call you."

"Okay, great."

"Hey, don't forget that black dress, a'ight?"

"Yeah, okay, get off my phone, crazy."

We hung up, laughing.

I stood there a few moments just trying to get a handle on what had just transpired, and the only words that came to mind, with my immeasurable sophisticated vocabulary skills, were, "Wow, what a nice guy." I thought handing him the note was hard enough. Now I was going to be sitting across a dinner table from him. I had no idea what I was going to do with myself. I was truly fit to be tied.

Of course, the week dragged on slowly. I almost hoped he would cancel. I was taunted by what I would wear, which black dress, flats, or high heels. How should I wear my hair—up or down? Would he take me seriously, or would the evening be successful?

It was 7:10 p.m. I was standing in front of the restaurant, starting to feel conquered. Slightly on the side of an idiot comes to mind. As I was about to turn and head toward my car, he walked up, looking even more striking up close, as if it were achievable, wearing white linen slacks, a melon-and-mango colored short-sleeve shirt, and Gucci shades. He spoke first.

"Hey, you. I'm sorry to keep you waiting. I got caught in traffic, and my cell phone—"

I cut him off and interjected politely. "But you are here now. You are safe, and I'm glad you could make it. I'm hungry. Let's eat," I said, nervously laughing.

I managed to force all of that from my lips and surprised myself. God is a brilliant artist to create a man so breathtakingly handsome, and tonight is a dream come true. I have before me the man I had fantasized about so many times. Wow, what a nice vision. Snap out of it, girl, it's only one dinner. He is being nice because it is flattering, but who cares? I'm going to enjoy every moment of it, I argued with myself. After this, I didn't think I needed to go back to the club for my fix; I thought I was healed. If I thought watching him perform was the ultimate mind-sex, then this would be a continuous orgasm that would last all night long.

The hostess led us to a cozy corner booth overlooking the water—a perfect isolated spot in just the right environment for quiet conversation. There weren't many people, just a few couples scattered around. As we settled into our seats, he hit me with that blinding, beautiful, angelic smile. The conversation flowed so easily that his tranquil demeanor relaxed my nerves. His deep voice was even with highs and lows. He had a great sense of humor and was extremely easy to talk to, even though it was "business." A thought hit me all at once. I didn't want this moment to end, sharing his space, breathing the same air, and talking to my dream man.

How crazy was this?

By the end of the interview and dinner, I had more than enough material to complete my research for my book. As we walked out of the restaurant, I broke the short silence.

"Thank you so much for giving me this time, because I know you are a busy man. I hope dinner was to your liking, and I wasn't too intrusive."

"No, not at all. I enjoyed it. It's not often that an attractive female is interested in me outside of performing and the obvious. It was refreshing."

"I'd like to see the final draft when you are done putting it together."

"Sure, I would love for you to read it. I can forward a soft copy once it is completed."

We walked out into the night air, which was a genuinely nice temperature of around seventy-nine degrees and a nice flowing breeze blowing off the water.

"You don't mind if I walk you to your car, do you?" he asked.

"Sure, it's right over there." I pointed. At that moment, I wished I had parked three blocks away. It didn't take but a second to make it to the car. "This is me. Thank you for walking me. That was sweet."

He reached out to hug me, and I thought I would collapse into his arms. He planted a kiss on my cheek as he pulled away. "Good night," he said.

"Yes, good night, and thanks again."

"The pleasure is all mine." He flashed that smile again.

I watched him walk away. I thought I had been released, and I had been cured. That night, I dreamed of an alternate ending to the evening.

We didn't see each other after the dinner meeting. I sent him a copy of the chapter, but he only sent back a reply via email, saying he liked what I wrote. I thought, "I'm cured," but I hadn't been back to the club yet.

Miami was calling, Tonya and I answered with a resounding "Yes!" Let me tell you about my girl Tonya—love her to pieces, but when it comes to finances, she's about as reliable as a bucket of water with a hole in it. Picture this: We're at Anne Arundel Mall, bellies rumbling, ready to dive into some Italian goodness. Tonya's wallet unknown. So, who's covering lunch? Yours truly. It wasn't the first time that occurred, thank goodness I could cover us.

Then there was that night at the sports bar in DC. Good vibes, great laughs, until her car decided to run on empty. Only one gas station in sight, and Tonya's pockets? They're playing hide and seek with her cash. So, it's me to the rescue—cab fare, gas money, the whole nine yards.

But you know what? We cackle about it now. Those mishaps? They're the spice in our friendship. Every outing with Tonya is a guaranteed adventure and I wouldn't trade those memories for the world.

Okay, back to the current situation.

We made it to Miami, dropped our things off at the hotel, and immediately did a 180 right to the streets for sightseeing. We were chillin' on Ocean Drive, just a stone's throw from Wet Willy's. Tonya and I were feasting on... well, who knows? The food's a blur, but the check? That's another story. My girl ordered up a storm and then played coy on the tip. But hey, no drama—your girl's got it covered. We're here to vibe, not quibble over coins. Annoyance is my middle name during that time, but I kept it cool. Tonya, all about that sun worship, wanted to bronze it up. Me? I'm more of a shade queen. "Go on, be Suntan Christie, if you want to," I said. "Catch you when the sun dips low." While she soaked up rays, I soaked in the view and poured my soul into writing my book.

Come twilight, we hit the strip, ready to own the night. And B.E.D. on Washington Avenue? That spot was something else. Beds everywhere, like a sleepover with a club twist—curtains fluttering, secrets whispering. Now that's what I call interesting, but not really my cup of tea.

The name of our Miami hotel hideaway? Lost in the sands of time, I can't remember. But the place? It was a slice of vintage heaven, talk 'bout a bathroom straight out of the '50s, with checkered tiles that had more stories than a library. The patio was my personal writing retreat, with a white wrought-iron setup that screamed old-school chic. There I was, pen in hand, soaking in the activities on Collins Avenue, while Tonya—bless her social butterfly heart—was glued to the phone. That's my girl, always connected, even when unplugged. The night was my muse, the pulse of vacationers' beach life playing the backdrop to my writing. There's something about the ebb and flow of foot traffic;

the symphony of laughter and chatter. I let it all wash over me. But even the most beautiful distractions must come to an end. As the sidewalk serenade reached its crescendo, I bookmarked my thoughts and closed the chapter on another Miami night. With the ink still drying on the page, I retreated to the sanctuary of our room.

On our last Miami night, we tried to go back to the beach and dip our feet in the ocean one last time, but baby, it was giving a Stephen King vibe. The beach was all cloaked in darkness. The hotel lights were doing their best impression of illumination, but child, that wasn't enough light for this city girl. That kind of pitch-black? It's the kind that'll have you speed-walking like you're in the final scene of a horror flick. So, we booked it back to the hotel pool, where the light was loyal, and the shadows weren't out to get me. There, with the patio lights humming, I could finally chill, letting the ocean do its thing without giving me the heebie-jeebies.

Tonya and I hit the pool bar like it was our job. The stars were out, the drinks were cold, and we were enjoying the music playing at the pool bar. We met a couple of decent guys. We swapped stories, clinked glasses, and laughed about everything from flip-flop tan lines to the mystery of beach sand ending up in places it had no business being.

As the night ticked on, the pool lights reminded us that Cinderella's carriage was about to turn back into a pumpkin. We wrapped up our poolside pow-wow feeling like we'd just starred in our own sitcom episode. It was the perfect end to our Miami script—just two gals, a couple of new pals, and a night that was more fun than a seagull stealing your sandwich.

Morning came too soon; I was dreading our flight back home. I get anxious about flying sometimes. The turbulence had me gripping the armrests, praying for solid ground. I tried to think about positive things. I thought we lived it up in Florida, but next time? We're bringing a treasure chest, meaning we need a lot of spending money. Miami, you were a wild ride, but you're officially kicked off the bucket list.

I was happy to be back in my own bed and off that damn plane with all that turbulence. The summer continued to be full of things to do. Between Tonya and my coworker Yvonne, I didn't have time to be lonely or play on BlackPlanet, which was a good thing. Ronnie was bringing Lexy home. They were braving the thirteen-hour trip to Maryland. It felt good finally having family in my home, especially Ronnie and his family. They didn't stay long; they had to get back, and I hated to see them go. It felt good to have their essence, laughter, and good vibes in my house.

It was just me and Lexy again. To tell you the truth, I think I got it out of my system, you know, trying to live the carefree life I thought I was missing out on. I was ready to embrace and accept just being a mom wholeheartedly, the simple life. I still wasn't crazy about structure and routine. I had to learn how to get excited about the small things, but it gave me such a secure feeling that I was doing the right thing. I surrounded myself with women who were doing the same thing—we were raising the future. Just being Lexy's mom was enough. Finding a mate to share my world was going to have to take a backseat.

Out of nowhere, the man I once shared my world with—the 'sperm donor'—rang me up. Three years gone, and here he was, asking for my forgiveness. He had a whole saga ready to spill, but

Homecoming

I wasn't buying a ticket to that show. Still, he went on, not catching my cues until I switched lanes in the conversation. But you know what? His words did something unexpected. They unlocked something deep inside, like a breath of fresh air in a long-sealed room. I felt lighter—like I'd shed a layer of the past that had been clinging to me. The chains fell away, and there I was, standing tall, feeling a sense of closure I didn't know I needed. And get this—he was about to tie the knot with the same woman who played a part in our split. Now, you'd think I'd feel some type of way, but nope, I was as blank as a fresh page. I even tried to stir up a little drama in my soul, but baby, the stage was empty. I wished him well, though. All I wanted was for him to step up for our little one, to be present, to let her know her siblings. That's what mattered. As for the back child support? Well, that's a song for another day.

With a heart washed clean by clarity and validation, I found myself at a crossroads of closure and renewal. It was time to lay to rest the old monikers, the labels that no longer served me. He would simply be "D" from now on—a single letter marking the end of an era.

It felt like life had conspired against me, a cruel game of emotional hide-and-seek where I was always 'it.' I was the butt of a cosmic joke, punked by fate and circumstance. But as I carved out a new existence, miles from where I started, they all popped back up, shouting, "Just kidding! We're right here!" It was a waking nightmare, a test of endurance and faith. Yet here I stand—battered, yes; weathered, certainly—but unbroken. A testament to resilience, the unwavering support from above. So, here's to the journey ahead, to the chapters yet written, and to the Almighty who's always had my back.

August rolled around, and with it came a curveball from my landlord—talk of selling the townhouse. My heart skipped a beat. Buy it? Me? With credit still healing from the debt left by D, which led me to bankruptcy. The idea seemed as far-fetched as a fairy tale. Lawyers, agents—the mere mention of them had my wallet trembling. I was a fish out of water, clueless about the first steps in the home-buying dance. Little did I know, I was holding a winning hand. The landlord, pinching pennies like they were going out of style, saw me as his easy out. No repairs, no fuss—just hand over the keys and cash out. But where would I go if not here? Marlton had been my haven, my slice of Maryland paradise. A three-bedroom sanctuary for less than a grand, with neighbors who'd become like family. Try matching that in the wilds of the rental market—mission impossible. The thought of packing up was enough to send me into an emotional tailspin. My cozy bubble was at risk, and the world outside was scary. It was a big unknown, a map I hadn't yet charted. But sometimes, life's about finding your footing when the ground shifts beneath you.

I was spoiled by the space of my townhouse, and I couldn't imagine moving into anything smaller, let alone an apartment. Listen, it's not like I hadn't lived in an apartment for part of my life, but I didn't want to go backward if I didn't have to. My survival skills kicked in, and thank God, I had Yvonne from work who helped me navigate through what I needed to do. She knew exactly what was going to happen with the buying process because she had been through it already. Tonya was in training to be a mortgage lender, so she helped me get a real estate agent. My stress level was at an all-time high, but having these ladies in my life brought me back from the cliff.

Let me break down this home-buying hustle for you—it was like stepping onto a rollercoaster with no seatbelt. First up, shelling out $350 for an appraisal. That's a chunk of change, but necessary. The verdict? A cool $125,000. For a townhouse in this neck of the woods in 2002, that wasn't too shabby. Now, on paper, with my $84,000 salary and that sweet raise, it looked like a done deal. But here's the kicker—I was about as good at saving money as a strainer is at holding water. Everything I earned was spent just as fast, a hand-to-mouth merry-go-round that never stopped spinning.

Securing that loan was like an obstacle course designed by a sadist. One of the hurdles? Proving I had a cool $3,000 lounging in my bank account. Spoiler alert: I didn't. The list of potential lenders in my life was shorter than a haiku. Mom? Please. Borrow five dollars from her and she'd be on you like white on rice come payday—and yes, that actually happened. Grandma was out of the question, too. Her retirement budget was tighter than a pair of skinny jeans. So, I shot my shot with Mellie, all the way out in Texas. And wouldn't you know it, she came through. That money hit my account, and I could've cried tears of joy. I was sending up all kinds of thanks to Mellie and my God. As soon as that sale was signed, sealed, and delivered, I would zip that money back to her faster than a tax refund. It's moments like these that remind you—that God will give you what you need, just when you need it.

The home-buying plot thickened with a termite inspection that cost me a cool $250. Then came the paper trail—half a year's worth of bank statements and two years of tax returns laid bare. I asked the owners for a laundry list of fixes: a new roof, doors, deck repairs, and those hefty closing costs. But here's the deal —I had to park $3,000 in the bank, untouched, while also footing the bill for inspections and appraisals. Rent money? It was there, but it had to play the part of a showroom car—look, don't touch. So when the landlord rang me up about the missing rent, I laid it out for him: "It's either the rent or the sale, buddy. Your call." I promised him a check on closing day if he chose wisely. And would you believe it? I clinched the deal! The house was mine, keys and all. Talk about a real estate rollercoaster, but I rode it out to the very end.

We finally closed in November 2002. I still felt like I was getting ripped off. I couldn't put my finger on why, but I didn't feel like I got a deal. I felt like the owner was getting over. My credit score sucked, so the interest rate was 6.75%, something crazy like that, plus that awful PMI, which is a type of mortgage insurance you might be required to pay for if you have a conventional loan. Of course, I had a conventional loan, so I didn't have the luxury of the first-time homebuyer advantage. My mortgage was $1,528 for a $125,000 old-ass 1979 townhouse. The PMI was about $450 baked in. If not for the nasty PMI, my mortgage would have been basically the same amount as the rent I was already paying. Hell, now it was basically my whole check.

There I was, spilling my heart out to a friend at work, the whole rollercoaster of becoming a homeowner. As we drove to grab lunch, the weight of it all hit me—I broke down in tears. Me, a homeowner! Can you believe it? A little piece of this Earth that was all mine. No more moving, no more uncertainty. Hallelujah! But let's keep it real—the switch from renter to owner was no joke. That mortgage payment? It was like a monthly mountain climb. I made it work, but it was a tightrope walk every time. The honeymoon phase of owning my place? It was short-lived. When things broke down, there was no landlord to call—it was all on me. Now I get why my mom and granny had a tool collection that could rival any hardware store. I used to breeze past those tools without a second thought, but now? I need to start a collection of my own.

We've got new bonding material, my family and I—DIY tales and home repair fails. It's a whole new chapter, learning the ropes of maintenance and the true cost of calling a place your own.

Changing gears, the upcoming holidays were great, even though I didn't go home. Tonya and I didn't do much at all. We spent Thanksgiving, Christmas, and New Year's together. Lexy was in preschool; she attended the pre-K program in our neighborhood. She had her first Christmas program. I didn't have any family here, so Tonya came. It was so cute seeing my baby on stage. I tried hard to keep the tears back. My family would have loved to have seen it. I recorded it so I could share it. I recorded all of her performances; she hates it when I play them now. I love them all, especially the first one. All she did was wave at me and say hi; she was the cutest little reindeer.

Tonya, with her heart set on a genuine pine, had us trekking to Walmart in Waldorf. Together, we wrangled that big-ass tree into her apartment like a pair of Christmas commandos. Meanwhile, I was giving my year-old artificial tree the glow-up treatment, decking it out in all its festive glory. Christmas rolled around, and Lexy's eyes sparkled brighter than any ornament under a mountain of toys.

As Dick Clark's voice filled the room, the final countdown of the year played out like a promise of fresh starts. We stood there, in my living room, ushering in 2003 with nothing but hope in our hearts and the sparkle of new beginnings in our eyes. We opened the champagne and clinked our glasses to a new year.

I was finding my groove, settling into the rhythm of normalcy. 2003 rolled in, and with it came my resolution. I'd be deliberate about love. That crown on my head?

New Year's rolled around, and with it came my resolution. I'd be deliberate about love. That crown on my head? It had been there from day one, and it was high time I started wearing it with the regal grace it deserves. I'm a prize, honey—a treasure. And I had earned the right to be choosy, to hold out for someone who saw the sparkle that had been there all along. Since landing in Maryland, I'd been on the up and up—a job that's more than just a paycheck, a home that was all mine, and a circle of friends that kept on growing. So, here's to intention, to knowing your worth, and to the journey of finding someone worthy of the crown you've been rocking all along.

Alright, so I sat myself down and whipped up a little manifesto, a recipe for my Mr. Right. He's gotta be fluent in the language of real talk, a trust fund of reliability, and a maestro in the sheets—see what I did there?—because let's keep it real, compatibility is key. This man? He's got to have his act together, family man, good to his mother, and a little Jesus in his soul. Respect? That's the seasoning that makes everything taste better. Riches ain't a must, but he better be standing on solid ground, with a crib of his own—no roommates, please, unless they're four-legged and furry.

I'm not asking for the moon and stars, just a grown-ass man who's got his life in order. It's that simple. I figured I'd meet someone when I wasn't looking, and that was exactly what happened. I had vowed to stay off BlackPlanet, but I couldn't help checking in on the weekends.

It was a Saturday afternoon. I was cleaning my house and doing the chores before I ran a few errands with Lexy in tow. Someone new pinged me on the BlackPlanet chat. It was blinking. I cursed it because I was so tired of the duds that had nothing to lose, but they would hit me up. However, he looked harmless enough, so I pinged him back. I sighed and shrugged in surrender. Maybe this time…(cursor blinking).

Homecoming Playlist

Scan the QR code to listen to the playlist.

Lonely—Glenn Lewis
Step in the Name of Love—R. Kelly
Butterflies—Michael Jackson
Always on Time—Ashanti
4ever—Lil' Mo
Put It On Me—Ja Rule
Round and Round—Jonell
Buddy—Musiq
Floetic—Floetry
This Love—Glenn Lewis
Break of Dawn—Michael Jackson
Halfcrazy—Musiq

NoNDicCuaL

Hey You—Floetry
Happy—Ashanti
I'm Real—J.Lo
Getting Late—Floetry
Foolish—Ashanti
Ifuleave—Musiq
Why Don't We Fall in Love—Amerie
Smoking Cigarettes—Tweet
Ice King—Res
Love of My Life—Erykah Badu
So Gone—Monica
Full Moon—Brandy
You Don't Know My Name—Alicia Keys
Love at First Sight—Mary J. Blige
My First Love—Anthony Hamilton
Sittin' Back—Res
I Cry—Ja Rule
Hello—Floetry
Sundress—CoCo Brown
Far Away—Kindred the Family Soul
The Way—Jill Scott
Love of My Life—Erykah Badu
The Light—Common
Better Days—Dianne Reeves
Grandma's Hands—Bill Withers
Unbreakable—Michael Jackson (my anthem)

Albums

Floetry—debut and second album
Musiq Soulchild—Juslisen
Jill Scott—debut album
Aaliyah—I Care 4 U
Michael Jackson—Invincible (I LOVE THIS ALBUM!)
Glenn Lewis—debut album
Res—How I Do
Erykah Badu—Mama's Gun
Ashanti—debut album

Goodie Bags

You are worthy to be loved!

You are **worthy** to be loved!

You are worthy to be **loved**!

Self-love is the best love!

God's love is **sufficient**!

Never compromise who you are!

Say it out loud when you feel insecure or discouraged…

Well, folks, we've hit that bittersweet note—Boyz II Men serenading us with "End of the Road" as we close the cover on this journey. You don't have to go home, but you can't stay within these pages. I hope you've had as much fun reading as I've had writing—and sipping on a little vino along the way. It's like the lights are coming up, and the last dance is done, but I can't let you go without a little something to remember our time together. So, here's a goodie bag packed with all the wisdom, laughs, and 'aha' moments we've shared. Take it with you, and whenever you need a pick-me-up, just reach in and grab a memory. Thank you for being the best guests a girl could ask for. Now go on—take a piece of this party with you, share it with friends and let's keep dancing through life. One chapter at a time.

Wear Your Crown With Pride—I spent ten years chasing a crown, seeking to recapture the glory of my first win—a superficial value determined by others whose judgment of me decided my worth. But I have always been a winner, and I didn't require anyone else's opinion on my accomplishments. Celebrate yourself. You did not make it this far without achieving goals. Never shortchange yourself. You have worked hard for everything you have done. Even if no one else has congratulated you, congratulate yourself. You got the job done. You finished the paper. You earned that degree. You lost weight. You raised your children. You finally took the trip you planned. You survived a breakup. You got the home you wanted. You started a business. I am celebrating with you. If no one else has said it, I'm saying it: CONGRATULATIONS!

The first gift is a crown/tiara. Wear it to remind yourself that you are worthy of being celebrated in this pageant called life.

Not on the Menu—Why be a snack when you are a full-course meal? Don't let anyone treat you like refrigerated leftovers. If you choose to live with your third eye open and legs wide shut—the NoNDicCuaL way—then sex is off the table for a bit.

Why copulate if it isn't leading to something? You are showing all your tricks upfront. You think you're impressing them, but they are going to wonder if you have done this with every person you've met. Equally, you would wonder the same. If you don't, you should. It's a fair thought.

In the times we're living in now, we must be more careful. Give yourself time to get to know the person as they get to know who you are. Allow them to earn your time and don't give it away.

You are the prize. Time will weed out those who are unworthy of you.

Do some old-fashioned courting. Let them open doors, pull out chairs, and pick you up. Make sure you spend time in the daylight hours. A lunch date in a park with a lake, horseback riding, a walk in the city, a winery visit, couples bowling—anything that allows you to get to know each other. It would suck if the sex was great, but you can't stand to be vertical in a room with them. Allow them to respect you. Slow the pace down and go at your own tempo. If they are truly for you, this will be effortless. Remember, you can't think with your legs open.

The second gift is a party game for couples.

Define the Relationship—Never start a relationship without a definition, even if it's a friend with benefits, work wife/husband, little sister, wifey, play cousin, or my favorite—situationship. I'm not talking about labels. I hate those, too. I mean, be in control of the narrative. Who will you be to me in my life? It needs to be communicated upfront. It takes out all the guesswork—fingers crossed—hopes, late-night analyzing with your close friend about what it means when they do this (insert the action). You know you will do it. We have all done it.

Never be afraid of the answer. Ask them! All they can say is no. We are all grown, and you need to know where you stand. There's no space for disappointment if you never waste your time.

Never compromise your line in the sand. Hold true to your principles. Believe them when they are being honest with you. You know how they are being honest with you? Here are some generic examples: "Hey, I gotta be honest," or "If we are keeping it one hundred," or "Hey, listen." Pay attention! Don't act like a girlfriend if they say, "We're just cool, right?" They will take advantage if you let them. They will turn on you and tell you with certainty, "We were just chillin'. Why you all serious?"

You teach people how to treat you by your reaction to any situation. It's okay to want a relationship, settle down, or just be exclusive. However, there is no value in holding your cards to your chest, hoping they will be the person you want if they don't even know your intentions. People are terrible mind readers. They need to be on the same page if you are going to be successful. There is no shame in vetting a potential mate. Ask the question! Be transparent with your intentions!

The third gift is a Magic 8 Ball. You can practice asking questions. *wink*

Family First—I took for granted what family meant by thinking I could live without them by my side. It was a heavy price I paid. I didn't consciously do it. I just didn't understand what I had until I moved away, and they weren't there. I'm able to appreciate them more because I'm not with them every day. I didn't realize it was bigger than me. I was concentrating on the dot, not the circle, and I missed the point. I don't regret my decision, but I wish I had options. Family over everything—never take them for granted!

The fourth gift is a set of beautiful gold and white picture frames—to remind you to keep your family first. Put your loved ones in frames.

Forgiveness—I am sure you heard the saying, "Forgiveness isn't about them; it's about you." It's really about the extra, needless weight you carry when your heart is heavy. Release it!

What is it doing for you when you decide not to forgive them? It's not hurting them. They have moved on with their life and haven't thought about you or your hurt feelings at all. Why hurt? The person you gave control to will never validate you the way you think you deserve. Listen, I forgave my daughter's father. I even hurt with him when he lost loved ones. It was very sincere, and my blessing was finding my husband. It is not easy! It will take some time, but don't let it take too long. I almost blocked blessings by not forgiving him. Let it go! Watch the blessings come.

The fifth gift is a personal journal so you can put your thoughts/feelings in writing to sort them out, so they don't have to continue to float around in your head or contaminate your heart.

Preserve Your Peace—Now, there are some folks out there who seem to have a PhD in Misery. Names? Oh, they shall remain nameless, but if you've been riding with me this far, you've got the guest list. My strategy? I hit 'em with the cut-off. Mid-conversation veers into the land of bickering. I'm out. "Love you, talk later," I say, and that's my mic drop. It's been a journey to this Zen zone. I had to study the patterns, get my degree in sign reading, and learn not to RSVP to their pity parties. You've got to build up that immunity, like a drama vaccine, or else they'll have you stressed to the max. But here's the real tea—if they matter to you, you've got to master the art of loving them from a distance. Keep their dark clouds away from your sunshine. And the golden rule? Never let their stormy ways dampen the way you love.

The sixth gift is a beautiful hand mirror. May you always stay focused on what's important: YOU!

Step Out on Faith—I will not preach. I am still a heathen, a work in progress, and this is my testimony. My story is about my choice to step out on faith. I listened to God. He said, "I've got you. Everything is going to be all right." I was worried about having this baby alone. I was so devastated when I didn't get the house, and the landlord ran away with my money. I ended up at Aunt Tina's house, who asked me if I had thought about moving to DC with my cousin, Mellie.

God sent me an angel: Mellie. She posted my resume, and I got a job the next day. I had left my baby with another angel: my grandmother. Mellie came to St. Louis and helped me move to DC. I stayed with her for two months. God found me a place of my own. When it was time to go get my baby, he sent Mellie once more to go home with me to get her.

God blessed me with a good job, more money, and a better position to provide for my child. Then God sent my husband to love and relieve me of my loneliness. He had it all worked out. All I had to do was step out on faith. Thank you, Jesus. Giving God all the glory.

Great things are waiting for you! Let nothing or no one hold you back, not even yourself. You are worthy. You deserve it. You can achieve it. You are a BOSS! Own it! Always know a Higher Power is guiding your steps. Please, pay attention to the signs and the little voice in your head. No one can define your worth. You own the narrative of your story. Live your dreams. Never let them go. Keep God in your life. He will never let you down.

The seventh and final gift is a candle to light your inner fire. Use it to meditate or pray.

My Last Thought...

Remember, trying to outdo your past self is like running a race against your own shadow—it's a chase with no finish line. Instead, stand tall on the foundation your former self built. Let every triumph, every stumble be the steppingstones to your next big leap. Be bolder, shine brighter, and soar higher than you ever thought possible. Celebrate your amazing journey. I hope you enjoyed reading mine. God bless! Always a drama club kid, I hear "Believe in Yourself" from *The Wiz* soundtrack playing in the background.

> "I am earning my wings, one feather at a time."
> —AR, aka 2n2me

www.ingramcontent.com/pod-product-compliance
Lightning Source LLC
Chambersburg PA
CBHW032032150426
43194CB00006B/240